P9-DCL-357

SECOND EDITION

From Indians to Chicanos

SECOND EDITION

From Indians to Chicanos

The dynamics of Mexican-American culture

James Diego Vigil

WAVELAND
PRESS, INC.
Prospect Heights, Illinois

For information about this book, write or call:
  Waveland Press, Inc.
  P.O. Box 400
  Prospect Heights, Illinois 60070
  (847) 634-0081

Cover mural:
Title: "Nuestra Vida." (Our Life). Painted by Creative Solutions, S.T.E.P. Jesus Julian Estrada, Karla, Shyrel, Lilian, Yionara, Oscar, Robert, Mario, and Sandra. Funded by Los Angeles Conservation Corps. Rodriquez & Sons Market, Fourth St. and Euclid in East Los Angeles.

Copyright © 1998 by Waveland Press, Inc.

ISBN 0-88133-976-8

All rights reserved. No part of this book may be reproduced, stored in a retrieval system, or transmitted in any form or by any means without permission in writing from the publisher.

Printed in the United States of America

7   6   5   4   3   2   1

To all my children, for the love
and joy they have given me
over the years (listed by age,
not favoritism!):

*Joanie, James, Jr.,
Nicky, Matthew, Nena,
Vivi, and Adriana*

Contents

**STAGE III   *MEXICAN INDEPENDENCE AND NATIONALISM,
1821 TO 1846***

Handwritten margin notes: "Beginning of Mexican Independence & Nationalism"; "Northern Frontier"

STAGE IV   ANGLO-AMERICAN PERIOD 1846 TO 1960S

Conclusion   285

Index   307

Foreword

To understand the history of the Chicanos is to understand the Chicano movement. It is this complex, multi-layered history that Diego Vigil has chosen to record. Chicano history is still being written, since the movement has not fully matured.

There is, of course, no typical Chicano; they are an amazingly diverse group even though they have certain common interests and associations. This text is of special importance, not merely for its scholarship and research, but because it reflects the intellectual evolution and maturing point of view of a representative Chicano, Diego Vigil, who first became interested in the Chicano movement in the middle-1960s. His interest has grown and deepened in the years since then.

The Chicano experience differs in significant respects from that of other ethnic minority groups. It has been affected by many influences that have changed with time and in different geographical and socio-economic settings. It is an experience that must be patiently unfolded, making allowances for regional and historical differences. Not surprisingly, it has created identity problems for those who have been caught up in it, for it involves racial, class, cultural, and national conflicts in the Southwest, a rapidly developing region of different interests and economies. The Chicano experience has accordingly been marginal and exceptional and has been given a variety of interpretations and definitions. To some extent, it reflects the same syncretic experience that occurred in Mexico but with different causes and results.

The diversity of the experience has spawned the so-called Chicano rebellion, which has altered the consciousness of Mexican Americans in ways that set them apart from their parents and the older generation of Spanish-speaking people, as well as the dominant Anglo majority. The movement seems to be guided less by ideologies and theories than by the Chicanos' determination to forge their own identity and to reject outside influences and imported schemes and ideas. The legacy of the Chicano movement has not yet been worked out; it changes and is constantly being analyzed and restated. The fact that Diego Vigil reflects this experience, in addition to reciting its history and causes, makes this text an important contribution to Chicano studies.

Carey McWilliams

Preface

This text has a dual purpose. It is an historical account tracing the formation of modern-day Chicano culture and lifeways, and it also examines key culture change dynamics of the Chicano past and present. Passing through two major wars of conquest and undergoing at least four cultural imprints make for quite a journey, a passage of five hundred years of complexity built on repeated controversies and confrontations. To simplify this long and deep account, two conceptual frameworks are utilized to identify key trends and developments. The first one, the six C's, shows how class, cultural, and color (racial) attitudes and practices were transformed under intense contact, conflict, and change sequences. The other framework addresses how major changes forged macrostructural identities over this time period. It provides insights on how indigenous lifeways were interrupted, turning Indians into peasants and still later into migrants and immigrants, as they lost control of land, labor, and wealth at the hands of "others."

The text is divided into four major historical stages. Stage I, "Pre-Columbian Period," describes the life of Mesoamerican Indians before European contact and ends with the initial phases of the Spanish conquest. Stage II, "Spanish Colonial Era," summarizes three hundred years of rule, documenting the dynamics of class inequality and intense cultural and racial discrimination leading to the early phase of peasantry. Stage III, "Mexican Independence and Nationalism," begins with the promise and fervor of social movements and independence with an autonomous Mexico struggling to achieve nationhood in the later period of peasantry, including activities in its northern reaches (now the U.S. Southwest), and ends with the Mexican-American War of 1846, which began the years of closer Mexican and American ties. Stage IV, "Anglo-American Period," examines the rise of the Mexican-American people, the effects of large-scale immigration in the twentieth century, the mobilization of the people culminating in the 1960s Chicano movement, and how that event has played out to the present. The text concludes with some comparative observations on the importance of understanding the culture change sequences that indigenous populations undergo. It was an especially strained process to be remade by "others" into macrostructural categories. The long, drawn-out episode considerably altered their cultural (tribal and regional) identities by transforming their economic bases. The latter takes on more significance because indigenous populations presently number in the hundreds of thousands in the United States (immigrants) and along the Mexican/U.S. border (migrants); peasant movements and unrest, such as the Zapatistas, now dot the rural Mexican landscape.

As with all works of such a broad and encompassing nature, so many people and events contributed to the formulation of the first edition and reformulation of the second edition of this book that there is not enough space to express my gratitude to all of them. First of all are the students who took my class, Culture Change and the Mexican People: North and South of the Border. Those from Chaffey College helped with the initial, innovative formulations, and students from the University of Southern California (USC) and the University of California at Los Angeles (UCLA) built on these ideas, adding many more facts and refinements. I owe these students a lot, for their receptive manner and enthusiasm as well as their critical feedback.

Over the years, several scholars have offered stimulating conversation and keen advice on some of the main issues of the text. Among them are Tom Weaver, Margarita Melville, Robert Alvarez, Steve Arvizu, Sam Rios, Ed Escobar, Juan Gomez-Quinones, Luis Arroyo, Guadalupe Friaz, Leo Chavez, Mauricio Mazon, and Rudy Acuna. The artwork was contributed by Jeffrey Huereque and Mary Nunez, and the maps by Charles Roseman. My son, Nick Vigil, is responsible for the graphics and final illustration of the six C's model; and Matthew, my other son, helped with the index and early reformulation of the book. My research assistant, Gisella Hanley, helped with the conceptualization of the six C's illustration and aided immensely on several chapters with new references and ideas to sharpen the focus. Special appreciation is offered to John M. Long, my longtime friend and research associate, who characteristically took the time to edit and refine major themes of the text and compile the index. Since so much of my thinking and writing has been influenced by the works of Carey McWilliams, his foreword still resonates and brings warm feelings of appreciation for the time and energy he took to write it.

Over the decades, my wife, Polly, has been my consistent supporter and defender, and when my spirits sag, she is always there to pick them up. To my mate, a hardy embrace and thanks. Although all of the aforementioned people are credited with helping me in this work, I readily accept the responsibility for all errors of fact, judgment, and interpretation.

Photo Credits

Chapter 1

17 Permission of the estate of Paul Mangelsdorf **21** Jeffrey Huereque **22** BAE Bulletin 170, Smithsonian Institution

Chapter 2

28 Jeffrey Huereque **30** Jeffrey Chouinard **34** *bottom* Jeffrey Chouinard

Chapter 3

47 Corbis-Bettmann **49** Courtesy Peabody Museum, Harvard University **51** Courtesy Department Library Services, American Museum of Natural History, Neg. No. 326597 **55** Library of Congress, LC-USZ62-33976 **59** Jeffrey Chouinard

Chapter 4

74–75 Library of Congress, LC-USZ62-33965 **78** The Bancroft Library **88** Jeffrey Chouinard **97** Jeffrey Huereque **102** *Cuijla: Esbozo ethnografico de un pueblo negro.* Gonzalo Aguirre Beltran. Mexico: Fondo de Cultura Economica, 1958.

Chapter 5

113 Corbis-Bettmann **114** Library of Congress, LC-USZ62-52186

Chapter 6

128–129 Commissioned by the Trustees of Dartmouth College, Hanover, New Hampshire. **132** From Turner, J. K.: *Barbarous Mexico*, Austin, 1969, University of Texas Press **135** The Bancroft Library **140** From Starr, F.: *Indians of Southern Mexico*, Chicago, 1899, published by the author.

Chapter 7

156 *top* Library of Congress, LC-USZ62-2727; *bottom* Library of Congress, LC-USZ62-2723 **158** *top and middle* The Bancroft Library **164** Library of Congress, LC-USZ62-11184 **168** *top and bottom* Reproduced by permission of The Huntington Library, San Marino, California. **169** Reproduced by permission of The Huntington Library, San Marino, California.

Chapter 8

181 From *A History of Mexico*, by Henry Bamford Parkes. Copyright © 1938, 1950, 1960, 1966, 1969 by Henry B. Parkes. Reprinted by permission of Houghton Mifflin Company. **183** Mary Nunez **184** Corbis-Bettmann **186** *top* Library of

Congress, LC-USZ62-30690; *bottom* Corbis-Bettmann **187** *bottom* Library of Congress, LC-USZ62-35239 **206** *top* Library of Congress, LC-USF34-32684-D; *bottom* Library of Congress, LC-USW3-1194-D **227** Jeffrey Huereque

Chapter 9

236 Courtesy United Farm Workers **237** UPI/Corbis-Bettmann **238** *top* From Nabokov, P.: *Tijerina and the Courthouse Raid*, Albuquerque, 1969. Reprinted by permission of University of New Mexico Press. **248** *top* UPI/Corbis-Bettmann **249** Mary Nunez **253** Mary Nunez **269** Mary Nunez

Introduction

With large-scale immigration in the last twenty years and a high birth rate, the Chicano people now comprise the second-largest ethnic minority in the United States. By 2020, they will have surpassed blacks in numbers. At present the population is anywhere from 18 million to 25 million, if one includes undocumented immigrant workers. When combined with other Latinos, primarily Puerto Ricans and Cubans, the total might be over 30 million. In several areas of the American Southwest, which some activists call Aztlan after the legendary Aztec name for the region, Chicanos are in the majority. Indeed, some of these people's ancestors inhabited the Southwest long before its incorporation into the United States. On the other hand, and because of the changes noted above, many more Chicanos are offspring of recent immigrants from Mexico and often maintain close ties with relatives in that country. Although the ethnic label Mexican American is still used by some people who take pride in being American, the recent trend appears to favor emphasizing the Mexican background and thus, using either the label Mexican or the label Chicano.[*]

Why a Dynamic History?

An ethnohistorical interpretation of the Chicanos is needed because there are many unique aspects to their background (Cline 1972). First,

---

[*] The ethnic label Chicano has many definitions (Munoz 1989:61–63). A strict colloquial usage suggests that it is a shortened form of Mexicano, which gained renewed popularity during the 1960s Chicano movement. In this text it is used to reflect the multiple-heritage experience of Mexicans in the United States, reflected in an Indian, Spanish, Mexican, and Anglo background. The political consciousness-raising events of the 1960s helped develop an appreciation of Chicanos' multicultural heritage. The term Chicano will be used throughout most of the text because the text is a look backward to trace the historical development of a contemporary people.

there are the multiple heritages and influences covering several centuries that need to be examined and assessed. What cultural and linguistic blending occurred? What new customs and traits were introduced, and why did some people adjust smoothly and others resist? Significantly, major upheavals and wars have abruptly and radically transformed their lives, causing repercussions that are still with them today. There are books on Mexico and works on the American Southwest, but few books attempt to grapple with and unravel the complex strands of Chicanos, as the "in-between" people who straddle both nations with a thin borderline separating the two. As we shall see, the Chicanos' experience is so complex and marked with the stigma of lower socioeconomic status that it has tended to blur their sociocultural traditions and lifeways.

It is in the last five centuries that the most radical and significant changes have taken place, but the movements, settlements, and revampments that have molded the Chicanos actually began thousands of years ago. Their early ancestors, the indigenous people, provided them with a rich cultural foundation. (The ethnic label Chicano is a derivative of the Aztec tribal name *Mexica,* with the *x* pronounced like *ch*.) The last of these people, the Aztecs, reached a grand plateau of civilization, and in some ways were more advanced than other peoples in the world of that time. The process of their displacement by first the Spanish, and later as Mexicans by the Anglo, has had serious effects on their historical evolution. Most of the facts concerning these historical influences are readily available and easily understood.

However, describing the outcome of the merging of Old and New World cultural styles presents a perplexing problem. What was the result of this merging? Were Chicanos forged from that experience? To what degree can one determine the contributions of each culture to the mixture? These questions continue to plague students and researchers alike, as they probe to uncover the complex issues shaping the Chicano people (Bernal and Knight 1993). Indeed, many of the contrasts, strains, and mergings rooted in these beginnings are still being played out.

This ethnohistorical account attempts to resolve some of these issues. Taking a dynamic approach that charts various time periods and peoples will help the assessment (Mirande 1985). The narrative begins with pre-Columbian Mexico and focuses on over five centuries of problems arising from the struggle for resources. Key to this engagement is how Europeans and their successors repeatedly battled with the indigenous majority population over land, labor, and wealth: who owned it, who worked it, and who benefitted from it (Wolf 1982; Frazier 1957). Not the least of the problems to be illuminated will be the psychological consequences of the suppression suffered by the Chicano people over these many years. The text will examine how indigenous peoples adapted to new social systems and how social systems also changed.

Macrohistorical Evolution and the
Six C's Model of Culture Change

To aid comprehension of such a long, complex epic, this text will look at the evolution of the Chicano people by focusing on questions of land, labor, and wealth, especially as they involved Europeans and their descendants and transformed indigenous people into peasants. As people's relationship to the land changed and control over their labor shifted, the peasants were further displaced and became migrants and immigrants. It is helpful to look at these changes macrohistorically and macrostructurally as a process of the capturing of energy with the aid of tools and technology (White 1949). The early evolution of Indian hunting and gathering cultures to dependence on agriculture paralleled changes elsewhere in the world, and with the growth of towns and cities, human energy was captured in new ways to aid expansion. Radical shifts in this independent processual evolution began to take place when Europeans entered the picture and captured most of the energy, relegating most natives to a life of peasantry. In time, as larger social and economic networks arose, the lands and other resources needed for economic expansion and exchange as well as political control increased. In many areas, peasants were uprooted and forced to immigrate to cities to find work. Both peasant and immigrant experiences amounted to a "supraclass" reality of people collected into a larger generic category.

A macrohistorical progression of the additive and cumulative change provides a clear picture of the process. It is a way of looking at land, human labor, and the control of productive energy in a grand conceptual way to understand, for example, why so much wealth today is in the hands of a small elite. It is useful to divide this progression into a series of historical stages or periods. The historical periods show the introduction of new cultural ways of relating to the resources, noting contests and accommodations where necessary, and suggesting future directions.

As we proceed, it will be made clear how different aspects of each historical stage interrelate and why a particular type of awareness is found in one stage and not another. While successive stages often are not qualitatively better, each is more complex than the last, if only from the incorporation of what has been learned in previous stages. Of course, there are instances where stages overlap or one takes priority over another, or when development is blocked or uneven. Nevertheless, the implicit goal here is the establishment of a conceptual framework to draw parallels and make comparisons. This macrohistorical and macrostructural perspective will facilitate discussion of whether mature, evolutionary progression characterizes various stages of Chicano history

Historical Periods and Macrostructural Identities

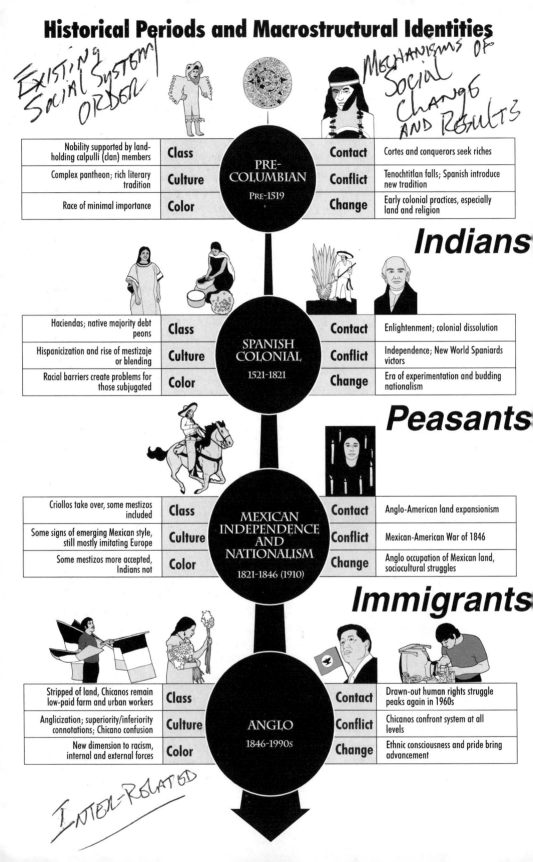

EXISTING SOCIAL SYSTEM ORDER (handwritten)

MECHANISMS OF Social CHANGE AND RESULTS (handwritten)

PRE-COLUMBIAN
PRE-1519

Nobility supported by land-holding calpulli (clan) members	**Class**	
Complex pantheon; rich literary tradition	**Culture**	
Race of minimal importance	**Color**	

Contact	Cortes and conquerors seek riches
Conflict	Tenochtitlan falls; Spanish introduce new tradition
Change	Early colonial practices, especially land and religion

Indians

SPANISH COLONIAL
1521-1821

Haciendas; native majority debt peons	**Class**	
Hispanicization and rise of mestizaje or blending	**Culture**	
Racial barriers create problems for those subjugated	**Color**	

Contact	Enlightenment; colonial dissolution
Conflict	Independence; New World Spaniards victors
Change	Era of experimentation and budding nationalism

Peasants

MEXICAN INDEPENDENCE AND NATIONALISM
1821-1846 (1910)

Criollos take over, some mestizos included	**Class**	
Some signs of emerging Mexican style, still mostly imitating Europe	**Culture**	
Some mestizos more accepted, Indians not	**Color**	

Contact	Anglo-American land expansionism
Conflict	Mexican-American War of 1846
Change	Anglo occupation of Mexican land, sociocultural struggles

Immigrants

ANGLO
1846-1990s

Stripped of land, Chicanos remain low-paid farm and urban workers	**Class**	
Anglicization; superiority/inferiority connotations; Chicano confusion	**Culture**	
New dimension to racism, internal and external forces	**Color**	

Contact	Drawn-out human rights struggle peaks again in 1960s
Conflict	Chicanos confront system at all levels
Change	Ethnic consciousness and pride bring advancement

INTER-RELATED (handwritten)

or whether the long experience has set Chicanos further back. The broader categories in these developments show the indigenous to peasant to immigrant transformations (Kearney 1996).

For the purpose of this text, Chicano macrohistory is divided into four major historical periods:

1. *Pre-Columbian, pre-1519.* For biological and cultural reasons, Chicanos are, in an evolutionary sense, tied to the Indians of Mexico and the Southwest. Aztecs, especially, impressed their culture on surrounding natives and for their time reached the highest level of indigenous civilization. In addition, they became the first large native group to be defeated militarily by the Europeans and to experience a life of subjugation and a radical change in status.

2. *Spanish colonial, 1521–1821.* This period is one of the most influential in the formation of the Chicano people. Although Chicanos received most of their genetic makeup from Indians, the Spanish were profoundly instrumental in shaping Chicano cultural life, for example, with Spanish surnames and language and the establishment of peasant lifeways. Their three-hundred-year reign was the longest and perhaps the most significant of all the postcontact stages.

3. *Mexican independence and nationalism, 1821–1846 for Mexicans in the United States, but up to 1910 for those in Mexico.* The experiences of Mexicans on both sides of the border differed markedly. However, there are important features that bind them together. On the whole, peasant cultural patterns remained similar, and there was some reciprocal immigration that tended to maintain that connection. Often the events in either nation affected affairs in the other. Thus, the awakening of an ethnic and national consciousness must include an awareness of activities in both regions.

4. *Anglo period, 1846–present.* By accident or design, the Anglo "assimilation" policy for foreigners was begun at the time that Chicanos entered the United States. This was the government's predominant cultural adjustment strategy until a massive, concerted effort to change matters began during the 1960s. Meanwhile, immigration increased substantially in the late twentieth century.

In each of these historical stages, the Chicano people were confronted with new realities and problems, but always there was a developing awareness and growth.

It should be noted that this division of dynamic historical changes into periods characterized by related structural changes is a technique for depicting the growth of a people. The technique could easily be applied to any one of the stages designated above, thus, for example, making a broad assessment of the Indian and Spanish experiences. Every sociocultural beginning is also in some sense an end or a middle, depending on the perspective one takes. Surely the Aztecs and colonial Spanish attained growth pinnacles in their respective eras. The purpose here is not to designate any of the earlier cultural patterns as complete, but to give emphasis to their role in the blossoming of the Chicano variant: to show how a preindustrial, localized people became integrated into an industrial, transnational entity.

A second method used in the text to clarify Chicano history is a model of sociocultural change, the Six C's: Class, Culture, Color, Contact, Conflict, and Change (table 1). This model provides a framework for understanding both the structure and the process of a social system. Anthropologists might say that the model aids synchronic and diachronic analysis and interpretation. A synchronic assessment refers to the functional approach to the study of culture in a given time, such as what occurs daily, seasonally, or annually. This can be likened to a photograph. On the other hand, a diachronic focus emphasizes the historical or developmental approach to the study of culture, such as the interpretation of an evolutionary or macrolevel cumulative change (Vancina 1970). The analogy here would be a series of photos that make up a bigger picture, a cinematic rendering.

Table 1   Six C's Model of Sociocultural Change

Functionally Intact and Stable Social Order

1. CLASS—land, income, occupation, home, neighborhood, prestige, and esteem; also includes factors from other sectors of the social system
2. CULTURE—language, religion, philosophy, values, beliefs, customs, and general worldview of the people
3. COLOR—emphasis, or lack of it, on physiognomic or racial traits in the social system in terms of racist ideology, prejudice, discrimination, segregation

Breakup and Evolutionary Transformation of Social Order

4. CONTACT—often military force, but also involves the spread of ideas, such as religious or revolutionary principles; often is guided by economic concerns
5. CONFLICT—a multiple experience, including military confrontation and resistance and rebellion efforts, as well as a host of religious, sociocultural, and psychological dimensions
6. CHANGE—all initial transformations that take place after contact and conflict and before a new class-culture-color system is firmly rooted

The application of the Six C's model to each historic period will provide a clearer understanding of the sociocultural change that occurred. It will simultaneously provide a framework for a synchronic perspective, or what is functionally operative at any given time, and a diachronic assessment of transformations over time (Park 1950). Issues and conditions of class (sociological or socioeconomic conditions and practices), culture (anthropological or sociocultural change and innovation), and color (sociopsychological problems caused by racism) are discussed first. To simplify the presentation, other subjects are included under the major headings listed above. The sequence in which they are presented is also important and emphasizes the mechanism of energy capture. Generally, the class factor is the foundation for developing an examination of the other sectors (Wolf 1982; Harris 1979), especially in light of the macrohistory and structural developments that reflect major changes. However, there are times when the discussion includes all of the features simultaneously, either because of similar time placement or because they are inextricably interwoven. The categories of class, culture, and color provide a vehicle to highlight the continuous social order and the way in which several major social features intertwine to make a a people's history (Marger 1994). The overarching macrostructural identities serve further to underscore the placing of people into large generic categories.

The second three categories of contact, conflict, and change aid in explaining the quality and nature of social evolution, the series of events and forces that kick-start macrolevel revampments. Contact refers to intrusions that upset an ongoing social system; conflict designates the nature of the subsequent struggle; and change denotes the reorganization of society in the aftermath, in both a short- and long-term view (Spindler 1984; Spicer 1962). A contact-conflict-change analysis enables one to determine how and why a stable social system is disrupted, transformed, and reintegrated. It does this by graphically showing how a people evolve from one historical period to another. The result in each stage is the establishment of a new social order, by which Chicanos are progressively shaped and molded according to the dictates of that period as well as the cumulative, incremental innovations that mark a changing people.

To summarize, each historical era begins with a relatively intact, stable, class-culture-color system, which in time is altered. A contact-conflict-change explanatory sequence clarifies the transformations that a fully functional social system undergoes, and pinpoints specific aspects of the upheaval. Thus culture change, conflict and continuity, acculturation and marginality can be viewed in specific moments of history and charted as they move through history. At another level, macrohistorical developments concurrently shape macrostructural identities.

Theoretical Implications for the Present Day

Application of the Six C's model to each historical period yields a categorical framework within which to describe and discuss similar social-system sectors. More importantly, it focuses on social, cultural, and psychological patterns on which to base a comparison for all the time periods. Another purpose the model fulfills is to document specifically the beginnings of certain modern traits and customs of Chicanos. The model has several dimensions that offer insight into different types of issues in a holistic fashion (Pitt 1972; Hodgen 1974).

With the use of the macrohistorical evolution framework and the Six C's model of sociocultural change, this sociocultural history should provide one with an appreciation of the complexity of all these transformations. If it is true that Chicanos have had a diverse contact and change experience, then it follows that there are diverse legacies from which to draw. This diversity underscores the difficulty in comprehending modern Chicano issues and problems. An understanding of the broader and deeper developments of these features will aid in identifying and underscoring the weak points as well as the accomplishments of a people.

It is important to base assessments and understandings on history, especially appreciating the depth and breadth of each epoch, but the central point of this work is to look deeper for the macrostructural identity. Uprooting Indian culture and lifeways to create a peasant society (with many varieties within this lifestyle) was a major shift for indigenous peoples. With the passage of time, new tools and technologies emerged to carry peasants to another era. In the last one hundred years, under the onslaught of industrialization, urbanization, and economic globalization, this change has again uprooted the peoples in this time of migration. Thus, an assessment of the Indian to peasant to immigrant sequence is warranted.

As situations of time and place dictate, Chicanos have been affected by many influences (Mirande 1985). In adapting and adjusting to a multitude of circumstances, they have had to change and rechange customs, values, and beliefs. Their experience is different historically from that of most other national minority groups because they were made to feel culturally and racially inferior by more than one dominant group. Hence, a "layered-on" type of oppression occurred.

Clearly, negative material conditions of land, labor, and wealth are germane to this history (Wolf 1982, 1969). Nevertheless, there are also positive inheritances. As one possible reason for their survival, Chicanos epitomize the ability of modern colonized people to fashion multiple-pronged strategies of adaptation. They have learned to integrate and synthesize past racial and cultural mixture experiences. This, in turn, has led to the development of a flexible and comprehensive approach to life, in which first one avenue and then another has assisted their perseverance. José Vasconcelo's reference to Mexicans as "La Raza Cosmica" (the Cosmic People) was an early assessment of how cultural diversity makes for strength and vitality. This description also pertains to the even more culturally diverse Chicano people, a legacy of Indian, Spanish, Mexican, and Anglo antecedents; what has been referred to as *personas mexicanas* (Vigil 1997).

References

Bernal, M. E. and G. P. Knight, eds. 1993. *Ethnic identity: Formation and transmission among Hispanics and other minorities.* Albany: State University of New York Press.

Cline, H. F., vol. ed. 1972. *Handbook of Middle American Indians: Guide to ethnohistorical sources.* Austin: University of Texas Press.

Frazier, E. F. 1957. *Race and culture contacts in the modern world.* New York: Alfred A. Knopf, Inc.

Harris, M. 1979. *Cultural materialism.* New York: Random House, Inc.

Hodgen, M. T. 1974. *Anthropology, history, and cultural change.* Tucson: University of Arizona Press.

Kearney, M. 1996. *Reconceptualizing peasantry.* Boulder, CO: Westview Press.

Marger, M. N. 1994. *Race and ethnic relations: American and global perspectives.* Belmont, CA: Wadsworth Pub. Co.

Mirande, A. 1985. *The Chicano experience: An alternative perspective.* Notre Dame, IN: University of Notre Dame Press.

Munoz, C. 1989. *Youth, identity, power: The Chicano generation.* London; New York: Verso.

Pitt, H. C. 1972. *Using historical sources in anthropology and sociology.* New York: Holt, Rinehart, & Winston.

Spicer, E. 1962. *Cycles of conquest.* Tucson: University of Arizona Press.

Spindler, L. S. 1984. *Culture change and modernization: Mini-models and case studies.* Prospect Heights, IL: Waveland Press.

Vancina, J. 1970. Cultures through time. In *A handbook of method in cultural anthropology,* ed. R. Naroll and E. T. Cohen. New York: Doubleday & Co., Inc.

Vigil, J. D. 1997. *Personas mexicanas: Chicano high schoolers in a changing Los Angeles.* Ft. Worth, TX: Harcourt Brace.

White, L. A. 1949. *The science of culture.* New York: Farrar, Straus & Giroux.

Wolf, E. R. 1969. *Peasant wars of the twentieth century.* New York: Harper & Row Publishers.

———. 1982. *Europe and the people without history.* Berkeley: University of California Press.

Stage I
Pre-Columbian Period
30,000 B.C. to A.D. 1519

Chapter 1

Human Evolution in Mesoamerica

Before the first Europeans arrived in Mexico, the Aztecs had constructed the most advanced civilization on the continent of North America. It is useful to examine the complex process by which the Aztecs came into being and shaped one of the most sophisticated societies in the Western Hemisphere. A look at the thousands of years of American Indian prehistory, the successive achievements of one people after another that culminated in the rise to prominence of the people who called themselves Mexica, will provide an understanding of how social institutions began and were refined and perpetuated by the Indian forebears of the Chicano people.

During this prehistoric period leading up to the Indian civilizations, indigenous people were able to experiment and develop their own way of relating to the land, dividing and allocating labor, and collecting and distributing the wealth in ways that benefit most or all of the participants. Every civilization represents the results of tens of thousands of years of human adaptation. Experimentation and innovation are at the core of this gradual evolution, as the foundation is being laid for later development. In the meantime, human intellectual and cultural powers and networks grow in sophistication and complexity. Later natives benefited from the adaptations of preceding peoples and thereby fashioned a more secure and variable style of life. This early development, like the lore and legend of a people, is remembered only in others' telling of it and in the foundations it has provided. Hence, it is illustrative of how past events, however distant or small, operate to shape the present.

Ecological Adaptation

The rise of great Mesoamerican civilizations was preceded by many prehistoric events. Beginning in 30,000 B.C. (some experts say it was earlier, around 50,000 B.C., while others support a more recent period, 12,000–14,000 B.C.), there were great migrations of people from Asia (Coe 1994).[1] According to archaeologists, they wandered across the Bering Straits, which during the last Ice Age was a land mass connecting Asia and Alaska, or perhaps arrived here by sea travel at an earlier date. These migrations brought hordes of people whose descendants, over several thousand years, established themselves throughout North and South America. They were the original Americans.

These early pioneers found their way down the streams and valleys of North America, seeking food and water, clothing to keep them warm and protect them from abrupt weather changes, and shelter for rest and protection from predators. These early hunters were forced to follow a nomadic path, restlessly pursuing game wherever it might lead them. This dependence on large herd animals affected other areas of life. Following herds of mammoth or musk ox over the landbridge, taking many routes in this prolonged chase, the hunters learned to fashion tools out of natural objects.

Over a period of time, as early humans adapted to their environment, crude flaked stone points gave way to more refined and useful technology. Techniques to aid in adaptation were consciously fashioned and tools were invented and perfected to aid in the acquisition of food and the manufacture of clothing. "We know that man controlled fire. . . . He also knew how to make spears, scrapers and knives. He had the *atlatl* spear thrower, he knew how to cook meat, he had domesticated the dog, wore skins to protect himself, and he probably knew how to make baskets" (Peterson 1962:19). Initially, this wandering human found temporary shelter in natural caves and ledges. Much of what we know about this time period comes from remains these ancient people left behind in that part of the United States now most densely populated by Chicanos.

As the years passed, the Ice Age receded and the climate became warmer and dryer. Groups of natives split off in different directions to find refuge in a variety of regions and climates. Accordingly, they fashioned new relationships to the environment. Some combined the gathering of edible plants with hunting but in time came to rely mostly on the former. Evidence of this relationship to the land, flora, and fauna is found with the literally thousands of querns and mullers, grinding platforms, and milling stones left behind by these people. In time, a reliance on plants for meals began to increase chances for survival, making big-game hunters in some areas a thing of the past (Coe 1994; Wolf 1959).

Other natives, who settled near streams or oceans, learned to subsist on the surrounding plant and animal life. Even those who were reluctant to experiment with new food sources eventually were forced to adopt new subsistence patterns through a process of cultural diffusion.

Even at this early date one can observe the human propensity to vacillate between conserving the old and creating or adopting the new. Many individuals are reluctant to test new ways of doing things, even if their own existence is threatened. Clinging to age-old traditions is common because familiar patterns are time-tested and thus verify what has been gained. Eventually, however, ecological pressures may necessitate changes to ensure survival. A conservative orientation is not all bad; many old traits and customs persist because they still fulfill important functions. However, certain innovative individuals play a strong role in readapting themselves to changing conditions, and they are at the forefront in selecting the inventive paths that hasten human evolution (Spindler 1984). Those individuals and groups who persist in clinging too long to outmoded and worn customs of the past face extinction.

Available natural resources—flora and fauna—determined for the early native peoples the time, place, and manner of eating, dress, and sleep, for the latter primary needs and drives help motivate humans to control and domesticate the world around them. Consequently, a secure environmental relationship developed as human social and cultural institutions evolved.

The connection between improved ecological adaptation and the blossoming of other human traits cannot be overemphasized. Time for activities other than securing the basic necessities is important in human evolution. The spiritual needs of humans arose to accompany the material needs. While the body finds nourishment in the material world, the soul strives to participate in life's spiritual and intellectual struggles. Spiritual considerations become involved in the everyday affairs of humans—perhaps to ensure that the environment is not abused as a result of selfish motives. The innate human tendency toward self-centeredness needs to be curbed; otherwise, total exploitation of the environment would result.

The early natives were able to reside in permanent cavelike dwellings only where there was an abundance of natural resources. Otherwise they continued the seasonal nomadic cycle. Over a period of time, however, there occurred a far-reaching change that shifted natives from a nomadic to a sedentary lifestyle.

Agricultural Revolution

According to some writers, women were in the forefront of the agricultural revolution, for they traditionally gathered fruits, nuts, and seeds near camps while the men were out hunting. It is hypothesized that over time the female seed collectors may have noticed that a grasslike plant with edible seeds at the tip had grown on the previous year's campsite. Where seeds had been haphazardly strewn in the past, there were now plants that could be eaten right on the spot, eliminating the need to go out and search for food. To test their inferences, the gatherers may have scattered seeds in a spot that had similar rich-looking soil but no plants, to find upon their return the following year that the seeds had grown into plants. Thus began the agricultural revolution (McGregor 1982; Coe 1994).

Around 7000 B.C., seed gatherers settled in the Tehuacan Valley, just southeast of present-day Mexico City. Here occurred a concerted program of plant domestication—or what is termed "evolution directed by the interference" of humans (Coe 1994:29). The first seeds produced an edible part the size of a copper penny. After fifty-five hundred years of gradual change, the Indians were able to increase its size and yield until they developed the present form of maize (modern corn).

Once this discovery was made, others followed. Beans and squash joined maize as the primary staples in the diet known as the American trinity. Other crops and products native to the New World are chile, which is high in vitamin C and useful in digesting cellulose products (see Andrews 1984, for a fascinating array of illustrations and information on a variety of chilies), pineapples, peanuts, potatoes, avocados, chocolate, tomatoes (which helped change a leavened bread and olive oil dish into pizza!), pumpkins, strawberries, tapioca, quinine, maple syrup, vanilla, cashew nuts, and pepper. These products were the major food sources for both natives and, later, Europeans; in fact, these foods add up to one half of the modern world's aggregate agricultural wealth (Coe 1994; Ruiz 1992).[2]

Most modern people are unaware of this early cultivation, and Indians have not been given full credit on this account. "Middle America, particularly in the highlands of Mexico and Guatemala, is one of the four or five primary centers of plant domestication in the world. Here . . . an array of other plants was gradually brought under cultivation" (Helms 1975:18). The reliance on these foods, along with small game such as turkeys, decidedly changed the Indians in most of Mesoamerica from meat-eating hunters to settled farmers.

One cannot overstate the importance of agriculture. Fertile valleys and water-filled streams were sought out by former hunters and plant gatherers. As so much in culture change, it was a process of diffusion that spread the techniques and tools to other areas and many heretofore hunters and gatherers, thus accelerating their cultural growth.

In this way humankind was brought to an important point in historical development. They had time now to expand on and improve other

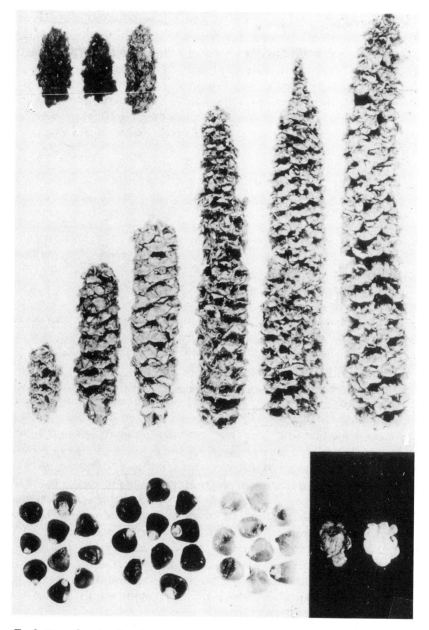

Evolution of maize (corn).

social and cultural practices. Moving from a nomadic life to an established, sedentary, agricultural one allowed for the development of many other artifacts and practices, including pottery and the arts, religious beliefs and rituals, and more elaborate tribal organizations.

By using technology to improve their ability to adapt environmentally, early natives rose to high levels of civilization. Crude tools were replaced by many more sophisticated ones, and more time was available to pursue other activities. Running and chasing were superseded by sitting, thinking, and creating.

Refinement of Sociocultural Life

At the outset, social and cultural features remained rudimentary, primarily because farming equipment and tasks were simple. Later, as farming practices became more elaborate and cultivation efforts intensified, sociocultural traits grew in complexity. In effect, advanced technology released human labor for other activities, especially the thinking and planning needed to secure these new ways of doing things. Organizing the new, larger community and establishing the different habits and newly-needed customs began to dominate human activity.

By at least 2000 B.C., among the ongoing transformations, religion and military patterns grew in importance. Nominal leaders among the hunters became warrior chieftains to help expand the territory for farming pursuits. Shaman-priests emerged and invoked the blessings of the heavens for the planting, irrigating, growing, and harvesting of maize. Raised earthen platforms were built for the shaman-priests to conduct rituals and ceremonies. Careful observation and scientific study of celestial movement—stars, sun, and moon—became increasingly important. The movements of the sun and other stars were keys to the development of calendars, the basis of knowledge of when to sow and when to harvest. Warriors and the military complex helped protect and preserve this essential activity as they also worked to expand the land base to support a larger population (Hassig 1992). Thus, the people of the community soon began to seek direction from both warriors and priests.

Crude earthen pit-houses were built as permanent residences. "The population grew as the cultivation of corn grew . . . men had time to make life more comfortable. They began to build better shelters, improve their preparations for food, and to accumulate possessions . . . families lived close together near good farming land in order to share in the field work and the protection of the crops, and so the first permanent tiny communities came into existence" (Peterson 1962:31; see also Fiedel 1992).

Several other factors were involved in the expansion of social and cultural features. They include, first, "the appearance of sedentary farming villages; second, the rise of small temples or ceremonial centers; third, the development of civilization with populations clustering around temple centers in true urban zones or living in temple-center-with-outlying-hamlet arrangements; and fourth, the formation of expansionistic civilizations dominating large territorial states" (Willey et al. 1964:488). This ordering corresponds in general to the sequence in which such events unfolded. To insure that the accumulated knowledge could be passed on to future generations, record-keeping devices, including written language, were developed. These in turn brought changes to art forms such as pottery, jewelry, and murals. Specialization in various trades and skills became the rule of the day. Religious leaders, warriors, healers, and potters were only the first in a long line of new occupations.

Religion became the most important profession for a number of reasons, not least of which was its effect on other roles and occupations. A large array of gods evolved whose perceived existence helped stabilize the relationship between humans and their environment. Rain gods were the most important among them, for they were needed to balance the forces of nature and insure that the agricultural system succeeded. Thus, deities constantly had to be nourished, sustained, and worshiped; monumental temples dedicated to them began to grace the land. As will be noted later, religious customs and duties dominated the life of the Aztecs, especially in their artistic expression.

Olmecs—Mother Culture

Around 1500 B.C., one group of Indians, the Olmecs—"people from the land of rubber" (Weaver 1993)—reached a refined and sophisticated level of cultural grandeur. Other groups learned from them and prospered. Because of this influence, they have been referred to as the *Cultura Madre*, or Mother Culture. They inhabited the lowland region south of Vera Cruz, along the eastern coast of Mexico, where the modern states of Tabasco, Campeche, and Yucatan converge. Their cultural glory lasted until 300 B.C. In subsequent centuries, other Mesoamerican groups inherited the Olmec tradition and readapted it to their own purposes. In different time periods, the Huastecas flourished in northeastern Mexico; the Mayas in the southeast, reaching as far as Central America; the Teotihuacanos in the central Mexican plateau; and the Zapotecs in the southwest. These groups "only represent different cultures within a civilization, just as western Christianity is but one civilization in spite of differences that exist between Spanish, German, or English cultures" (Bernal 1969:187–88; see also Cantrell 1984).

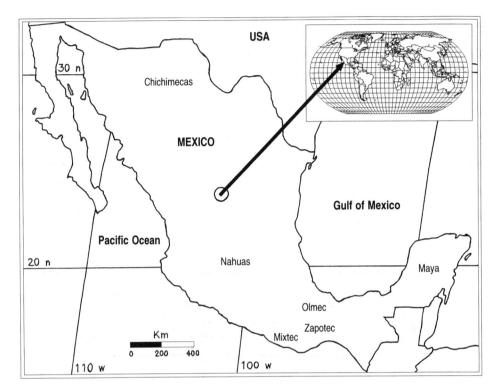

Major cultural groups in Mesoamerica.

The Olmec era is a watershed in the growth of ancient indigenous civilizations. It emerged suddenly as the culmination of all the contributions made by earlier, unnamed peoples, and it blossomed beyond compare (Weaver 1993). Many of the significant cultural achievements identified with ancient Mexico stem from Olmec innovations, such as the development of the calendar, the invention of the zero concept, and the creation of a system of writing. Other features of Olmec life included stone temples and pyramids, ornate personal dress for the budding elite, commercial networks, defensive fortifications, and sea travel. Hence, this early civilization provided the basis on which the following general cultural foundations were laid.

Some of the features shared by native groups were "hieroglyphic writing ... books ... maps ... a complicated calendar ... astronomy ... a team game resembling basketball ... markets and favored ports of trade; wars for the purpose of securing sacrificial victims; large-scale human sacrifice; private confession and penance ... tobacco smoking; and a pantheon of extraordinary complexity" (Coe 1962:17–19). The many basalt stone heads and jaguar art forms found on Olmec sites are a further testimony to the growth of human culture, especially underscoring organizational ability and social structure (Sharer and Grove 1989). The gigantic heads seem to suggest the development of a higher consciousness and awareness and advancement to a more profound level, thus a head with no neck or body. The jaguar, in contrast, was considered a cult animal, a type of guardian of the spirit that endowed a person with special, mystical powers. Every person had such a *nagual* (spirit) to accompany them through life.

It is relatively unimportant whether religious-philosophical beliefs were imported from Asia or conceived in the New World. What is significant is that natives early developed a mythological basis for spiritual endeavors. That spirituality represents a recognition of the contrasting forces all around them: The external, material reality was joined by the internal spiritual world, and this vision of duality permeated other aspects of life. They assigned "the original foundation of the world to a supreme dual principle, Our Mother—Our Father, which was the origin

Olmec basalt head.

of everything which exists" (Leon-Portilla 1969:30). The Olmecs believed, for example, that the jaguar's spots symbolized day and night, fire and ice, heaven and hell; the rest of the world was also viewed in this way. Life-death, sun-earth, light-dark, fire-water, male-female, father-mother are but a few of the dualities of the real and imagined features of life (Cantrell 1984).

Dual existence was the abiding hallmark, the teaching that ordered their life. One side of any duality could not be embraced or thoroughly understood unless its counterpart was acknowledged. Mother-earth took on more meaning when joined by father-sun. Similarly, an appreciation of water-heaven could occur only when fire-hell was introduced. Generally, those who adhered to this spiritual orientation, accepting and integrating these oppositions into their very being, charted a broadened life path.

Cache of Olmec jade figures from Gulf Coast plain.

Tens of thousands of Indians over a long period of time participated in the building of Mesoamerica. Like the ocean tide, surging and ebbing, each Indian group took the lead and then lost it to another group through internal decay or foreign encroachment. Of course, progressive changes transpired during these millennia as groups added their particular contributions to the sophistication and complexity that accompanied an agricultural base. However, it is in the nature of human technological and sociocultural evolution to have ups and downs. The periodic moving forward and standing still are universally shared human patterns of evolution. As Will Durant once stated, human and cultural evolution can be compared to the accelerator and brakes of an automobile: One is for moving forward at any speed and the other is for slowing down and stopping when it is appropriate (Durant 1983). In any event, after about A.D. 500 Mesoamerica remained on the same cultural plane.

Chichimecas—Migration from Aztlan

Beginning in A.D. 900, about four centuries into this cultural plateau, a wave of migrations lasting several centuries swept the valley of Mexico and upset the stability of the area. The Chichimecas (meaning "lineage of the dog," a proud appellation like the valued "dog soldiers" of the Plains Indians) came from the far desert northwestern region. Interestingly, the historical and cultural connections between these northern groups and the resident, central valley Mexican indigenous peoples was quite old and deep. Many architectural features, cultural habits, language (the Uto-Aztecan family), and trade routes show how geography (or "geopolitical" catchment, where the coterminous northern Mexican desert and southwest American desert join) influences cultural evolution and diffusion (Mathien and McGuire 1986; Suarez 1982).

Chichimecas were from a desert culture in the intermediate area between tillable lands in the modern United States and Mexico. They were forced into a cyclical nomadic pattern that fluctuated with the climate, sometimes farming with limited productivity, but more often food gatherers and "communal" hunters of rabbits. In time, they began to raid the northern reaches of the central valley of Mexico (Coe 1994, 1962). The Chichimecas either forced their way into the region or simply filled the vacuum left by others, or both. According to legend, they had migrated from Aztlan, their mythological homeland, which is now either northern Mexico or the southwestern United States (Townsend 1992).

The Chichimecas later absorbed many of the cultural traits of previous residents of the area, but "warfare and military expansion on the one hand, intensive agriculture and the appropriation of surpluses

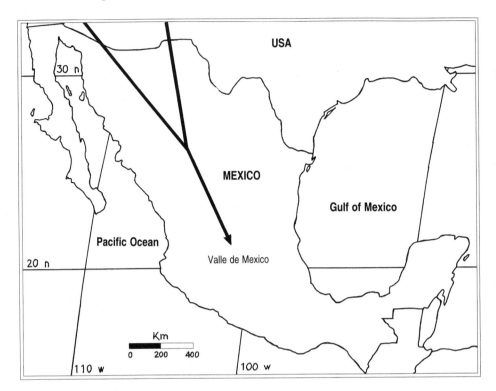

Chichemeca migrations.

through tribute payments on the other, are the hallmarks of this new period" (Wolf 1959:117; see also Hassig 1992).

The Toltecas were the first of several subgroups within the generic Chichimeca population to establish hegemony in Central Mexico; they were closely linked to indigenous groups that remained in the Aztlan region (Molitar 1981; Riley 1987). Borrowing from earlier people, especially the Olmecas, Teotihuacanos, and Mayas, they settled at Tula in A.D. 968. Here blossomed a cultural epicenter from which Toltec rulers could dominate others in the valley. Borrowing and readapting the culture and lifeways of the settled inhabitants, the Toltecas soon fashioned a grand "high" culture, to which subsequent groups looked back with admiration (Mathien and McGuire 1986; Riley 1987).

Many other Chichimeca subgroups eventually found a niche in the area. Most of them spoke the Nahua language and generally followed a militaristic way of life. Before incorporating the cultural habits of the valley, they filled active roles as mercenaries in the power struggles that were under way.

Toltec ruins of warrior pillar in Tula. ▶

After Toltecan rule ended in A.D. 1156, another wave of migration brought a group later to gain power and fame: the Aztecs. With most of the tillable farmland already occupied, the Aztecs at first wandered about, hiring themselves out as mercenaries. Later they found a temporary refuge in Michoacan in western Mexico. Still not satisfied with that location, they finally moved to a most undesirable spot in A.D. 1325 (Ruiz 1992).

According to myth, the Aztec warrior-god leader Mexitli followed explicit instructions from heaven to find a spot suitable for his people. This location would be visibly apparent. They were to look for an eagle with a serpent in its mouth, stationed on a lone cactus in the middle of a large lake. And so it happened as foretold. "The place was called Tenochtitlan, in token of its miraculous origin, though only known to Europeans by its other name, Mexico City, derived from their war-god, Mexitli" (Prescott 1931:16). This miraculous sign notwithstanding, it was not until A.D. 1430, after much intrigue and warfare, that the Aztecs were able to secure a stable foothold in the area. With this beginning, they established themselves as the last Indian group to reign over the central plateau.

Notes

[1] Mesoamerica refers to a cultural region encompassing an area just north of the central plateau of Mexico City and all the way down to the northern nations of Central America.

[2] Major nonfood agricultural products first domesticated in the Americas include cotton (a similar species was domesticated separately in the Near East), rubber, chicle (chewing gum), tobacco, and cocaine, among others.

Chapter **2**

Intact and Stable Social Order

Most of the basic attributes of civilization were firmly established during the Aztec period, laying the foundation for further cultural and intellectual refinement. Thousands of years of ancient developments preceded the Aztecs, who both benefited from the past and built for the future. As indigenous inhabitants, inheritors of a separate and independent evolution, they followed a communal and agricultural tradition.

It is clear that Aztec society facilitated the satisfaction of human drives such as hunger and thirst, cemented the willpower to satisfy needs, and steered the populace in the preservation of time-honored customs and habits. Further innovation and growth was made possible by the solid grounding of Aztec social and cultural institutions. This period reflects the indigenous stage of social and cultural evolution, and underscores these factors: (1) biological drives were better met; (2) learning through trial and error and emulation of others was becoming increasingly important to societal maintenance; (3) as more and more energy was captured with the aid of larger numbers of humans over a wider expanse of territory, other difficulties and strains arose; and (4) in spite of these accomplishments, a sense of uncertainty still pervaded the scene, as impending flux and ferment filled the air. The comparison of Aztec cultural attainment with this stage of cultural evolution is generally valid for pre-Columbian life.

Class: Nobility Supported by Commoners

Aztecs organized a social stratification system that was a bundle of contradictions. One interpretation is that it was a nonegalitarian aristocracy (Berdan 1982; Coe 1962, 1994), while another rendition seems to support a basically democratic situation (Morgan 1963). Because the social system was based on past communal traditions that were breaking down under the weight of complex changes, it appears that both views are correct for different times. "The Aztec nobility . . . began to grow. . . . The continual expansion of the aristocracy undoubtedly diminished the importance of the tribal organizations—the calpullis [groups of houses]—which comprised the common people" (Villegas et al. 1974:39). The system was initially egalitarian and had, over a century, gradually become less so (Berdan 1982, 1989). Yet there were moments when older practices prevailed in the midst of the new ones. While this was not exactly democratic in the purest sense, it did seem to incorporate elements of equality (Townsend 1992; Padden 1967).

Life of Indian nobility.

Recognizing that role-class assignments were necessary, the Aztecs sought to prevent social conflict and disintegration with a community-oriented ideological framework. This was undertaken at the expense of the individual, who now was taught to integrate his interests and direct his duties to those of the total group. In a sense the Aztecs put much effort into developing a political system that mirrored and indeed supported the unificatory nature of their culture and economy (Coe 1994; Soustelle 1967). Thus, as a state-level society, they took on the responsibility of developing a collective ideology and destiny.

Land System

The basis of Aztec society was a land and agrarian community that evolved around the most important natural resource: the people. In general, land belonged to the people in common; their labor built a sophisticated *chinampas* (irrigation agriculture, floating gardens) system and produced basic necessities (Berdan 1982; Townsend 1992). Consequently, a large share of the wealth was returned to them. However, as noted earlier, this arrangement had undergone important transformations with the rise of a ruling elite, and with the gradual eroding away of a people-oriented land system there arose a new practice, perhaps an incipient form of *latifundia* (large landed estates).

The backbone of the earlier arrangement was the *calpulli*, a socioeconomic unit based on kinship (blood and social relations) and territoriality (ownership of the land required for subsistence) (Coe 1994; Berdan 1982). Some even state that it was a "big house" of families with a common ancestor (Leon-Portilla 1988, 1992). Each calpulli possessed a set amount of territory for its own use. Rights of land tenure and ownership were carefully outlined, as were water and irrigation rights, timberland rights, hunting privileges, and farming for household consumption and market bartering. Each calpulli set boundaries with maguey plants, stone walls, and worn footpaths. Trespassers from other calpullis were subject to prosecution and punishment (Berdan 1989; Whetten 1969).

Social Classes and Life

The members within each calpulli were known as *macequales* (commoners, or citizens of the confederacy), who comprised about 85 percent of the population. Most macequale household heads, working on about a ten-acre plot, had enough food to support themselves and their families. Ambitious individuals who labored harder and longer each day were granted the right to farm untilled calpulli land. This added incentive and investment allowed them to use surplus earnings for bartering at the marketplace. The macequales also were periodically called upon to provide labor service to ruling elites or for public works.

Family life was well ordered, with each member learning about and carrying out his responsibilities. Children were taught to respect their parents, grandparents, and aunts and uncles. Living arrangements followed a pattern: "each house was surrounded by a little garden. . . .

Figurine of a standard-bearer.

These more modest homes had foundations made of stone; their adobe walls supported a flat roof of beams. . . . One rectangular room sufficed to lodge an entire family; for the kitchen, granary, and bathhouse were separately installed in the garden" (Villegas et al. 1974:37). Their primary staple was maize, and fields of small hillocks planted with maize dotted the surrounding countryside. When it came time to harvest, the women would gather the maize and grind it into flour, which would then be used to make tamales, or else they pounded the maize dough into flat tortillas and baked them over slow-burning fires. Beans, fruits, and vegetables were also grown in abundance, as well as various types of tasty chiles (Foster and Cordell 1992; Andrews 1984). "The Aztec diet was basically vegetarian, supplemented by fish, wild fowl and game; they raised no domesticated animals as significant food resources" (Townsend 1992:172). Most of the food and cooking techniques were native creations and were named with Nahuatl words: *metate* (grinding stone), *mano* (stone hand grinder), and so on.

In addition to the macequales in social class status, there were two other groups: the *mayeques* and the *tlacotin*. The mayeques, never more than 2 or 3 percent of the population, were like marginal persons, that is, without certain rights held by the macequales. They worked the fields for the rulers on a permanent basis. Similar to serfs, they received only enough to maintain their households. Another slave-type class, the tlacotin, consisted of those who sold themselves to the rulers for a set amount of time and lived on their land as permanent laborers, some of whom improved their lot by gambling or criminal activity. Their tenure could last a few years or a lifetime, but their offspring could not be born into slavery. They comprised 3 or 4 percent of the people, and when coupled with the mayeques never rose above 10 percent of the total population.

It is important to note that the growth in numbers of these two groups increased in direct proportion to the steady expansion of a ruling elite—the latter being former calpulli members who had left agricultural work for positions of political and cultural leadership. Thus, it was a status system based on both ascription and achievement, combining caste (or birthright) and class (mobility) elements (Berdan 1982).

Each calpulli was composed of a group of families related by kin and residing together (Leon-Portilla 1988, 1992). Some observers question the importance of "blood" in the kinship network; in other words, kin ties may have been fictive (Wolf 1959), but it is nevertheless clear that the emphasis on "social" kin relations functioned to make the calpulli a cohesive unit. Often the members of a single calpulli would number into the thousands. "In addition to its function as a localized, land-holding corporation, the calpulli also had ritual functions in that it had its own temple, and gods, and an association. . . . There were approximately twenty calpoltin [plural of calpulli in Nahuatl] in Tenochtitlan, some of which have actually persisted as traditional barrios near the center of modern Mexico City" (Coe 1994:167).

Several local *tlatoques* (speakers) would be elected to serve as a "natural" calpulli high council, and from their ranks one person would be designated the calpulli "speaker" (Townsend 1992). All the supreme calpulli leaders met as a council to advise the head of government (Berdan 1989). However, this egalitarian practice of allowing calpulli leaders access to the higher echelons of government was increasingly being phased out.

Rise of the State

Since the Aztecs profited from earlier technologies and thus were able to support a larger population, it similarly followed that social relations would also change. In early Aztec society, tlatoques were selected from the ranks of the people. These natural leaders knew the people well, for they were of the people and made decisions with their consent. The gradual replacement of a grassroots democracy with an aristocracy was one of the major social changes. This did not mean, however, that the achievements of individuals from the lower classes were no longer recognized and duly rewarded. Although the aristocracy was protective of its exalted position in society, class boundaries were permeable enough to allow worthy lower-born men to ascend into and invigorate the elite (Soustelle 1961).

It can be postulated that a particular calpulli eventually became entrenched as the leading group. Perhaps it became all-powerful because of its military prowess. At first its actions benefited the total community, but before long it had become a hereditary ruling body and no longer took the interests of the community to heart. Coe states that "a society evolved from a primitive organization in which all lands were originally held by the clans . . . [and] there was no higher authority than clan chiefs, into a fully fledged state with the appearance of a privileged class . . . . Given time, the clans would have certainly declined to total insignificance" (Coe 1962:165). Hence, having initially been seen as merely the extension of the tribe, the city-state had become a force for the acquisition of neighboring territories and resources. The consequences of this development were unfortunate, as class differences grew more pronounced, and animosities between the aristocracy and the lower classes began to surface. Natural leaders, tlatoque, gradually gained control over their own private lands and had the tribute and labor of mayeques at their disposal (Berdan 1982).

The members of this ruling group became known as the *pipiltin* (rule by the elite, nobles), presumably descended from Toltec lineage and thus, because of that lineage, superior to other natural leaders. Never more than 2 to 10 percent of the populace, they directed religious and political concerns from the center of the city. Although power was concentrated in their hands, they still were charged with the duties of administration, government, and religion. Because these responsibilities were typically handled fairly and efficiently, the people generally supported their rule. As a matter of fact, the rule of Texcoco, one of the neighboring city allies, was very democratic. Here, the bureaucracy consisted of a number of neatly organized tribunals of varying degrees of influence. The most significant governing event occurred in the capital, where a general meeting or convention was held every eighty days (Prescott 1931).

The primary support for the pipiltin came from the tribute of the macequales. This was paid in two ways: contribution of a set amount of produce and labor service for a certain number of days on pipiltin land. Thus, it would have behooved the pipiltin to keep an open ear to macequale demands so long as the latter remained dutiful and productive. After all, it was the macequales' extra efforts that released the pipiltin from working the land, allowing them to devote their energy to civic and religious chores.

Priestly duties were closely linked to the pipiltin rule. For example, the emperor Motecuhzoma (Coe 1994) ruled over a very complex and multifaceted society. His powers were immense and absolute, and his word was the law. Since he also was technically the high priest of the state religion, his person was seen as being divinely derived and not of this earth. The early chronicler Fray Bernardino de Sahagun describes the great array of deities and the priests who served them, but especially noteworthy in his account was how priests were selected. "These two pontiffs were equal in standing and honor, even if they should be of very low birth and of very lowly and poor parents; the only reason why they were elected to be the high pontiffs was their having faithfully complied with and followed all the customs, rules, exercises and teachings" (Sahagun 1932:202).

Occupations other than those based on agrarian life also were held by the macequales. Their organization of society was based on social status, and depending on a person's occupation, they lived either in the town or in the adjoining settlements. Those who dwelt in the city were the warriors who made up the standing army (*tectecuhtin*), those who sold and traded goods (*pochteca*), and skilled artisans such as goldsmiths and featherworkers. The merchants and artisans were organized into hereditary guilds located in the residential sections of the town. In short, the pipiltin held the leadership positions in the city and the macequales filled the agrarian roles in the country and skilled occupations in the city.

The class of merchants known as pochteca came into being as trade with other Indian groups throughout Mesoamerica developed. They provided a dual service when away on trading expeditions. They gathered foreign information as spies and they represented Aztec commercial interests. However, because Aztec leaders feared the potential power of the pochtecas, they were watched very closely. Some pochtecas harbored entrepreneurial ambitions and desired to build a separate business dynasty. Wolf (1959:140) suggests that if the pochteca were discovered to be independently accruing wealth, they were put to death and their wealth was redistributed; as a result, they "made a special effort to appear humble and poor." In contrast, recent interpretations appear to show that the pochteca also participated in

Temple ruins in Tulum, Quintana Roo, Mexico

Chac-Mool statue in Chichen Itza, Yucatan, Mexico.

"potlatch feasts" as a way to redistribute resources and wealth (Berdan 1982).

Caution should be taken here to avoid perceiving the pochteca and pipiltin as bourgeois and aristocratic classes comparable to those of Europe. Although there are some similarities between the two, the feudal system of Europe had its own characteristics that simply do not exist here. Prescott (1931:22) chided Spanish historians for being too "fond of tracing analogies to European models" and argued that the Aztecs should be evaluated on their own terms. Nevertheless, one cannot resist the temptation to compare the macrohistorical and evolutionary paths characteristic of the two continents.

Every civilization that has grouped over one-half million citizens in one location, as the Aztecs did, has had to establish and maintain a system of law and order. The people of Tenochtitlan were guided by a code of laws ordering behavior, and if they deviated or were remiss, well-defined methods of enforcement ensued. One supreme judge, chosen for life with veto powers over the king, interpreted the law and meted out decisions for all the people. Lesser judicial officials were appointed for each calpulli district and for the remaining outlying provinces of the confederacy, or league of states. A network of higher and lower courts guaranteed that all citizens, no matter where they resided in the central region, would receive a swift and fair legal decision when a law was broken. Social stability was maintained also by a police force.

Confederacy and Trade

To further the interests of the people, it was necessary for the Aztecs to establish diplomatic alliances and commercial relations with other groups. Interpretations of the Aztec means of doing this continue to generate controversy. In 1430 they created an alliance that was later to expand into a confederacy, or empire, as some experts have suggested that the Aztecs were military imperialists (Berdan 1982). Two other Nahuatl-speaking cities, Texcoco and Tlacopan, joined the Aztecs to share obligations and increase their security. During the later expansionist wars, both cities aided in the Aztec military campaigns: Tlacopan provided supply carriers, and Texcoco sent warriors. This triple alliance was able to gain and maintain control over the whole central plateau of Mexico.

In the process of expansion and conquering other tribes, the prevailing type of rule was not that of a single consolidated state but the coexistence of many loosely knit state-like provinces, which retained a modicum of self-rule. Indeed, it was an organization composed of many cultures and languages, with the Nahuatls speaking their own tongue along with the Otomis, Mazahuas, Maya, and many more (Soustelle

1967). This ruling system benefited the Aztecs, for they could not afford to station a permanent military force in the outlying provinces. Nevertheless, in comparison to most imperial systems, it was rather egalitarian. As in the transition between an egalitarian calpulli and an incipient ruling elite, this confederacy may have been part of an evolutionary phase toward a centralized system in which even more energy was controlled and dominated. Nevertheless, one sixteenth-century observer noted that the native rulers of conquered lands were left in place, as were local languages and cultural practices (Zorita 1963). Berdan (1982:109) maintains that "after a conquest, Aztecs usually refrained from pillaging or destroying the city. The imperial Aztec goal was to add provinces to their empire, to provide them with continuous and assured supplies of goods through tribute, not the spoils of a one-time sacking."

On the whole, in spite of some rivalry among the main allies, the confederacy was able to function fairly smoothly. Under this political unit, far-reaching trade activities were undertaken with other regions north to the modern state of Durango, east and west to the Atlantic and Pacific Oceans, and as far south as Nicaragua. Tenochtitlan, as the leading city of the triple alliance, provided these conquered regions with military protection from other warring tribes and in return received tribute from all thirty-eight provinces that constituted the Aztec empire. This tribute—paid yearly—took on many forms. Usually it was paid with basic foodstuffs such as maize, beans, amaranth, dried chile peppers, and maquey honey, but the giving of other items such as cloth, pottery bowls, and native paper was not unusual (Helms 1975). Groups that were unable to contribute agricultural products gave tribute in the form of labor.

Tenochtitlan reigned supreme over the entire valley. Tlatelolco, its twin marketplace city, served up to sixty thousand people daily. There the shoppers would purchase the innumerable items and services available and pay for them by bartering or with money, the latter being either cacao beans or quetzal bird quills filled with gold.

Generally, then, the socioeconomic and political practices of the Aztecs were shaped to benefit the total community. Interestingly, although the pipiltin were the elite group, macequales who showed talent and intelligence were given the opportunity to attend their schools. Thus, some egalitarianism yet remained.

Culture: Pantheon of Gods, Moral Order, and Literary Tradition

Like most peoples, the Aztecs had their positive and negative traits, ranging from a tendency toward military oppression to their cultivation

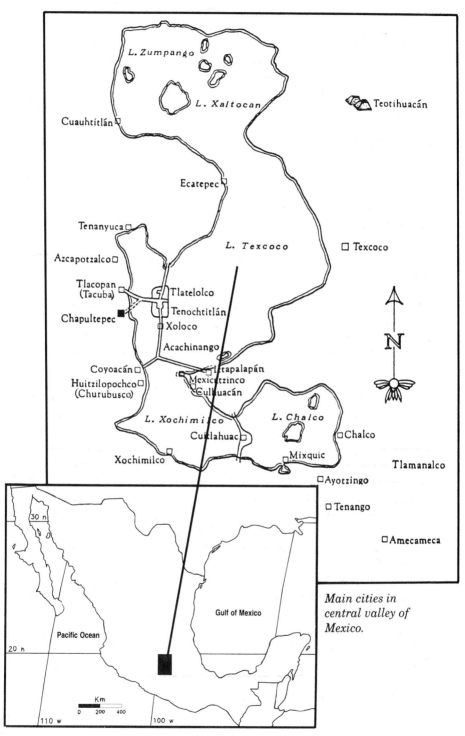

Main cities in central valley of Mexico.

of a very refined, sensitive, and morally based culture. This cultural theme embodies all that the Aztecs represent. Learning from the world around them and from the contributions of earlier Indians, they embraced the dual nature of reality. They were similar to the Greeks, who combined the body (materialism) and soul (spirituality) in their paideia: A man should become a speaker of words (soul) and a doer of deeds (body). Here is how the Aztecs phrased their ideal (Leon-Portilla 1963:135):

> The mature man
> is a heart solid as a rock,
> is a wise face,
> possessor of a face,
> possessor of a heart,
> he is able and understanding

To this end, all people from youth onward were taught by their parents and teachers to develop their "heart" (soul) and "face" (body). Always uppermost in their mind as they pursued this goal was how best to serve the community, and religion was the glue for this communal goal (Leon-Portilla 1992). Importantly, females fared relatively well with "an ideology which stressed tribal identity over gender, and the common plight of humankind over tribe, [and] allowed them to escape definition as 'other'" (Clendinnen 1991:206).

Religious principles encompassed this view of humankind and guided the people to be as one with nature. The breadth and scope of their religious beliefs, based on set, formal practices and the internalization of their legends, encompassed and permeated nearly every facet of a person's life. The nation itself was marked by the constancy of its religion, and it governed all levels and aspects of society. It was a major determinant in people's lives from the moment they were born to the time of their passing, dominating even the realms of art and sporting (Scarborough and Wilcox 1991). In fact, there was nothing that existed that did not have the heavy imprint of religion on it (Berdan 1982; Soustelle 1961).

Education

The educational system was structured to fulfill the lofty goal set forth by the guiding religious tenets. Accordingly, regardless of socioeconomic background, all male citizens were entitled to participate in a universal system of education. Females were socialized for domestic duties and affairs, which oftentimes included artistic and craft activities, and for that time enjoyed a relatively high status and prestige as wives and mothers. As noted previously, many intelligent children of humble origins were placed in the higher schools, where all the spiritual and intellectual knowledge was found in great books. "The priests were in charge of educating the young people; they were custodians of esoteric knowledge, wisdom, and tradition, of the two calendars, and of the art of writing in painted books and inscriptions" (Leon-Portilla 1969:4). All instruction was conducted in the Nahuatl language.

This constant, daily struggle to balance the dual human drives of environmental adaptation and spiritual betterment was not always successful. There were numerous instances when either material or spiritual practices, or both together, failed completely. And yet, in spite of the many failures, there were more successes, and this undoubtedly stemmed from the almost obsessive religious devotion of the Aztecs. It appeared that the guidance they sought from the heavens enabled them to change and readapt on a continuous basis.

School life was built around two types of learning environments. The *calmecac* (higher college) was devoted to the intellect and spirit, and there the leaders and priests received training. In the *telpochcalli* (arsenal), the crafts of the military warrior were taught. Because military prowess was a highly valued skill, most young men attended the telpochcalli (Hassig 1988). As a military power, the Aztecs had to maintain control of the valley of Mexico, insuring that the resources and people remained under their domination. Many liberties were granted those trained at this institution, but a rigorous upbringing under the aegis of religion instilled physical and mental discipline for the production of hardy warriors. In brief, one might say that the calmecac was an intellectual and spiritual school (perhaps analogous to the best of Harvard and Notre Dame), while the telpochcalli was strictly military (like West Point) (Peterson 1962). Although formal education was geared primarily toward the males, females had occasion to attend the *cuicacalli* (house of songs), and some noblewomen were allowed to become priestesses (Berdan 1982).

Official state instruction began at about six years old, when parents would take their sons to school. However, education was initiated much earlier in the home, the father ministering to the sons and the mother to the daughters (Berdan 1989). Such an urgent emphasis was placed on quickly preparing the children for the assumption of adult responsibilities, that teaching was begun as early as three years old, after the child had already been weaned. The case of females in this instance appears to support a somewhat egalitarian role for them, as marriage obligations and domestic duties were accorded high status and importance, especially given that a strong military flavor permeated Aztec society (Clendinnen 1991).

Religious Practices and Moral Code

As noted previously, religion was more than a segment of Aztec life. Accordingly, every day was a holy day and every member of the community was a part of the collective worship. "It was by religion that the city and tribe were one, and by religion that variety was unified" (Soustelle 1961:93). Charged by such a spiritual force, they viewed poetry as a way of gaining an ultimate understanding of reality and as a way of expressing the results of their inspirations (Leon-Portilla 1992). Much of their artistic and creative activity centered on religious beliefs and practices (Carrasco 1990, 1992). Agriculture products and activities were never far from religious ceremonies and rituals, for maize consumption and farming routines were essential to the preservation of the community.

Aztecs believed that beyond mortal life were heaven, hell, and purgatory (these differed in many particulars from the Christian counterparts, however) (Markman and Markman 1992). Warriors who died in battle were rewarded with heaven, a serene place of flowers, birds, clouds, and sunshine. Those who died in sin fell to a dark forbidding hell. A neutral, intermediate purgatory awaited those who had not given service to the community. Forgiveness for one's sins was possible through confession, in which both spiritual and temporal absolution were granted. As Aztec law allowed only one confession for each individual lifetime, not surprisingly, most waited until old age to confess their sins.

There were many other rituals and ceremonies in which citizens actively participated, including baptism with holy water to ward off evil spirits, and dozens of supplicatory prayers—incantations, poems, or songs—directed to one of the many deities, a commemorative holy day, or for a cure for a particular ailment (Berdan 1982; Leon-Portilla 1963). The people's faith in these practices equaled the height of fervor and devotion reached by other world religions.

Worshiping the gods by prayer was not enough, for the community also undertook large-scale projects in building pyramids (and, for lesser deities, smaller buildings). A whole pantheon of deities was honored in this way, each with his or her own temple of a size to reflect the patron god's importance or insignificance and reflective of the syncretic nature of the Aztec religion that borrowed and absorbed from others (Berdan 1982). Among the most important of the pantheon figures was Huitzilopochtli, the sun god, who had evolved from a mixture of many deities the Aztecs had incorporated on their journey to central Mexico (Townsend 1992). According to tribal myth, the Aztecs were now in the fifth world of creation—the previous four had been destroyed by wind, water, fire, and the earth. This fifth world was named *El Quinto Sol* (the Fifth Sun). According to one source, "When the world was still in darkness the gods resolved to make a 'sun' that illuminated the earth and. . . . this sun ate hearts and drank blood, and for this [it was necessary] for them to create war where hearts and blood could be had" (Florescano 1994:9).

Symbol of Aztec god of death.

Because of the failure of past worlds through one catastrophe or another, the natives feared the destruction of this one. Thus, they took it upon themselves to conduct ceremonies to keep the sun alive. These earlier cycles of rain and drought, feast and famine, peace and destruction, had instilled a fear of the unknown, and as the famous philosopher/poet/king Nezahualcoyotl suggested, the transitory character and absolute ephemerality inherent in all that exists cannot be ignored (Coe 1994; Gillespie 1989; Leon-Portilla 1992).

Every day, with the rising of the sun, the priests would sacrifice human beings, cutting out their hearts. Offerings of hearts made at the top of the temple dedicated to Huitzilopochtli guaranteed his daily return. This important act of creation, the rising of the sun, kept the people from total darkness and had to be propitiated. Thousands of people were sacrificed in this manner, for their precious blood, *chalchihuatl*, was the only suitable nourishment for the sun (Padden 1967). Mostly a ritualistic rather than a bloodletting affair, the Spanish later overemphasized its barbaric elements to excuse their own behavior (Coe 1994). In any event, many of the intended sacrificial victims faced the affair in a solemn manner, and often they received special treatment. Leon-Portilla depicts the austere ceremony in this way: "There were dialogues between different choirs, solemnly recalling myths and religious beliefs. . . . They were all trained to act just once in the cosmic drama of the Aztec perpetual theater. They were messengers from the people, collaborators with the Sun, carefully chosen to begin their journey to the beyond" (Leon-Portilla 1969:98–99). Many of those chosen for sacrifice received royal attention and were granted special privileges for weeks prior to the event. On the whole, like most people who die for a cause, these sacrificial victims bravely served their community (Gillespie 1989).

Other victims were not so blessed. This was especially true of the many prisoners captured in actual or acted-out "flower wars" (Berdan 1989). Mock battles were organized with neighboring tribes, and the captured prisoners were later sacrificed to each tribe's respective gods. Like contemporary wars, this practice was brutal and savage but can also be seen as adaptive. In keeping with expansionism and military logic, "the killings were explicitly about the dominance of the Mexica and of their tutelary deity: public display to overawe the watcher, Mexica or stranger, in a state theater of power, at which the rulers of other and lesser cities, allies and enemies alike, were routinely present" (Clendinnen 1991:92; see also Townsend 1992). According to one writer, from this state of war "arose the strange institution of the war of the flowers, Xochiyaoyotl, which seems to have come into being after the terrible famines which ravaged central Mexico in 1450" (Soustelle 1961:101; see also Hassig 1992).

This overview of cultural life highlights the most striking customs. Other activities worthy of mention are the arts and music, architecture and stone carving, and the many fine crafts, such as sculpture and gold and silver jewelry making. One can observe that here were the recipients of the traditions of an ancient people, the human cultural repository of all that came before, barely beginning to indigenously form their own brand of civilization. According to the evidence, and despite certain paradoxes, Aztec life was both culturally sophisticated and generally contoured to the requirements of the total population. Among their most lasting accomplishments are their foods and cuisine (Sokolov 1991) and folk medicines and remedies (Ortiz de Montellano 1990).

Color: Intragroup Racism

The emphasis on racial features, or racism, as we know it today, did not exist in Aztec society. Of course, there were physiognomic differences between Indian tribes: some were taller than others, higher cheekbones characterized Mayas, broad noses appeared to be an Olmec trait, and so on. These intraracial differences are similar to the heterogeneity found among Caucasian Europeans. Presumably, the French fit the Alpine mold, Swedes are typical Nordics, and Italians are Mediterranean, at least in a general way. In the main, this is also true of pre-Columbian Indians. Certainly, the Aztecs oppressed and exploited other groups in Mesoamerica. In some respects their rule was as severe as that found elsewhere in the world, then and now. Nevertheless, it was not purely racial criteria that determined who was to be subjugated and kept that way.

Culture as a Basis for Oppression

Indeed, racial appearance was not enough to prevent a capable person from rising to the highest position, although higher class status, as we have seen, was beginning to make a difference. Generally, cultural cues—dress, gestures, language, and so on—shaped Aztec thinking and behavior regarding opportunities for social mobility and betterment. The situation was more relaxed within the Aztec group but changed dramatically when outside Indian groups were encountered, with allies faring better than strangers. Enemies, of course, caught the unmitigated wrath of the Aztecs. In these instances, race and racial appearance take a second seat to ethnic nationalism and territorial contests.

So, in brief, the whole notion of racial superiority and inferiority and the attendant psychological ramifications were not present in the social system, at least not in the same way and on a large scale. This was a system in which the conquering peoples maintained control for as long as possible, dominating the hinterland from an urban center. In the case of the Aztecs, and because they were relative newcomers to the valley, theirs was a trail of conquest that absorbed and integrated what existed there. This was an already established pattern, culture makers replaced by culture seekers, and so on. Myth was then used to legitimize the successors' claims to dominance. Aztec leaders, for example, claimed Toltec heritages. "Some Toltec were undoubtedly real; but others were Toltec through myth-making, . . . all conceptions of Tollan and Toltec soon passed into the realm of myth. Those who came after [including the Aztecs] regarded these mythical original Toltec as a race of supermen, taller than ordinary men and able to run faster than decadent later breeds. They were the master artificers, the first scientists, the first astronomers" (Wolf 1959:120). Ruler designation and legitimacy, then, were inconsistent and usually had a cultural basis and, increasingly over time, a class bias.

Chapter 3

Breakup and Transformation of the Social Order

Contact: Conquerors Seek Riches

After years of scouting various parts of the Caribbean basin, the Spanish accidentally discovered Mexico. Directed by Governor Diego Velasquez of Cuba, early expeditions to that land failed, but they returned with rumors of fabulous wealth and set the stage for an enterprise that succeeded, the expedition of Hernando Cortes. In February 1519, Cortes set out with 11 ships, over 600 Spaniards, 16 horses, 10 brass guns, several large dogs, and over 200 Indian and African slaves of both sexes (Berler 1988:13–14; Diaz del Castillo 1956:40–41).

European exploration of the Caribbean region had begun with Columbus's voyage in 1492, and his discovery was not so much of a New World but of contact between two worlds that were already very old. By 1519 the Spanish had subdued many natives in the Caribbean islands and established a strong colony in Cuba. From there they moved north, west, and south, seeking other territories to incorporate into their expanding empire. Aiding them in this exploration and discovery were the recently vanquished natives and many imported African slaves.

Background to Exploration and Discovery

The background to these events begins in Europe. The European desire for goods from the Orient ignited an age of expansionism. The defeat of the Moors, who controlled Mediterranean sea commerce, opened the door for further commercial relations. Spain's interests then turned to building an empire. Tardy in the European rush for new lands and access to resources, the Spanish had their own house to set in order. Belatedly uni-

45

fied in 1469, when the kingdoms of Aragon and Castille were joined through the marriage of Ferdinand and Isabella, they then embarked on casting the Moors out of Granada in 1492. Serious expansionist efforts followed these events (Ruiz 1992; King 1985). In the aftermath, nationalist consolidation was speeded up. Navigational science developed because of the search for riches and commercial ties with the East and made possible the age of discovery and exploration. Adventurous expansionism became fashionable, and many Spaniards were swept away with get-rich-quick schemes.

Spanish success can be attributed to several factors:

1. The tension brought about by the establishment of a centralized government under Ferdinand and Isabella, which encouraged Spanish nationalism and expansionism
2. The control of the strategically located continental gateway between the Mediterranean and the Atlantic
3. The evangelical Catholic zeal and nomadic adventurous ambitions born during the Reconquista (expulsion of the Moors)
4. The obsession to become rich, particularly on the part of dispossessed *segundones* (second sons not entitled to a full share of the family estate because of inheritance laws favoring senior sons), who sought to become *hijos de algo* or *hidalgos* (noblemen, "son of something or someone") through military achievements (Vives 1969:315–16).

The last two influences were particularly instrumental. Many segundones were eager for adventure and enterprise. Joined by other commoners and soldiers of fortune, they set out for the New World. One writer says that the messianic missions were a carryover from earlier times: "These Spaniards were all imbued with the sense of common fellowship fostered in Spain as in all the Latin world by the twofold tradition of Rome—the Imperial and the Christian" (de Madariaga 1947:6).

The motivation provided by fellowship and adventure was strongly augmented by personal ambitions. Spanish soldiers of fortune also sought to become landed aristocrats, along the lines of the old Roman principle of *occupatio,* or occupancy. This concept was based on a complex set of laws that translated into a natural "possession is nine points of the law" way to expand and control new territory. This acceptable practice of the Reconquista set the ground for the takeover of the Western Hemisphere (Padden 1967). Thus, *conquistadores* (conquerors) had reason to expect a prestigious title and landed estate in the Americas. Garnering wealth for the Crown and themselves, the conquistadores pushed discovery and colonization efforts to exploit new resources and establish new systems of control even as they disseminated Christianity.

Cortes Begins Conquest

Upon setting foot in Mexico, the Spaniards under Cortes immediately established themselves as conquerors. In the first encounter over fifteen hundred Yucatan Mayas died, while the victors lost only thirty-seven men. Moving toward the center of Mexico, the Spaniards repeated this bloody pattern. To maintain military superiority, they often wiped out whole Indian groups. Numerous tribes were met and dealt with summarily. Some small disorganized tribes were quickly subjugated. Others, larger and more socially united, required more time and effort. Cortes directed this process with skillful (although unfeeling) military genius.

Cortes and his men were initially ignorant of Indian languages. As a result, most of their early contacts with natives lacked any exchange of information. However, luck was on the Spaniards' side. Early in the expedition the army met Aguilar, a shipwrecked Spaniard who had learned the local Maya dialect (Diaz del Castillo 1956; Prescott 1931). This chance meeting enabled Cortes to use Aguilar as an interpreter, or interrogator, of Indians in the area. Later, as Cortes marched closer to

Reception of Hernando Cortes by the Emperor Montezuma.

the heart of Mexico, he encountered more good fortune. It was an Indian custom to present gifts to any conqueror, and the offerings often included young maidens. One such woman, Malinche, known to the Spaniards as Dona Marina, played a crucial role in the conquest (Diaz del Castillo 1956). Her life has become a pivotal point in which to examine the conquest (Paz 1961). More recently, attention has been focused on her role as an early "feminist" (Candelaria et al. 1980; Soto 1987). Malinche was originally bilingual, speaking the Nahuatl Aztec language and the Maya dialect Aguilar had learned, but she soon learned Spanish. Consequently, although Cortes understood only Spanish at the outset, he quickly utilized the two translators to become totally apprised of Indian thinking and designs. He used this tactical tool to speed up the march and to guard against attack.

Other tactics benefited the Spanish military juggernaut. For example, some dissident Indians welcomed Cortes as a liberator and assisted in the conquest. Having lived under the thumb of Aztec hegemony for many decades, these subjects (or confederates?) were only too eager to support Spanish military maneuvers, ignoring for the moment what their long-term economic and political designs might have been. Tlaxcala was one of these groups; more than twenty thousand Tlaxcalans aided campaigns against other Mexican Valley Indians. In some instances Cortes resorted to psychological ploys to prove the power of his Christian God. Once he had cannon sharpshooters blow up an Indian statue of a god gracing the top of a temple. Thus, by exhibiting a technological advantage, in one stroke he demonstrated the superiority of the Spanish deity and the impotence of Indian gods (Townsend 1992).

When all else failed, Cortes turned to the simple and time-proven practice of rhetorical bravado, inspiring his men to extraordinary acts of military prowess. Cortes, his oratory replete with references to Caesar, Pompey, and Hannibal, transformed each military mission into an act of super-human purpose, enhancing the morale of his troops (Wolf 1959).

Montezuma and the Legend of Quetzalcoatl

It appeared that the Indian gods had forsaken the defenders. At every turn Cortes undermined native plots and intrigues. Paradoxically, a most curious legend apparently furthered the Spanish cause and explained to a degree why many Indians openly received the Spaniards. The legend concerned a tall, bearded, white god, Quetzalcoatl (the Feathered Serpent, or Kukulcan to Mayas). This legendary character had gained prominence several centuries earlier, during Toltec rule. According to the legend, the beneficent Quetzalcoatl left the valley because of troubled times—mainly the downfall of the Toltec empire—with the promise that he would return. The Indians inferred that Cortes was

Temple of Quetzalcoatl at Teotihuacan, near Mexico City.

Quetzalcoatl incarnate, returning from the East intent on bringing back the good, moral, and just life (Coe 1994; Padden 1967; Leon-Portilla 1962). However, recent writers stress that this explanation came into vogue after the conquest and served as an Aztec *apologia* for the Spanish victory (Gillespie 1989).

Cortes exploited this legend when he discovered that the Indians connected him with the returning Quetzalcoatl. Like many other Indian groups, the Aztecs had already incorporated this god into their pantheon. As a result, the Aztec ruler Montezuma believed that Cortes was a god-man as well as an ambassador from a foreign land. This belief made him waver and vacillate, delaying action, even as he negotiated and tried to bribe Cortes.

Montezuma had made a fatal mistake in misreading the motives of his opponent (Padden 1967), and he ignored the advice of the royal family. Such men as Cacama and Cuitlahuac early advocated the extermination of foreign interlopers. The legend of Quetzalcoatl notwithstanding, they felt that Cortes's intent was evil. But growing despair weighed heavily on Montezuma as he followed the inexorable advance of the Spanish from his capital at Tenochtitlan. As the leader of his people, he did not have the luxury of contemplating escape into the hinterland.

Instead, a malaise of inactivity overwhelmed him (Leon-Portilla 1962). Meanwhile the conquerors moved ahead, tribe by tribe, province by province.

At first gifts of gold and other rare objects were offered to placate the Spanish. These were to no avail, however, and only whetted conquistador appetites. As Cortes himself said, the Spanish suffered from "an affliction of the heart, and gold was its only remedy" (Diaz del Castillo 1956). The more offerings to the Spaniards in return for their retreat, the more they pushed forward. Finally, an Aztec retinue escorted them into the great city of Mexico-Tenochtitlan.

Mexico-Tenochtitlan

Cortes's men viewed the central urban area of Mexico-Tenochtitlan with awe, for they had never seen such a splendid place. Spaniards "had seen nothing better during the twenty-five years of exploration of America than the houses of poles and thatch of Indian tribes, none of whom had risen above a state of barbarism" (Diaz del Castillo 1956:202).

Although Europeans were skeptical of creations made by "barbarians," they agreed the city was beautiful. In all their previous contacts with regions and cities of the Old World, nothing had impressed them more. All the buildings of the central plaza were plastered a brilliant white, and the streets were lined with trees and flowering shrubs at regular intervals. At night, well-tended braziers in wall brackets illuminated the streets. Canals were filled with canoes carrying passengers to and fro, and after dark the light from crude lighthouses guided them (Berdan 1982; Zorita 1963).

The city was dominated by the main ceremonial precincts, and a huge marketplace was located in the neighboring community of Tlatelolco (Adams 1996). The temple enclosure itself held twenty-five pyramids, several palaces, two ball courts, and many civil buildings. Activities abounded throughout the city: policemen made the rounds, anxious crowds gathered near medical and dental facilities, teams played on the ball courts, and schools bustled with children. Tlatelolco, the greatest Indian trading center of the Americas, offered a variety of services and goods: tattooers, barbers, leather tanners, jewelers, healers, basket and pottery makers, tailors, storytellers, magicians, wood carvers, cotton, turkeys, bells, slaves, edible dogs, sweets of all kinds, fish, tomatoes, tortillas, rubber, lentils, peanuts, pineapples, iguanas, firewood, perfume, toys, pumpkins, mate, tobacco, vanilla, parrots, pepper, sweet potatoes, strawberries, meal, jade, turtles, and much more (Townsend 1992).

Main temple complex of Mexico-Tenochtitlan.

Conflict: Destruction of Tenochtitlan

There were many sources of conflict. Some caused more friction than others, yet in one way or another all reflect the results of Spanish-Indian contact. The conquistadores sought wealth, in whatever form, and this ambition generally brought problems. Their motives were very basic, aimed toward accumulation of wealth, acquisition of territory, and enslavement of the indigenous population. Conversion of the Indians to the Christian faith and making a name for themselves were coinciding objectives. After the available supply of mineral wealth dwindled, the Spaniards turned to other sources of support. This caused the escalating conflict between Spaniards and Indians to reach its climax.

Cortes entered Tenochtitlan and was welcomed by many of the inhabitants. Fearing reprisals from the antagonistic Aztecs, and to secure his own tenuous position, he made Montezuma a prisoner in his own land. Cortes believed the Spaniards needed a hostage to prevent their annihilation. What better hostage than the main leader, who was respected and obeyed by all the people—and who, of course, stumbled into their hands? At the outset, relations between the two groups remained steady. Only after Cortes left for the east coast of Vera Cruz did warfare break out in the city. His departure was prompted by an invasion of other Spaniards, sent from Cuba by Governor Velasquez to reassert control over Cortes and to appropriate his gains. Although many Indians were uncomfortable with the Spanish presence in the city, it was the Spanish who initiated the fighting. One of the captains, Alvarado, was charged with maintaining order while Cortes was away. Instead, fearing a plot, he viciously attacked the Aztecs during a dance ceremony. The Indians retaliated mainly to protect themselves from being massacred (Leon-Portilla 1962). On Cortes's return everything worsened and turned to chaos. There was nothing for the Spanish to do but flee, and so they did, driven from the city by angry warriors. In the words of the eyewitness Bernal Diaz del Castillo: "Had it been in the daytime, it would have been far worse, and we who escaped did so only by the Grace of God. To one who saw the hosts of warriors who fell on us that night and the canoes full of them coming along to carry off our soldiers, it was terrifying" (Diaz del Castillo 1956:315).

While the Aztecs celebrated that night, it was *La Noche Triste* (the Sad Night) for the defeated Spaniards. Many of the conquerors tried to escape with gold but succeeded in saving only their skins. Others, not so fortunate, drowned because of the heavy weight of the gold they carried. Obtaining sanctuary and aid from friendly Indians, the Spanish nursed their wounds and regrouped. Afterward, they returned, laid siege to the city, and eventually subdued the defenders.

Causes of Aztec Defeat

The Spanish victory over the Aztecs stemmed from a combination of factors: their technological superiority (weapons), their psychologically astute diplomatic strategy, and their temporary alliances with dissident Indians (Clendinnen 1991). Many Aztec customs weakened the Indian cause and added to the Spanish advantage. For instance, Cortes was captured by Aztec warriors on several occasions but was not slain. This transpired because the Indian goal in warfare was to capture, not kill, so that the prisoners could later be ceremonially sacrificed to the gods (Hassig 1992). Spaniards were able to recapture their leader in the heat of a battle. In addition, fighting against mounted men was new to the natives. Since the Aztecs had never seen horses before, the animals naturally terrified them (the prototype of the smaller horse had become extinct in North America earlier).

Most important of all were the eager Indians who helped Cortes, reasoning (incorrectly, as it developed) that they would benefit in the aftermath. When the Aztecs realized that certain defeat was ahead, it was already too late to foster alliances with other similarly besieged Indians. Hence, the conquistadores conquered the tribes piecemeal, without facing coordinated resistance. Perhaps, like so many other peoples who are convinced their way is right, the Indians felt that the gods would not abandon them. The following comment describes the Aztec view of the fall of the city:

Indian portrayals of the Spanish invasion.

Nothing but flowers and songs of sorrow are left in Mexico and Tlatelolco, where once we saw warriors and wise men. . . . We know it is true that we must perish, for we are mortal men. You, the Giver of Life, you have ordained it. We wander here and there in our desolate poverty. We are mortal men. We have seen bloodshed and pain where once we saw beauty and valor. We are crushed to the ground; we lie in ruins. There is nothing but grief and suffering in Mexico and Tlatelolco, where once we saw beauty and valor. (Leon-Portilla 1962:149)

Following the downfall of Tenochtitlan in 1521, over twenty years passed before most major Mesoamerican tribes were conquered. Spanish expeditions were sent out in all directions to ensure the subjugation of other tribes, as well as to reveal the locations of gold concentrations. As a result, Spanish population centers of various sizes sprang up, some of which were to serve as starting points for subsequent forays (Helms 1975; Wagley and Harris 1958). The Mayas, despite their defeat in a number of earlier skirmishes, in 1846 were the last important group to be subdued. Some groups such as the Yaquis of the northwest resisted the Spanish much longer and were only subordinated in the twentieth century by the Mexicans (Spicer 1962). The Spaniards usually sought out groups living in heavily populated settlements, with plenty of resources to capitalize on. The Aztecs fit this criterion in two ways: dense groupings and strategic location. This settlement pattern made it possible to bring the area under immediate subjugation with a few heavy battles. Those who fled to the hinterland and mountains were more fortunate, for they escaped the worst excesses of contact and conflict.

Friction over Land and Religious Practices

Land and religious practices were serious conflict issues, often affecting other areas of life. With the defeat of the Aztecs, the Spaniards replaced the old elite and became the new collectors of tribute, which directly involved the land system. However, the most serious and intensely observable confrontation emerged in the area of religion (Lockhart 1992). The Spanish earnestly focused attention on the Indians' minds and hearts. They reasoned that control over the natives' laboring bodies would be assured after a new ideology was implanted. Their program of implementation, reminiscent of the heated European holy wars and inquisitions, was calculatedly vicious and effectively merciless. "It is easy to see why the phobia about heresy that raged in Spain was exaggerated in America among the religious who were perpetually in contact with a pagan civilization" (Ricard 1966:35).

A well-organized campaign led to the destruction of many religious sites. Native religious roles and activities of all types were banned. All resisters discovered secretly upholding the old "pagan" way were punished or exterminated. Not surprisingly, many Indians responded to the Spanish campaign pragmatically, interpreting elements of Christianity "as things they might make their own" (Lockhart 1992:443).

Missionaries, beginning with the Franciscans in 1524, followed by the Dominicans and Augustinians, were charged with the Indian Christianization policy. Many ascetic, humanistically inspired clerics undertook the Christian salvation of Indian souls and worked against great odds to convert them. The missionaries' protective intervention softened the cruel impact of military contact. No matter how lofty their goals, though, the church fathers actually further aided the Spanish crown by opening the Indians up—soul as well as body—thus, speeding up the process of integration into the new order. They also placed a wedge between generations, causing intratribal conflict. Church schools taught Aztec children the catechism to combat Indian religious beliefs. Children were instructed to spy on their elders and report parents who continued in the old ways (Madsen 1967).

The missionaries initiated a campaign of indoctrination to make Christianity and "paganism" appear incompatible to the neophytes. Some of the frictional contrasts were these: Aztecs believed in multiple creations, and Christians in one beginning and one God; Christians spoke of the pains of hell for sinners, whereas such explicit afterworld punishment was unimportant to the Aztecs. In addition, clerical sects competed for Indian souls, each with its own conversion program and all

How the Spanish viewed Huitzilopochtli.

with the intention of rescuing them from damnation. Vine Deloria, a contemporary Native American, pithily puts it this way for all Indians: "It has been said of missionaries that when they arrived, they had only the Book and the Natives had the land; now the Natives have the Book and they (missionaries) have the land. An old Indian once told me that when the missionaries arrived, they fell on their knees and prayed. Then they got up, fell on the Indians, and preyed" (Deloria 1988:101).

On the whole, Indians underwent a traumatic period because of these conflicting religious philosophies (Markman and Markman 1989). Missionaries constantly preached that individual salvation of the soul resulted from practicing Christianity. Eternal hell awaited those who rejected Christianity. Significantly, one early observer was already laying the groundwork for both their conversion and subjugation: "These Indians are free of almost all the impediments to salvation that hinder the Spaniards, for they are content with very little. . . . they are incredibly patient and long suffering, and meek as sheep. I do not once remember having seen one of them nurse a grudge. They, the humble and scorned, live only to serve and work" (Zorita 1963:164; see also Schwaller 1987).

As a result, many Indians attempted a balancing act, worshiping both the old and the new religions and symbols simultaneously. Many priests working with the Indians began to notice a laxity—in some an outright refusal—to conform to the impositions of Christian belief and worship. Meanwhile, the continuing practice of old religious customs by the Indians worsened the tensions that existed between them and the priests (Padden 1967).

Religious conversion programs brought superficial native acceptance, sometimes elicited with torture in the name of God. One such example of a common conversion method for that time is "the water torture, in which the mouth was fastened open with a stick and water was poured in until the abdomen swelled up, after which the investigator stood on top of the victim until water mixed with blood came out of the mouth, nose, and ears" (Madsen 1967:385).

In giving its blessing to the "higher-purpose" of converting the heathens to the Christian faith, the Catholic church provided the Spanish with the legitimacy to carry out their policy of conquest.

Change: Colonial Practices Begin

Sixteenth-century Mexico, and for that matter the New World, was probably among the fastest-moving transitional societies ever, and was the stage for one of the most dramatic cross-fertilizations of cultures then known to humankind. Contact, conflict, and change between the peoples of the Old and New World raised havoc in all sectors of life. Centuries passed before any semblance of stability was established. During that time an empire grew. Owing to the Spanish initiatives, the period bore the earmarks of their culture, even though Indians also participated in the events (Lockhart 1992; Wolf 1959).

Adoption of Christianity

At first Christianity was accepted grudgingly; therefore, the Spanish resorted to other ways of teaching religion. These approaches proved more successful, although Spanish leaders no doubt considered such innovations a retreat from the original goal. They were especially unhappy that such a "demonized" religion had to be accommodated in bringing about changes. The Indians had always accepted good and bad, for in their view, life came from death and creation from destruction and all were parts of the human drama (Cervantes 1994). This the Spanish disliked, for they viewed reality as an either/or choice, good or bad. To speed up the conversion and the accommodation, the conquerors began to learn and adopt native language practices and cultural images, which enabled them to put the new teachings in books for the natives (Ricard 1966).

Despite such efforts, conversion went slowly. In part, this was due to the conquistadores who had become *encomenderos* (landowners and tribute collectors), for they held responsibility for Catholic conversion of the natives even though clerics actually administered the program (Behar 1987; Ruiz 1992; Whetten 1969). Making it doubly difficult, native religion was highly developed and was an integral part of the sociopolitical system (Lockhart 1992). While the crown sought to mediate here, government officials, far from Spain, often found themselves in competition for the same resources. These recently arrived gentry often took much more interest in the Indians' labor than in their souls.

A unique and far-reaching incident became the turning point of this era. In 1531, Juan Diego, a recent Indian convert, had a vision affecting all of Indian Mexico's future. According to legend, his miraculous experience occurred on a former Indian holy site dedicated to the Aztec mother goddess Tonantzin ("Little Mother of the Earth and Corn"). (Madsen 1967; Smith 1983). Juan Diego reported that he had seen the embodiment of the Virgin Mary in a saintly, brown-skinned apparition (Mosqueda 1986). At first skeptics dismissed the report as the superstitious preachings of an Indian, but to prove his point, Juan Diego returned to the same place and the vision reappeared. This time he allegedly brought back evidence: roses and the facial imprint of the Virgin on a shawl. Bishop Zumarraga, who at this time played a vital role in the Christianization program, was finally convinced and, recognizing the significance of the event, sanctioned Juan Diego's vision. Thus began the

"Virgen de Guadalupe cult" (Ricard 1966:188; Johnson 1980; Taylor 1987).

This miraculous affair built on native pride and hastened the Indians' acceptance of Christianity (Guerrero 1987). They found it easier to embrace the Catholic faith, if for no other reason than that one of their own kind was accorded a saintly status and God could be reached through this intermediary (Wood 1991; Johnson 1980). One might also suspect that this was an Indian way to reclaim and reestablish the importance of the female in their world and bring back old beliefs and practices that placed women at a higher level. In some ways, that reasoning has survived to the present, as Chicanas look to this image for strength and affection (Rodriquez 1994). In time, the effect of the Virgen de Guadalupe spread throughout Mexico, growing in popularity in the sixteenth century and gaining its full momentum in the seventeenth century (Wolf 1982; Taylor 1987). What began as a cult figure was more firmly institutionalized as Queen of Mexico in 1895 and Patroness of Latin America in 1910.

During this time the same bishop, Zumarraga, participated in wiping out other vestiges of Indian religion. In a letter of June 12, 1531, he bragged of destroying more than five hundred temples and twenty thousand idols (Prescott 1931; Ricard 1966; Padden 1967).

Altogether, clerics burned over four hundred thousand manuscripts. The Spaniards considered written words too powerful in supporting the religio-philosophic beliefs of the Aztecs. They reasoned that destroying books would somehow rub out the spiritual ideology in Indian minds and hearts. (Again, book burning also took place among Europeans who were vying for their particular brand of Christianity, mostly Catholics against Protestants.) Most unfortunately, almost all the knowledge the Indians had accumulated was lost. Moreover, human lives were destroyed—several million died in the decade after the conquest.

Many clerics taught the liturgy and catechism in the native Indian languages in order to contribute to a better understanding of the doctrine. "The friars of Mexico, from the moment of their arrival, recognized that the knowledge of Indian languages was the essential prerequisite of serious evangelization" (Ricard 1966:46). Patterning themselves after Jesus Christ, many also gave an excellent example in their daily lives. This further influenced native adoption of Christianity. Some outstanding, humane priests (Bartolome de las Casas, for one) felt that the Indians should learn all that European education could offer. Because this goal did not coincide with Spanish interests, it was unfortunately eliminated (Padden 1967; Ricard 1966). Other reasons, to be discussed shortly, will clarify the reversal of Spanish policy.

The Virgen de Guadalupe. ▶

Religious Syncretism

An apparently unexpected outcome of the conversion program was the merging of Indian and Spanish religious features—words, symbols, and so on (Lockhart 1992). This phenomenon was indeed also part of the Spanish experience, for there is no such thing as "pure" Catholicism. In the New World case, certain Indian ceremonial dates were retained with Christian symbols being commemorated. In some respects this adaptation eased native adjustment, gaining their cooperation by showing respect for their culture. Naturally, it also aided the dissemination of Catholicism, although some would argue that the Indians "have not really accepted" Catholicism (Ricard 1966:276). In any case, it is clear that they have mixed both ancient Indian and Catholic rites and cults into something new that they regard as Mexican Catholic ideology.

This kind of religion is known as "syncretic." Syncretism is a process whereby different cultural elements are combined into an entirely new system. In this instance, previous Indian forms and novel Spanish religious conversion techniques made the recombination easier (Ruiz de Alarcon 1984). This occurred in Mexico because: ". . . indigenous and Spanish patterns reinforced each other" (Lockhart 1992:26), and ". . . [since] two complicated societies were intermeshing, opportunities for new combinations continually arose" (Gibson 1964:404). By blending the Indian and Spanish views of the world, the Spaniards clearly advanced the colonization program. This innovation sparked overall cultural changes and interactions to fuse, in time, a new culture.

This cultural and biological cross-pollination is sometimes referred to as *mestizaje* (mixing). Mexican culture is especially known for this, although few can pinpoint with accuracy what portion of the culture was Spanish or Indian, except to state that this was the initial phase of a process where several other cultural layers were added later (Schryer 1993). Furthermore, the process was dynamic and unfolded differently for different people. Some were able to avoid total immersion into Spanish culture by retaining their own traditions. However, others were assimilated almost overnight, becoming Hispanicized Indians. In short, "the transformation of native society under Spanish rule was neither uniform nor pervasive" (Spores 1993:91).

Initial Changes in Land, Labor, and Wealth

There was a quantum leap into a new system in terms of how social labor was captured and deployed. "Cultural change or cultural evolution does not operate on isolated societies but always on interconnected systems in which societies are variously linked with wider 'social fields'" (Wolf 1982:76). The people's relationship to the land remained essentially the same. What did change was land ownership: who controlled the land, why, and how and for whom resources were extracted. The introduction of large-scale mining enterprises required the relocation of many Indians. Calpulli members once tied to the land were forced to change residences and work in the bowels of the earth (Wolf 1982; Vives 1969).

As the new "minority" group in the Spanish colony, the Indians became a source of cheap labor (Wagley and Harris 1958). Thus, the early decades of the colonial period began with a series of changes in the labor and landholding system, each change having a new name—*encomienda, repartimiento,* or *hacienda.* The name might change and so might the social relations, but the result was always the same: The natives remained oppressed as they were securely rooted in this new social system. In short, "a number of Indians were 'entrusted' or 'distributed' to Spanish settlers to be educated in the Christian life in exchange for their services" (de Madariaga 1947:17). According to Lockhart (1992), this was the first stage (1519–1545 or 1550) of the three stages that took place in the colonial period.

A new socioeconomic system was introduced and gradually transformed Indian society. Aztec society was built on local tribes and political units and became progressively more complex with larger and higher networks and strands of control, but the conquest eliminated the bigger units and allowed the local and less comprehensive ones to survive (Gibson 1964). The basis of it was the *altepetl* (an organization of people controlling a set territory) (Lockhart 1992). The calpulli kin- and territory-based system was no longer the primary land-ownership unit, though. Colonial authorities ignored kin networks and all the symbolic and social relations that kept people working together for a common cause and purpose (Wolf 1982). In doing so they broke up and separated families, calpullis, and even whole villages and effectively forced their members to far-flung regions to labor in new occupations for the ever-expanding colonial empire.

However, Spaniards preserved many calpulli land boundary lines, creating encomiendas or haciendas (landed estates) from them. The Spaniards reasoned that the calpulli kin system was in the way; it made for a united Indian group socially and thus had to be reformed into a new social labor group. Therefore, they broke up the calpulli to better exploit workers. The motto of the new overseers was, "Just give us some hands and backs." The important fact is that Indians no longer controlled or owned their land. The Spaniards had appropriated it, making the natives subjects in their own land. According to Wolf (1982:86), "The European merchants engaged in overseas operations brought surpluses into mercantile exchange in a number of different ways. . . . They grew directly out of the operations of the tributary mode and long remained intertwined with it."

Missionary Program

To offset these abuses, the missionaries entreated the crown to establish separate Indian and Spanish towns. These efforts shielded many Indians from ambitious colonists who aggressively pursued lucrative careers on landed estates, and protected and preserved some Indian land rights and cultural traditions. This plan was not altogether successful, for later colonists were still able to partition Indian lands, a process that continued in a different form until just before the 1910 Revolution. Furthermore, during this period the colonists' struggle over the control of Indian subjects reached tremendous proportions. First the encomenderos gained the upper hand, followed by the clerics, then the crown, and the cycle was repeated in a continual battle. This rivalry over natives consumed the energies of each competing group in New Spain: Should they emphasize that Indian souls be Christianized (church)? That their labor be exploited (encomenderos)? That they be made into good Spanish subjects (crown)? The three factions agreed, however, that it was all for the natives' benefit to become Christianized laboring subjects (Ruiz 1992; Villegas et al. 1974; Gibson 1966).

To achieve this objective, many Indian leaders (former pipiltin and local *caciques,* or chieftains) who collaborated with the Spanish were absorbed as minor colonial administrators—about one tenth of the Indian population. This indigenous aristocracy initially helped the Spanish gain and maintain power through traditional practices and tribute networks. They were feared and hated by the indigenous majority and considered traitors. But as the Spanish stabilized and particularly as they grew in numbers through immigration and their new mixed offspring, these native elites were gradually phased out (Gruzinski 1988; Wagley and Harris 1958; Wolf 1982). By assisting in the subjugation of their fellow Indians they became *endonado* (Hispanicized, entitled to use the gentlemanly "Don" before their names), but this conciliatory treatment was short-lived and by the eve of independence these "dons" had lost their minor influence.

Beginnings of Instability

There were several stages to the unfolding colonial system, and Lockhart (1992:428) has suggested three historical periods: (1) 1519 to 1545/50, (2) 1545/50 to 1640/50, and (3) 1640/50 to 1800 and after. Clearly, the postconquest period was chaotic, especially when contrasted with the relatively more stable indigenous system that had existed previously, although as Wolf (1982:71) notes, "conquest, incorporation, recombination, and commerce were also characteristic of the pre-Columbian New World" (also see Gutierrez 1991). As will be noted, the colonial period introduced a host of phenomena that radically altered society. These include: (1) Spanish, Indian, and African racial intermixture (known as miscegenation, or mestizaje in Spanish); (2) incipient racist practices, a peculiarly Mesoamerican type affecting both social class and mobility; (3) a program of Spanish racial and cultural superiority, which made the native and darker-hued people feel inferior; (4) the beginnings of a new syncretic culture, part of a wide-ranging mestizaje that still defies a simple definition; and (5) racial and cultural marginality, in which the masses found themselves torn between Old and New World cultural patterns and racial appearance. The Aztecs called this mental state *nepantilism* (marginality). These conditions brought economic and sociocultural problems and generally a native pattern of thought and action best termed a "psychology of colonization."

> Their culture, so suddenly destroyed, is one of those that humanity can be proud of having created . . . our common inheritance is made up of all the values that our species has conceived, [and] it must take its place among our precious treasures—precious because they are so rare." (Soustelle 1961:244)

Thus ended the indigenous period in Mesoamerica. Although the Indians suffered from the human imperfections that pertained to all groups, they had established a great tradition, one in which they took pride. To them it was a time when a closer rapport with nature prevailed, when their decisions, right or wrong, determined their common destiny. Now that came to an end. Previously they had been the captors of energy. Now they became captured in a new system that was bigger and just taking off (Sanderson 1995; Wallerstein 1974; Frank 1969). In the metaphor of Wolf, Indians, like so many other peoples in other continents, are a part of the larger picture: "We are back in a world of sociocultural billiard balls, coursing on a global billiard table" (1982:17).

The original humans in Mexico no longer had control of society. Their autonomous, indigenous years were interrupted by the arrival of the Spaniards and the subsequent contact, conflict, and change. Now a stern socialization of rigidly enforced conformity to new Spanish-based social rules awaited them, as they were transformed into a new peasantry and changing way of life. Without the Spanish, the Indians would presumably have fought wars to capture more energy, fashioned new technologies to improve and broaden their lives, and generally reordered and remade the lives of other indigenous peoples like themselves. But the usurpation of this stage of development by the Spanish made the process and outcome quite different from what would have otherwise occurred.

References

Adams, R. E. W. 1996. *Prehistoric Mesoamerica*. Norman: University of Oklahoma Press.

Andrews, J. 1984. *Peppers: The domesticated capsicums*. Austin: University of Texas Press.

Behar, R. 1987. Sex and sin, witchcraft and the devil in late-colonial Mexico. *American Ethnologist*, Special Edition, "Frontiers of Christian Evangelism" 14(1)(February): 34–54.

Berdan, F. F. 1982. *The Aztecs of Central Mexico: An imperial society*. New York: Holt, Rinehart & Winston.

_____. 1989. *Indians of North America: The Aztecs*. New York: Chelsea House Publishers.

Berler, B. 1988. *The conquest of Mexico: A modern rendering of William H. Prescott's history*. San Antonio, TX: Corona Publishing.

Bernal, I. 1969. *The Olmec world*. Berkeley: University of California Press.

Candelaria, C. et al. 1980. *Chicanas en el ambiente nacional*. Boulder, CO: Frontiers Editorial Collective.

Cantrell, J. P. 1984. *Ancient Mexico: Art, architecture, and culture in the land of the feathered serpent*. Dubuque, IA: Kendall Hunt Pub. Co.

Carrasco, D. 1990. *Religions of Mesoamerica: Cosmovision and ceremonial centers*. San Francisco: Harper and Row.

_____. 1992. *Quetzalcoatl and the irony of empire: Myth and prophecies in the Aztec tradition*. Chicago: University of Chicago Press.

Cervantes, F. 1994. *The Devil in the New World: The Impact of Diabolism in New Spain*. New Haven: Yale University Press.

Clendinnen, I. 1991. *Aztecs: An interpretation*. Cambridge, England: Cambridge University Press.

Coe, M. 1962. *Mexico*. New York: Praeger Publishers.

_____. 1994. *Mexico: From the Olmecs to the Aztecs*. New York: Thames and Hudson Inc.

Deloria, V. 1988. *Custer died for your sins: An Indian manifesto*. Norman: University of Oklahoma Press.

de Madariaga, S. 1947. *The rise of the Spanish American empire*. New York: Macmillan Inc.

Diaz del Castillo, B. 1956. *The discovery and conquest of Mexico: 1517–1521*. New York: Farrar, Straus & Giroux, Inc.

Driver, H. E. 1969. *Indians of North America*. Chicago: University of Chicago Press.

Durant, W. 1983. *The story of philosophy: The lives and opinions of the great philosophers of the Western world*. New York: Simon and Schuster (originally published c. 1933).

Fiedel, S. J. 1992. *Prehistory of the Americas*. Cambridge, England: Cambridge University Press.

Florescano, E. 1994. *Memory, myth, and time in Mexico: From the Aztecs to independence*. Austin: University of Texas Press.

Foster, N. and L. S. Cordell, eds. 1992. *Chilies to chocolate: Food the Americas gave the world*. Tucson: University of Arizona Press.

Frank, A. G. 1969. *Capitalism and underdevelopment in Latin America*. New York: Monthly Review Press.

Gibson, C. 1964. *Aztecs under Spanish rule*. Stanford: Stanford University Press.

_____. 1966. *Spain in America*. New York: Harper & Row, Publishers.

Gillespie, S. D. 1989. *The Aztec kings: The construction of rulership in Mexico history*. Tucson: University of Arizona Press.

Gruzinski, S. 1988. The net torn apart: Ethnic identities and Westernization in colonial Mexico, sixteenth–nineteenth century. In *Ethnicities and Nations*, eds. R. Guidieri et al. Austin: Rothko Chapel Book, University of Texas Press.

Guerrero, A. G. 1987. *A Chicano theology*. Maryknoll, NY: Orbis Books.

Gutierrez, R. 1991. *When Jesus came, the Corn Mothers went away*. Stanford: Stanford University Press.

Hassig, R. 1988. *Aztec warfare: Imperial expansion and political control*. Norman: University of Oklahoma Press.

_____. 1992. *War and society in ancient Mesoamerica*. Berkeley: University of California Press.

Helms, M. W. 1975. *Middle America: A culture history of heartland and frontiers*. Englewood Cliffs, NJ: Prentice-Hall, Inc.

Johnson, H. L. 1980. The Virgin of Guadalupe in Mexican culture. In *Religion in Latin American life and literature*, eds. L. C. Brown and W. F. Cooper. Waco, TX: Markham Press Fund.

King, J. L. 1985. *Ancient Mexico, an overview*. Albuquerque: University of New Mexico Press.

Leon-Portilla, M. 1962. *Broken spears: The Aztec account of the conquest of Mexico*. Boston: Beacon Press.

_____. 1963. *Aztec thought and culture*. Norman: University of Oklahoma Press.

_____. 1969. *Pre-columbian literatures of Mexico*. Norman: University of Oklahoma Press.

_____. 1988. *Time and reality in the thought of the Maya*. Norman: University of Oaklahoma Press.

_____, ed. 1992. *The Aztec image of self and society: An introduction to the Nahua culture*. Salt Lake City: University of Utah Press.

Lockhart, J. 1992. *The Nahuas after the conquest: A social and cultural history of the Indians of central Mexico, sixteenth through eighteenth centuries*. Stanford: Stanford University Press.

Madsen, W. 1967. Religious syncretism. In *Handbook of Middle American Indians*, ed. R. Wauchope. Vol. 6. Austin: University of Texas Press.

Markman, R. H. and P. T. Markman. 1989. *Masks of the spirit: Image and metaphor in Mesoamerica*. Berkeley: University of California Press.

_____. 1992. *The flayed god: The Mesoamerican mythological tradition: Sacred text and images from Precolumbian Mexico and Central America*. San Francisco: Harper.

Mathien, F. J. and R. H. McGuire. 1986. *Ripples in the Chichimec Sea: New considerations of Southwestern-Mesoamerican interactions*. Carbondale and Edwardsville: Southern Illinois University Press.

McGregor, J. C. 1982. *Southwestern archaeology*. Urbana: University of Illinois Press.

Molitar, M. 1981. *The Hohokam-Toltec connection: A study in culture diffusion*. Greely, CO: Museum of Anthropology, University of Northern Colorado, Archaeology series no.10.

Morgan, L. H. 1963. *Ancient society*. New York: Meridian Books.

Mosqueda, L. J. 1986. *Chicanos, Catholicism, and political ideology*. Lanham, MD: University Press of America.

Ortiz de Montellano, B. 1990. *Aztec medicine, health, and nutrition*. New Brunswick, NJ: Rutgers University Press.

Padden, R. C. 1967. *The hummingbird and the hawk: Conquest and sovereignty in the Valley of Mexico; 1503–1541*. Columbus: Ohio State University Press.

Paz, O. 1961. *The labyrinth of solitude*. New York: Grove Press Inc.

Peterson, F. A. 1962. *Ancient Mexico*. New York: G. P. Putnam's Sons.

Prescott, W. H. 1931. *History of the conquest of Mexico*. New York: Random House, Inc. (originally published in 1842).

Ricard, R. 1966. *The spiritual conquest of Mexico*. Berkeley: University of California Press.

Riley, C. L. 1987. *The frontier people: The greater Southwest in the protohistoric period*. Albuquerque: University of New Mexico Press.

Rodriquez, J. 1994. *Our Lady of Guadalupe*. Austin: University of Texas Press.

Ruiz, R. E. 1992. *Triumphs and tragedy: A history of the Mexican people*. New York: W.W. Norton and Co.

Ruiz de Alarcon, H. 1984. *Treatise on the heathen superstitions that today live among the Indians native to this New Spain, 1629*. trans. and eds. J. R. Andrews and R. Hassig. Norman: University of Oklahoma Press.

Sahagun, B. 1932. *A history of ancient Mexico*. Glorieta, NM: The Rio Grande Press, Inc.

Sanderson, S. K. 1995. *Civilizations and world systems: Studying world-historical change*. Thousand Oaks, CA: AltaMira Press.

Scarborough, V. L. and D. R. Wilcox, eds. 1991. *The Mesoamerican ballgame*. Tucson: University of Arizona Press.

Schryer, F. J. 1993. *Ethnic identity and land tenure disputes in modern Mexico*. Wilmington, DE: A Scholarly Resources Inc. Imprint.

Schwaller, J. F. 1987. *Guias de manuscritos en Nahuatl*. Mexico City: Universidad Nacional Autonoma de Mexico.

Sharer, R. J. and D. C. Grove, eds. 1989. *Regional perspectives on the Olmec*. Cambridge, England: Cambridge University Press.

Smith, J. B. 1983. *The image of Guadalupe: Myth or miracle*. New York: Doubleday & Co.

Sokolov, R. 1991. *Why we eat what we eat: How Columbus changed the way the world eats*. New York: Simon & Schuster.

Soto, S. A. 1987. La Malinche: 16th century leader. *Perspectives* (Spring): 13.

Soustelle, J. 1961. *Daily life of the Aztecs*. Stanford: Stanford University Press.

Spicer, E. 1962. *Cycles of conquest*. Tucson: University of Arizona Press.

Spindler, L. S. 1984. *Culture change and modernization: Mini-models and case studies*. Prospect Heights, IL: Waveland Press.

Spores, R. 1993. Spanish penetration and cultural change in early colonial Mexico. In *The Indian in Latin American history: Resistance, resilience, and acculturation*, ed. J. E. Kicza. Wilmington, DE: A Scholarly Resources Inc., Imprint.

Suarez, J. A. 1982. *The Mesoamerican Indian languages*. Cambridge, England: Cambridge University Press.

Taube, K. A. and M. E. Miller. 1993. *The gods and symbols of ancient Mexico and the Maya: An illustrated dictionary of Mesoamerican religion*. New York: Thames and Hudson.

Taylor, W. B. 1987. The Virgin of Guadalupe in New Spain: An inquiry into the social history of Marian devotion. *American Ethnologist*, Special edition "Frontiers of Christian Evangelism" 14(1) (February): 9–33.

Townsend, R. F. 1992. *The Aztecs*. London: Thames and Hudson.

Villegas, D. C. et al. 1974. *A compact history of Mexico*. Los Angeles: University of California, Latin American Center.

Vives, J. V. 1969. *An economic history of Spain*. Princeton: Princeton University Press.

Wagley, C. and M. Harris. 1958. *Minorities in the New World: Six case studies*. New York: Columbia University Press.

Wallerstein, I. 1974. *The modern world-system: Capitalist agriculture and the origins of the European world-economy in the sixteenth century*. New York: Academic Press.

Weaver, M. P. 1993. *The Aztecs, Maya, and their predecessors: Archaeology of MesoAmerica*. San Diego: Academic Press.

Whetten, N. L. 1969. *Rural Mexico*. Chicago: University of Chicago Press.

Willey, G. R. et al. 1964. The patterns of farming: Life and civilization. In *Natural environment and early cultures*, ed. R. C. West. Handbook of Middle American Indians. Vol. 1. Austin: University of Texas Press.

Wolf, E. 1959. *Sons of the shaking earth*. Chicago: University of Chicago Press.

_____. 1982. *Europe and the people without history*. Berkeley: University of California Press.

Wood, S. 1991. Adopted saints: Christian images in Nahua testament of late Colonial Toluca. *The Americas* 47(3): 259–93.

Zorita, A. 1963. *Life and labor in ancient Mexico*. New Brunswick, NJ: Rutgers University Press.

Stage II
Spanish Colonial Era
1521 to 1821

As the indigenous way of life gave way to a new one forged in part from their old customs and in part from newly learned patterns, what would later be referred to as a peasant society, there were many unhappy and harsh experiences. The Indians of Mexico were ill-prepared for what they had to undergo, an experience that was repeated in other parts of the world as Europeans incorporated more and more territory and people into their ever expanding empires. The peasant society that resulted from such major upheavals was a strange yet interesting amalgamation, and as noted, there were several stages to it (Lockhart 1992). In Mexico, particularly, it was a fascinating agglomeration of bits and pieces that coalesced from culture contact and change reverberations. One way to look at peasant ways of life is as fragments from the past—part societies and part cultures—that remain integrated into the present. In many ways, peasant life shows how indigenous peoples clung to the past to preserve some aspects of their identity. A cultural lag thus was always present in the resounding transformation of tribal societies and indigenous states into a subordinate system that became connected with larger political economic systems. In time, the Mexican peasants grew to be an insulated, protective society; perhaps because they were denied significant economic power in the new order, peasant groups were concerned more with social power and prestige.

Not all of the experiences of the colonial period were negative. The sequence and degree of contact and change were not the same for everyone nor were the outcomes entirely predictable. Many natives benefited during the transition phases, sometimes well into the colonial era. Nevertheless, colonial directives were forceful enough to restrict the range of behavior; the majority of Indians were subjected to a cruel pattern. "The colonial relationship . . . chained the colonizer and the colonized into an implacable dependence, molded their respective characters and dictated their conduct" (Stein and Stein 1970:vii). In the end, indigenous society broke down because of an experience that was largely damaging and unrewarding, especially since matters (i.e., independent cultural evolution, innovation, and so on) were taken out of their hands. In some ways, the natives became subservient to cruel, overbearing, and demanding masters; duties and accomplishments dictated by others now ruled the day. A new type of evolution emerged, as reaction to these intrusions eventually called for social movement and radical revolution to bring about change.

Since the Spaniards were the masters of the environment, they largely determined the extent of autonomy and coercion—who would do what, when, where, and why. This arrangement decisively affected the character and health of each person in the social system. Learning experiences and therefore all lives were effectively shaped by Spaniards.

As a tribute to the human character, many native peoples strove to liberate themselves from such harsh and inhumane conditions, if only temporarily. Moreover, Spanish cultural lifeways were not entirely embraced by natives. Still, the Indians were taught how to respond to events (beliefs), to know the difference between good and bad events (values), to integrate the details of proper or improper performance (rules), and finally, to understand that their behavior would be rewarded by positive or negative treatment (sanctions). These directives and regulations were unevenly impressed upon the indigenous population, causing many maladaptions. With all its vicissitudes, the colonial period was extremely significant because it was a macrohistorical imprint that lingered in the people's minds and guided their actions long after it officially fell apart.

Chapter 4

Intact and Stable Social Order

Class: Haciendas and Debt Peons

The Spanish used what they could of indigenous practices; but piecemeal, over several hundred years, they revamped the socioeconomic system—in their favor. With variations reflecting the respective time periods, modern problems involving the relationship between developed and underdeveloped societies often echo those generated by the Spanish colonial system in Mexico. One country develops by exploiting another country, leaving it underdeveloped; thus, development and underdevelopment can often be viewed as two sides of the same coin. Political and social actions support this system. This is the story of Spain's colonization policies—mercantilism and imperialism—and of how Indian society became underdeveloped (Frank 1969).

Spanish Motives

The motives behind the socioeconomic class structure that emerged can be briefly summarized. Conditions in Spain, even before contact with the New World, had led to the establishment of a centralized, crown-controlled economy. Ferdinand and Isabella sought to establish a monopoly on gold and silver resources. This led to consolidation by maintenance of a favorable trade balance and control of the colonial economy, in order for the crown to retain strict control of American metal exports. These monopolistic ventures follow the principles of mercantilism, that is, merchant wealth and the exchange of commodities under the centralized direction of the state (Wolf 1982; Haring 1963).

At the outset of the occupation of the New World, the Spanish seized and sent to Spain the most readily available sources of liquid wealth. Indian jewelry, often including fine works of art, was smelted into bullion. After the available supply of Indian gold and silver was depleted, the Spaniards forced the natives to work the mines. Since the Indians had only begun to labor in a few mines, the Spaniards strove to locate new ones. The exploration for new mines was an integral part of each step of the conquest and the gradual occupation of Mexico's territory, and it was silver mining that drove the engine of economic growth (MacLachlan and Rodriquez O. 1980; Raat 1992).

Indigenous labor was always the crucial resource for mining, but additionally, new techniques for extraction, production, and shipment evolved. More than 185,000 kilograms of gold and silver were transported from the New World (including Mexico as well as other areas) to the Old World during the period from 1503 to 1660. Calculated at twentieth-century prices, the value of the gold alone amounted to billions of dollars. Silver would bring the total worth close to five billion dollars in mineral resources (Wolf 1982; Vives 1969). This economic activity was an important feature of mercantilism, the precursor to capitalism in which merchant wealth is developed and regulated in a more or less tributary system.

One would assume that Spain's future was secure with all these riches. However, the Spaniards were concerned with establishing a non-laboring, genteel, aristocratic life as *gente de razon*—people of reason (Wolf 1982); they sought to continue a feudal tradition from the middle ages in which prodigality and extravagance were considered lofty human qualities (Haring 1963). To maintain this lifestyle, they generally used their liquid wealth to purchase manufactured products from others. Spain actually aided the rise of manufacturing in other European nation-states while unevenly developing her own industries (Elliott 1963; Stein and Stein 1970). Nevertheless, since Spain still had an abundance of colonial land and labor to exploit, its decline was gradual.

Encomienda

As one observer has noted, "The real treasure was the Indian. So Cortes distributed Indians" (Sierra 1969:97). Private property and large feudal landholding units were European practices that guided how the Indians fit into the new colonial social organization. Mining activities eventually slowed when mineral resources became scarce, and thus a turn to land made sense. Since mere land ownership does not produce a commodity, there had to be means whereby Indians could work the land to benefit those who controlled it. Thus, land and laboring natives were immediately brought under Spanish control. In the first decades, Indian slave labor worked the mines and performed other hard tasks, and Indians became rapidly integrated into the tribute system of the *encomienda* (MacLachlan and Rodriquez O. 1980; Zavala 1943).

The encomienda grew out of another Spanish custom during the Reconquista, the granting of land to reward a faithful conquistador. It only made sense to continue this practice in the Americas, and the encomienda system additionally added Indian tribute (or labor) to the arrangement. This trusteeship of land, together with the granting of Indian subjects to military leaders (known as encomenderos), was the basis of the encomienda system (Himmerich y Valencia 1991). Since the encomenderos only replaced Indian overlords, accepting tribute from native labor, at first the transition was relatively easy (Ruiz 1992; Gibson 1984; Simpson 1966). However, the encomenderos and other Spaniards who arrived late but eager to exploit, accelerated the acquisition of land and labor to force other difficulties. The encomenderos abused Indians by forcing them to work harder and longer, and many were uprooted and sent to northern mining and lowland plantation regions. In addition to these pressures, there were a great many Indian lives lost due to exposure to European diseases for which the native populations had no inherited protections (Himmerich y Valencia 1991).

Many humanitarian clerics influenced the crown in limiting the worst excesses of encomienda. It became obvious to them and others that there would be few Indians left under the present practice and hardly any souls to convert (Sierra 1969). Royal authorities mostly agreed, but they, too, were motivated by self-interest, as the crown must receive its *quinto* (one-fifth) of the take (Ruiz 1992). So that they would share in the profitable arrangements themselves, their representatives undermined growing encomendero power, which was increasingly dominating Indian land and labor, and thus wealth. Many encomenderos were challenged for this reason. For example, Cortes, now the Marquis de Oaxaca, was the biggest landowner in Mexico, controlling an Indian population of over twenty thousand. "His tremendous riches—it is likely that he was at one time the wealthiest person in the entire Spanish world—depended chiefly on encomienda, which furnished him a large annual tribute income and labor for his various enterprises" (Gibson 1966:55; see also Ruiz 1992), including distributing *peonias* to his foot soldiers to help cultivate interest in agriculture (Florescano 1984). He was recalled to Spain to answer charges of treason, for the crown feared his growing power (Chevalier 1966).

Repartimiento

The crown sought to prevent the decimation of the natives, as occurred in the Caribbean, and initiated a twofold policy: Save the natives from total exploitation, and restructure the colony to provide a broader Spanish ruling elite in place of a few enterprising individ-

The city that was built on the ruins of Tenochtitlan.

uals. This new program was called *repartimiento* (distribution or allotment of workers). It was intended to provide wages for Indian labor—but due to the human drive to maintain power and control of resources, it did something else (Gibson 1966).

Under this policy, laborers were to work for wages a limited number of days per year and thus have time for their own needs and enterprises. Not surprisingly, the results were otherwise. Self-interest guided the adoption of repartimiento, for exploitation of Mexico's resources would stop if native labor disappeared. Consequently, the crown's acceptance of pagan Indians as worthy of Christian salvation (as urged by the missionaries) was something of a subterfuge for preserving labor services. However, it was not very successful in this: The indigenous population fell from twenty-five million in 1519 to a little over a million by 1650 (Borah and Cook 1960; Skidmore and Smith 1992; Stein and Stein 1970; Gibson 1966). One writer stated that for every sixteen Indians in 1519 there was only one left in the next century (Sanchez-Albornoz 1988).

From the beginning, repartimiento was almost totally ignored by the colonists, and the Indians were unhappy because it was obligatory labor. In just a few decades, the conquistadores were joined by lawyers, merchants, doctors, government officials, and some enterprising missionaries in a continuing program of native exploitation (Chevalier 1966). As a general practice, colonists either casually avoided the repartimiento policy or tactfully manipulated it to their advantage. By controlling large parcels of good fertile land, land required for the necessities of life, the landowners held the Indians at their mercy. The latter, in turn, accepted any wages the Spaniards deemed fair. Usually the wages were low, for the Spaniards were interested in high profits. The practice of buying cheap and selling high took precedence over human need. Moreover, as the Spanish dictated the time and wages of work, they also began to introduce specialized craft and occupation sectors (Florescano 1984).

Most natives wound up working more days than the number specified by repartimiento. These specified days were a safeguard to allow them time to work their own land, but generally they had little land and were rapidly losing what remained. Instead, laborers sought more work on Spanish-held land for subsistence, and especially to acquire the new medium of exchange to pay the tribute, money (Florescano 1984). Because of this need and the landowner's demand for low-paid laborers, the owner-worker relationship turned sharply in favor of the former. The landowners enthusiastically participated, for their empire would quickly crumble if labor demands went unmet. Denied the right to leave the farm, the laborers were bound to the land in a very duplicitous way. Goods and money were advanced to them and they became obligated to work off this debt. This was a legal tactic that led to another more solidly institutionalized system known as the Mexican hacienda (Ruiz 1992; Israel 1975; Zavala 1943). Oddly, the initial push was to allow them the right to participate in a "free market" system, but it ended up the opposite (Florescano 1984).

Hacienda System and Debt Peonage

Undoubtedly, the mechanism that established a bonded landowner-laborer network leading to the hacienda system was the practice of advancing Indians money or credit for future work (Wolf 1982; Chevalier 1966). Offering advancements, landowners or their emissaries scoured the countryside for prospective workers, even infringing on mission domains and free Indian communities. The temptation was too great for Indians who lacked resources, for they still had to survive. If the contract was accepted, the worker fulfilled his part by working for a set period. Indians who defaulted were sought by the authorities and punished. In this way, they were bonded to the land as debt peons, and the landowners became their overseers and creditors.

With the available labor pool thus anchored to the land, the hacienda system burgeoned. Its evolution and the gradual consolidation of the native work force became the socioeconomic features that marked the colonial epoch. Peonage, and specifically debt peonage, was the trademark of the hacienda system. It grew slowly but strongly and lasted until the twentieth century. At first Indians were given money or credit to work a specified time, but later, with meager wages and *hacendado* (landowner) demands for a permanent workforce, the relationship changed. For example, workers frequently extended their stay on a job by accepting more credit or money. A vicious circle resulted in which they seldom completed the contract without asking for more credit ahead of time. They found themselves as poor at the end of the contract as at the beginning and signed on again for more credit. Whenever a family need or crisis required extra money, they might mortgage away a year or two of the future. If the household head died before fulfilling the contract, the sons would inherit the debt. In effect, "heritable debt" (Wolf 1982) weighed heirs down even before they could start their own families.

Other hacienda practices besides debt peonage affected the Indians. Bound to the land, the peons were also required to benefit the hacendados by buying on credit from *tiendas de raya* (hacienda stores). Also, they had to live in dwellings provided by landowners that were poor in quality, since good homes cost money and might lower the hacendado's profits (Chevalier 1966; Whetten 1969).

The hacienda itself was an offshoot of the medieval feudal system. Many Dark Age customs flourished in the New World. In the readaptation to the new setting, however, there was a flexibility and resilience that allowed the hacienda to be the production unit for mining, livestock, farming, and other craft and specialty trades. Nevertheless, the 1500 to 1700 era marked the formation of the landed estate, and while local units and networks are important, it was the macrolevel, world developments that generated a peasant class. While they differed somewhat in central and eastern Europe, in Mexico, these regional transformations took the forms of encomienda, repartimiento, and gradually debt peonage and outright slavery (Wolf 1982; Stein and Stein 1970; Israel 1975).

Still, there were many instances when natives escaped the worst effects of a hacienda-type system. This was especially true in mission, *republicas de indios* (Ruiz 1992), communal towns in southern Mexico (Chance 1978), where natives were either in complete control or assisted

Patron on landed estate.

the church fathers; in these cases they avoided debt peonage. Recent research has also shown that many peons willingly moved from villages to haciendas when times were hard (Gibson 1984). Despite these exceptions, the native majority, and especially the growing mestizo population, came under the hacienda system in the other regions.

Social Role of Hacendados

The quasi-medieval manor complex of the hacienda became the cornerstone of colonial society, although with significant variations from region to region (Wolf 1982). In an almost knightly fashion, the hacendado patron protected and cared for the native peons, a patronage/peonage social world efficiently and obediently structured to serve the interests of the empire.

Key to Spanish rule was the role of individual and personal initiative. Each of the strong-willed hacendados—whether conquistadors, late-arrival civilians, lawyers, or merchants—established a mini-empire based on a strong hand and indomitable will. A patronage system of social relations prevailed, in which the hacendado opted for the parent role and forced the peons to play children (Hewes 1954). If they misbehaved, he sternly upbraided them; if they were hard working and respectful, he solemnly patted their heads in a gesture of assurance. The patron hacendado was a god-figure on the landed estate, regardless of how well or badly Indians conducted themselves (Paz 1961).

Much of this paternal quality stemmed from the strong assertive manner of the conquistadores. From the start they used the vanquished race and depressed their spirit to take advantage of the new possessions. Being soldiers rather than workers, they fashioned unjust privileges to acquire wealth (Ruiz 1992; MacLachlan and Rodriquez O. 1980; Ramos 1962).

Colonists who followed adhered to this type of manly behavior. Spanish tradition supported this strong, lordly male image that was readapted to New World conditions. *Caudillismo* (charismatic leadership) was the offshoot of this inclination. Beginning on a small scale on haciendas or in minor military engagements, many *caudillos* rose to high positions of national leadership. Caudillismo is associated with the drive to acquire an economic empire and, later, political leverage. The Indian population served as the backdrop for this scenario.

The Spaniards continued to use Indian labor for farming, now turning to cash crop commerce. Sugar, coffee, maize, rice, bananas, wheat, tobacco, chocolate, and other crops were the mainstays of a growing economic empire. In most instances each of these crops and related enterprises constituted a monopoly (cf., tobacco, Deans-Smith 1992). Much of the harvest was processed for export to the Old World (Raat 1992; Stein and Stein 1970), and some became sources of immense wealth, Cochineal (a red dye from an insect that feeds on cactuses), for example, became second only to silver in importance (Wolf 1982). Although there was a gain for the natives in having pigs, sheep, goats, and so on incorporated into their subsistence system, they actually lost with these changes in their environment (Florescano 1984).

Specializing in sugar and pulque in the central region and cattle hides in the north, the haciendas supported the colony. Moreover, as self-sufficient estates, the haciendas provided the landowner and peons with all the necessities of life. On some of these estates, particularly the *mestas* (cattle or livestock ranches), the hacendados ruled on horseback. Accompanying the conquest, occupation, and settlement by Europeans was the introduction of livestock and the various related enterprises associated with it: cattle, sheep, *vaqueros* (cowboys), sheepherding, processing and distribution of products, and so on. Such activities speeded up culture change among the population and accelerated Spanish imperialism. In short, the long workdays and exploitation of families and peasant communities were behind the economic success of the hacienda (Florescano 1984).

Hacendados who controlled the largest parcels of land sought higher rewards, such as prestige and esteem from their fellow citizens. Consequently, social life revolved around the *gentil* (genteel) population, who maintained city residences along with their landed estates—the city for living and the country estate for supporting that lifestyle (Raat 1992; Florescano 1984; Morse 1989). Many enjoyed leisure and recreation in both urban and rural settings. Colonial society was based on hacendado-peon relationships, which included a complex of feelings, attitudes, and activities that demonstrated and reinforced superordinate/subordinate and superior/inferior relations and behaviors. Today, even though the hacienda system has presumably ended, this climate of feeling persists in a large part of Latin America (Kicza 1993; Wagley and Harris 1958).

Life of the Debt Peons: Mechicanos

As previously noted, the ethnic label "Chicano" was probably derived from the word "Mechicano," a sixteenth-century pronunciation of Mex(ch)icano. After the conquest and subjugation of central Mexican natives, the Spaniards generally referred to them as Mechicanos and later used the term for other similarly vanquished Indians. The word finally became synonymous with the dispossessed lower-class peons. It is interesting and somehow symbolic that the Aztec tribal name, Mexica, became fixed in this way. Because of the social class relationships of the colonial period, an ethnic label for the lower class became cemented in the minds of a people to remind them of their station, presumably so that they would remain there.

All of the pre-Columbian Indian classes—pipiltin, macequales, and so on—were compressed into one: peons. Limited exceptions were members of the Indian nobility who cooperated during the early sixteenth century and whose families, in some instances, maintained their *cacique* (local chieftain, an Arawak word brought from the West Indies by the Spanish [Gibson 1984]) role near the end of the colonial period (Gruzinski 1988). Although some remained in leadership positions, most eventually found themselves in the lowest class. According to the thinking of that time, the "doctrine of natural slavery was entirely applicable to the Indians on the grounds of their inferiority" (Elliott 1963:71–72; see also Knight 1990). Noble collaborators assisted in the maintenance of an empire and often mixed with the Spanish racially, but over time, social class barriers hardened and most were eased out of their higher status.

As the natives acculturated (learned about and adjusted to) Spanish culture, they also realized that moving up socially came with it, especially if they joined in the system that kept most of them down. In other words, they became cogs and springs in the wheels that ran the colonial enterprise, helping in the oppression.

Rationale of Social Classes

Spanish colonial authorities defined socioeconomic class rankings simply. Usually, "color-class became . . . to a certain extent entangled with labor-class" (de Madariaga 1947). In addition to race, place of birth and occupation determined social status. Spaniards born in Spain were at the top. Known as *gachupines* ("those who wear spurs"), they occupied the highest positions of religious, political, economic, and social life. Gachupines were primarily responsible for curbing overexploitation of Indians by *criollos* (Spaniards born in the New World) and maintaining control of the colony for Spain.

Below gachupines in the social order were criollos, some of whom carried a slight amount of Indian or African blood, a fact they preferred to conceal (Knight 1990). The criollos adopted the attitudes and behavior of gachupines, but most were artisans, mineowners, parish priests, merchants, and landowners. They were unable to attain the higher-status businesses or occupations and came to resent the Spaniards. There were close to one million of them by the end of the eighteenth century, and by then, British expansionist threats had opened opportunities for them in the military. Before this military calling (which also offered social advancement for many mestizos and Hispanicized Indians), criollos were barred from the highest church and state offices.

Commoners in the city of Puebla.

An interesting group of this period, almost as unfortunate as the Indians, were the mestizos, individuals defined as racially mixed, whose fortunes waxed and waned by virtue of how closely their color matched that of the Europeans (Ruiz 1992; Knight 1990). Many racial and social-class subdivisions, based on various combinations of Spanish, Indian, and African descent, existed within this category. Birthright (parentage of a higher status) and racial appearance were the determining factors of group membership. The mestizos' rise was woefully slow and generally filled occupations in the new colonial enterprises as "rootless" men (Florescano 1984:168). In this period they were mineworkers, vaqueros, craftsmen, soldiers, hacienda peons, and small-store owners. A few could be found in the lower clerical ranks.

Then as today, Indians and Africans were at the bottom of the socioeconomic ladder in Mexico. According to colonial law, Indians were given a high legal status, but social practice placed them below almost everybody else (Morner 1967; Kicza 1993). In some respects their treatment was similar to that of Africans, who were without legal rights and remained peons/slaves throughout this time. A small proportion were able to rise in their status by "raising color" through intermarriage with criollos or mestizos. To escape the grasp of land-hungry Spaniards, and aided by protective clerics, a sizable minority of Indians established communal villages, or *republicas de indios* (Zavala 1943). However, the majority worked on estates or in enterprises owned by others. High positions in any realm of society were outside their command, with the exception of those individuals who migrated to the cities and became part of the craft and *obraje* (woolen cloth workshops) system (Gibson 1984).

An additional explanation based on hegemony (nested and interrelated levels and processes of power) may clarify this social-class system (Mallon 1995:6–7). At the apex were people living in urban areas (mostly gachupines, criollos, and some mestizo workers) as the beneficiaries of the hegemonic socioeconomic network, especially the merchant class, who sat above all and controlled the capital and credit (Florescano 1984). The Indians, mestizos, and Africans making up the population of the satellite rural enterprises (agrarian or livestock haciendas, mines, small Indian communal farms, or towns specializing in particular crafts) increasingly fell behind economically because they functioned primarily to provide urban areas with the products of their labor, which they had little power to control. This arrangement deprived them of a fair share of production and forced them to live a hand-to-mouth existence. Esteem, prestige, and power were retained by the Spaniards. This invidious social structure, which developed one group by underdeveloping another, lasted for three hundred years. Even today, Indians, as well as other indigenous groups worldwide, have good reason to feel that they are the victims of uneven capitalist development and have been so for centuries (Frank 1969).

Wolf's words are reminders of colonization and imperialism: "The conquering Spaniard became a mining entrepreneur, a producer of commercial crops, a rancher, a merchant . . . he wanted to organize and press the human resources under his command, to enlarge his estate, to take his place among the other men grown rich and powerful in the new utopia" (Wolf 1959:176; see Wolf 1982).

Culture: Hispanicization and Mestizaje

Cultural life during this period was complex, full of contrasts and loaded with strains. Imagine the earth-shattering effect of the initial conquest, followed by a systematic and pressured expansion into other territories and encounters with new indigenous groups. The natives varied in their reactions and responses, in part depending on the intensity and duration of their exposure to the Spanish presence. Many natives quickly absorbed the dominant culture; however, even to this day others remain

Boy hauling wood in
Guatemalan highlands.

Girls carrying water.

Man weeding maize field.

Men playing native flute and drum.

Indian. Escape from Spanish jurisdiction usually meant moving to the hinterland or hidden mountain valleys (Gibson 1984). A few refused to leave and somehow retained strong elements of Indian culture. Spanish efforts to impart their culture, whether to assimilate or acculturate Indians, were also very uneven and incomplete. In large part this stemmed from the conflicting goals of different groups and interests that set upon the natives, often working at cross-purposes. This variance also stems from the diverse roots of Spanish culture, especially the Iberian regional differences (Hewes 1954).

Shift in Cultural Orientation

Colonial life was such a hodgepodge of cultural themes and activities that it is impossible to cover all aspects of it. Certain phenomena should be mentioned, however, especially in regard to the larger Indian entities or states who changed in a more uniform way (Gibson 1984). Such a time of cultural replacement involved the Spanish elites reserving the high culture to themselves. Spanish language and some technology—whatever was essential as well as the "leftovers" of culture—were imparted to Indians and later, mestizos. Contributing to a shifting cultural orientation, this lack of a stable cultural adaptation ensured their permanent placement in the lower classes. In addition, many cultural maladaptations—drinking, fighting, suspicion and distrust, and so forth—eventually became norms for thought and action, further guaranteeing low-class status. A discussion of Spanish colonial culture necessarily involves the process by which the dominant group made the learning of their culture the gateway to success, and conversely, the way in which the subordinate majority was moved to cultural disorientation, instability, and confusion. These impediments to learning "high" culture thus reinforced the almost castelike system designed to prevent social mobility.

Ironically, early in the colonial period, Indians and mestizos became the carriers of either Spanish culture or a hybrid version, what is referred to as a "Hispanicized, institutionalized Indian" way (Gibson 1984:394). For example, Spanish conquistadores and settlers moved north after the pacification of most Mesoamerican people. Many Hispanicized Indian and mestizo settlers accompanied them to the legendary Aztlan, home of the Chichimeca tribes. This area, known as the Spanish borderlands by writers focusing on the colonial period, is now the United States Southwest (Gerhard 1993). As noted, it is an area with ancient Mesoamerican connections (Ericson and Baugh 1993; Wills and Leonard 1994). There, as early as 1539, the Spaniards searched for gold and silver (Weber and Rausch 1994). The earlier contact-conflict-change scheme was repeated, but with substantial modifications, as the newcomers initiated other enterprises. In 1598, the "silver king" Juan

D'Onate moved north from the mines of Zacatecas and founded the first permanent colony in New Mexico (Gutierrez 1991). Thus, Indians and mestizos came to play a cultural role in the further expansion of the colonial empire. Many of them oppressed and exploited the Indians in the new territories. Others became settlers, often merging with the natives as had been the practice in Mexico, thus remingling blood lines based on ancient traditions. Thus went the expansion and incorporation of new northern territories, New Mexico followed by Texas and eventually California and Arizona, all mostly occupied by the "new" Mexicans. The pueblo of Los Angeles, known then as the Indian community of Yang-na, was settled in 1776 by two Spaniards, one mestizo, two Africans, eight mulattoes, and nine Indians from Mexico (McWilliams 1990).

During the territorial expansion, both Spanish and native culture changed. Many new patterns emerged, but three basic types stand out: (1) a culture taken directly from Spain, but reconfigured and altered under New World demands and pressures; (2) a culture primarily native to the New World with slight, mostly technological, influences from Europe; and (3) a wide, variable cultural spectrum derived from the merging of Old and New World traits. As noted, the Spanish utilized selected Indian political and economic practices in imposing their rule in the New World. The merging of late Spanish medieval hierarchies with indigenous structures brought about a peasant society that affected the bulk of the indigenous population.

Introduction of Catholicism

Religion provides an example of cultural merging. Church leaders attempted to integrate Indian elements—especially from larger, more influential groups' cultures—into the Catechism, finding success especially with saints and saint worship that paralleled icons and spiritual imageries already well developed by natives (Lockhart 1992). Cults centered on natural forces were particularly utilized to effect this end. Acceptance of external signs of Catholicism also became common even as many now unlawful Indian practices continued to be conducted in secret (Haring 1963).

Religion and Spanish language instruction influenced the shaping of a new Indian view of life. At least one author traces the beginning of Indian bilingualism to early religious rites; "It was baptism that started the process of change in the indigenous naming system" (Lockhart 1992:119). Clerics admonished neophytes who failed to serve their hacendados faithfully. While teaching the Indians religion, the missionaries taught respect for authority (Simpson 1966; Haring 1963). Natives were continually reminded that, no matter how bad the conditions or difficult the times, they would surely go to heaven if they remained obedient and dutiful; however, hell was the certain destination if they disobeyed and rebelled (Burkhart 1989). Furthermore, they were told that the Christian God favored especially those who suffered and remained strong in the faith. According to the teaching, earthly experience was merely a testing ground to determine where one would go after death. Missionary success stemmed from the power held by conquistadores who helped make sure that Indian children learned Catholic dogma.

Because the Indians were deeply religious anyway, they followed many Christian teachings perfectly (Lockhart 1992). Further, it made sense to the colonial powers to substitute a new thinking process in the minds of the new workers. Thus, religious worship was the most open area of colonial life to Indians. If they were not devoting time to church-related activities, as in the civil-religious hierarchy, they were consciously attempting to follow new teachings and practices in their daily lives. In addition, many Indians built and maintained missions and churches and established permanent residence there. They were very devout subjects indeed, just as they had been when they controlled the world.

Only one God was placed before them, but the many Christian saints, and especially the Virgen de Guadalupe, found ready acceptance by a people accustomed to a pantheon. Baptism, rituals, ceremonies, prayers, fasting, confessions, heaven, hell, and purgatory were not new concepts to the Indians and were thus easily adopted (Madsen 1967; Lockhart 1992; Burkhart 1989). Oddly, the symbolic sacrifice of the Catholic mass, with bread and wine representing the body and blood of Jesus Christ, was also reminiscent of Indian rituals. According to some writers, the sacrifice in the Catholic mass is a legacy of pre-Christian ceremonies when a lamb was slain and offered to the gods. Such similarities simplified the enforced transition to a new spiritual reality.

When possible, missionaries incorporated Indian practices to teach Catholic dogma (Gibson 1966). For example, in pre-Columbian times, towns honored a patron deity with a processional. The clerics staged the affair on the already established day but replaced Indian idols with Christian saints; thus, a mixed Indian-Spanish ceremony evolved (Ruiz de Alarcon 1984; Ricard 1966). As noted, "The Indian . . . embraced Catholicism but in his own fashion" (Ruiz 1992:70). This is most obvious in how peasant religion has evolved, become institutionalized, and lasted, in some places, even to the present (Foster 1990; Chinas 1983; Ingham 1986; Gossen and Leon-Portilla 1993). This syncretism, the combination of two distinct cultural styles into a wide-ranging new one, also occurred in other areas of life.

Every city and town had its church.

Mestizaje: Cultural Blending

"And here a new culture is coming into being, a mixed culture derived not only from the Spain of colonial times, but also from the aboriginal cultures of America. . . . Not only do the mode of life and point of view appear to be emerging as a fusion of diverse elements from other cultures, but, in the process of synthesis, local adaptations and innovations have been added, so that the total configuration of the culture seems to be developing aspects of uniqueness" (Gillin 1957:158–60). While this mestizaje process affected each group differently, depending on how close and familiar they were with Spanish culture, it was most clearly reflected in the emergence of a peasant social and cultural life in the Indian communities as well as the new *casta* (half breed) or *cholo* (racial and cultural marginal) populations rapidly becoming a part of Mexico.

Neither totally Indian nor Spanish, Mexican culture today is largely the result of this merging (Reck 1986). With the clash of civilizations, recounted by participants then and by ethnographers today, Spanish elements and Indian traits have been fused, blended, or simply juxtaposed, and have evolved to the present cultural ethos of the Mexican people (Gruzinski 1988). "It is precisely this success [of cultural blending] which sets Mexico apart . . . in Latin America" (Madsen 1967:370; Vasconcelos and Gamio 1926). Saying this, it is still an "inadequately studied" and poorly understood phenomenon (Gibson 1984:414).

Even the Spanish language underwent a syncretic change. Indian words aided the transmission of European concepts. Some words were integrated into the Spanish language because they represented a feature of Indian reality that was totally alien to the Spaniards. Language borrowing, creating, and synthesizing developed a linguistic spectrum of native and Spanish patterns (Hill and Hill 1986). "Some 5,000 Nahuatl words—like *metate* (from Nahuatl metlatl, 'quern'), *chiquihuite* (from Nahuatl chiquihuitl, 'basket'), *tepescuingle* (from Nahuatl escuintli, 'little dog', in Mexican Spanish, 'little boy')—came into everyday use among speakers of Mexican Spanish" (Wolf 1959:46). Moreover, many Indians who learned Spanish fashioned a new sound and style. This resulted in the many regional patterns and intonations found today. Some Indians became well versed in Spanish and shed their Indian idioms. Others even today speak mostly the Indian dialect. Either through design or accident, these tribes avoided heavy Spanish influence and remained isolated (Ricard 1966; Hewes 1954). Unfortunately, this linguistic diversity has led to critical adjustment problems for many people.

One of the most fascinating and creative examples of syncretic development is in the area of diet, medicine, and health practices (Ortiz de Montellano 1990). Indian food, basically the American Trinity of corn (maize), beans, and squash, with a dash of chili, was revamped and embellished with wheat, rice, and various other ingredients (Sokolov 1991). With a reliance on domesticated animals imported from Europe, many new dishes and flavors emerged. In short, Indian and Spanish food evolved into Mexican food; and when corn was unavailable for tortillas in the northern mining regions, wheat flour (*harina*) substituted and became a new favorite for many (Gonzales 1997). Even the evolution of liquor is traced from pulque to mezcal to tequila, each increasingly a refinement of juices from the maguey plant. This syncretism is evident in many medical practices and cures, with ancient ailments (*susto, mal de ojo*) and cures mixed in with modern knowledge and treatments, and even the persistence today of *curanderos* (folk curers) (Foster 1990).

A syncretic style also pertained to art and architecture, although perhaps these were more dominated by Spanish traits. "Hispanic American arts and crafts, while owing much to Indian developments, reveal profound and far-reaching European influences" (Foster 1960:4). The European culture of that time, including Moorish elements (which go back to the early Middle East), was reflected in official buildings, churches, and domestic dwellings. Indians made their biggest contribution in their labor and construction materials. Adobe materials and designs are both indigenous and Spanish, but the red tile roof has obvious Moorish influences. Conversely, many traditional Spanish customs began to be altered by native forms and practices as in, for example, poetry and ballads. In particular, religious syncretisms generated a diverse and interesting host of developments to make the new Mexican rituals and ceremonies festive and colorful. This mixing process also occurred in other creative activities: philosophy, jewelry, pottery, and music.

Numerous social customs and cultural perspectives evolved through syncretism. Equally important, though, is that many of these traits were adaptive reactions, fashioned for survival reasons, or "defensive reactions" (Gibson 1984:415). For instance, the Indian emphasis on kinship, family, and neighbor relationships persisted for several reasons. For one, kin ties became a valuable social resource in time of need. Furthermore, Catholic tradition maintained that a baptized person must have godparents, who would assume child-rearing duties if anything happened to the parents. Indians used *compadrazgo* (coparenthood) to establish social ties with nonfamily members, replacing in part the traditional calpulli networks that the Spaniards were breaking up.

Close ties between brothers and sisters continued long after they married and established separate households. They actively participated as uncles and aunts in raising each other's children. Grandparents represented the top level of the authority hierarchy in extended families. Children were taught to respect and honor their elders at all times. In the absence of an adult, supervision fell on the shoulders of the eldest child. (With adulthood, however, the male members, even those who were younger than female siblings, usually assumed a higher status [Chinas 1983].) The civil-religious hierarchy and associated ceremonial patterns, so prominent in Mexican village life today, also began as a syncretic sociopolitical practice (Foster 1990), especially in the republicas de indios (Ruiz 1992). Gathering together on a small town's patron saint day with fanfare and celebration, and with high social status and religious significance accorded the participants, these *cofradias* played a strong role in keeping natives on task. They helped cement a peasant society and gave the natives the form of power without the substance, thus fitting in very well with the new hacienda and ruling network.

Cultural Resistance and Marginality

It was during this period that the word *cholo* (from the Spanish solo, alone, but generalized to mean marginality in different ways) came into use. Initially applied to persons of "mixed" race, but later also to cultural marginality, choloismo became a mainstay in a land of conflicting and competing cultures. As pressure for Indian assimilation to Spanish ways intensified, forcing Indians into a mold, many rejected Spanish culture entirely at the same time their own was being destroyed. As a result, they were without solid roots in any culture. In contrast to those who had undergone a cultural syncretism—that is, adopted Mexican or mestizo culture in a new bilingual-bicultural way—there were many who remained culturally indecisive. This led to widespread anomie—cultural marginality and normlessness, or the equivalent of the Aztec nepantilism.

Rigid class biases limit movement between the two cultural worlds in an effort to freeze members of the subordinate cultural group in their places. The merging of cultures is never a smooth or even amalgamation, and sometimes takes rough turns and twists in the mind of an individual. Racial intermixture contributed to this difficulty (Ramos 1962), because mixed parentage created a mental confusion, with one parent representing the rulers and the other, the ruled. Significantly, "what the colonial society feared was not the creation of mixed offspring but the growth of a large mass of unattached, disinherited, rootless people in its centers and along its margins" (Wolf 1959:237).

For people in this quandary, certain problems arise when selecting one cultural world or another. One kind of problem comes when members of the dominant culture reject members of the subordinate culture who seek to join them. Another occurs when subordinate members remain in their original cultural milieu but are totally dissatisfied with its offerings. Thus, the group to which they aspire rejects them, and they despise the group to which they belong. Furthermore, such individuals are often members of groups that are themselves set apart on the periphery of social and political institutions and relations, and notably separate from the primary elites and other racial or cultural groups that have attained more favor.

It is precisely in this class and cultural setting that revolutions and revolutionaries are made (Friedrich 1968). Outside the mainstream of economic and political power, bereft of their original cultural moorings, and forced into changing cultural cues and forms, many people are quickly galvanized to push for "greater change or transformation" (Mallon 1995:6). Many Indians, and especially mestizos and cholos, reacted to Spanish contact, conflict, and change in this fashion.

Problems of Adaptation

The colonial period reflected a number of sociocultural problems. One that seriously affected demographic conditions stemmed from the diseases brought to Mexico by Europeans. Smallpox, typhus, measles, typhoid fever, and diphtheria epidemics wiped out whole towns. This was referred to as "the Great Dying" by Eric Wolf (1982:133). Because they were "isolated from the rest of the world . . . Amerindians had developed no resistance at all against these diseases" (Morner 1967:32). As noted previously, the native population suffered radical losses, particularly near the middle of the sixteenth century (1540s) (Lockhart 1992; Gibson 1966). Yet this was only the immediately observable part of the destruction—the aftermath had similarly dire effects.

For example, certain calpullis lost 80 percent of their people through disease, but those who remained still were held to the same tribute quota. "Of more importance is the fact that the recounts and reassessments consistently lagged behind the rapid shrinkage in the number of tribute payers, with the result that the survivors had to bear the tribute burdens of those who had died or fled" (Zorita 1963:12). How were these tribute quotas met? Simply by having survivors work harder and longer, with little time for anything else, to fulfill the tribute goal (Gibson 1964).

The colonial social structure was established to benefit the Spanish materially. It is important to stress, though, how the inclusion of new cultural habits complemented new social relations. Programs for Indian cultural awareness were designed to help them take their place in the new social order: ideas about life fitted in with one's position in the social structure.

Even with much resistance and the preservation of Indian lifeways, such as speaking their native language, the long colonial period wore down the population and took its toll, peasantization took hold, whereupon the bulk of the Indians became Catholic (albeit with a Mexican

Catholic ideology), joined community organizations (such as the cofradias), and generally adopted many Spanish beliefs and habits (Wagley and Harris 1958; Ingham 1986). Indian acceptance of Spanish authority also meant alteration of their attitudes and behavior toward leaders, and the introduction of the patron-peon complex (Foster 1990). To help natives in acting the "right way," their value system was revised to include highly formal rules of etiquette—all, of course, denoting a superordinate/subordinate relationship. Since Indians were already instilled with a respectful demeanor, they learned the new terms and actions quickly. The preexisting Indian humility was part of their philosophical view, which stressed the immensity of the world and de-emphasized egoism or self-importance. Humans were only a small part of the vast universe; they must coexist with other elements in it.

According to one expert, there were many factors that affected Indian acculturation. "Apart from agriculture, the accelerated migration to the cities, the further penetration of Spaniards into the hinterland, the unrelieved expansion of *mestizaje,* the many Spanish goods that found their way into Indian markets, were all factors inducing a progressive Indian acculturation" (Gibson 1984:416). Of course, in some places these alterations also included new reactions to the imposed and profound changes underway, such as the defensive strategies of (1) repression; (2) symbolic creation of an ideal environment; (3) self-disparagement; and (4) individualism (Kearney 1986). Most of these show the flip side of this type of rapid, intense culture change and its aftermaths.

While Indians fulfilled their part of the bargain, remaining honorable and dutiful, the Spanish skirted theirs. In the words of an early colonial Indian: "You have deprived us of our good order and way of government. . . . Now all is confusion and without order and harmony. The Indians have given themselves to fighting because you have brought it upon them . . . those who are not in contact with you do not fight; they live in peace" (Leon-Portilla 1963:151). The native people are still patiently waiting for the successors of the Spanish to lead in a way beneficial to all.

Political Structure

The Spaniards dominated the political institutions, which were linked to economic practices; and strangely, with the fragmentation of the Indian state, they reestablished the small political units that existed in pre-Columbian times (Gibson 1984). This was not a simple, routine arrangement, but rather one of "factionalism, infighting, and often complicated alliances of political and economic power" (Altman 1991:417). Conquistadores-turned-encomenderos initially dominated all aspects of the situation, although political power was supposedly concentrated in the hands of the Spanish king. Beginning with the introduction of the encomienda system, 20 percent of all production extracted by a colonist was paid to the king—the crown's fifth. Thus, the king was at the top of the political hierarchy. Situated in Spain, and directly under the king in authority, was the Council of Indies. They approved subordinate leaders and groups, made general policy decisions, and curbed the power and influence of ambitious colonists (Skidmore and Smith 1992; Gibson 1966, Elliott 1963).

The various *audiencias* (advisory and judicial bodies) in the New World were next in importance, particularly the first *cabildo* (town government) organized by Cortes and others. It was from this center that authority spread out into the countryside (Raat 1992). Each of these was composed of *oidores* (justices), whose number varied depending on audiencia land size. Each audiencia controlled its separate domain, serving as the supreme court, council, and executive and legislative bodies; at first these were notoriously corrupt and acquisitive (Ruiz 1992; Altman 1991). Depending on the time period and individual personalities, the audiencias were often more powerful than the Council of Indies. Since an ocean separated the council from the colony, it was easy for the audiencia to control affairs. The viceroy was the only barrier to audiencia dominance; he was appointed by the king to protect royal interests in the New World. Although the audiencia legally had the final word in checking the viceroy's actions, the viceroy had the imprimatur of the king, so political power often was determined by the personal strength or weakness of the viceroy.

Corregidores (governors) and *alcaldes mayores* (mayors) were in charge of smaller administrative units. By collecting tribute, they also could assign Indians to public works. In keeping with the innovative way the Spanish ruled, many local Indian ranking tlatoque were integrated into this network and referred to as *cacique* or *gobernador* (Lockhart 1992), apparently maintaining some semblance of this role until near the end of the colonial era (Gruzinski 1988).

Local town government followed a Spanish pattern that was a legacy of Roman times. New World natives filled positions in this framework, however, under the aforementioned cofradia or *cargo* (Kearney 1986) system that utilized indigenous ruling forms but sharply limited the range of their powers. The town leader, usually a criollo, was the municipal secretary. His authority was paramount. Indians served under the secretary as a council of elders (*principales*), or one was selected by the elders as the alcalde mayor. Others filled lower positions as *aguaciles* (constables). The Indians provided administrative and judicial services under the secretary's continual supervision. The secretary dictated policy and could veto native political decisions (Cancian 1967; Foster 1990).

The Spaniard's use of Indian cultural tradition to govern town members was very effective. This innovative strategy was based on the Indian practice in which leaders carried out duties in both the political and religious sectors (Carrasco 1965). For example, if a man became an aguacile, later rising to the higher rank of principale, he would have a dual role; he would perform civic duties and also lead group participation in religious ceremonies, especially during yearly patron-day celebrations. Different roles made up the civil-religious hierarchy, almost like a stepladder. This tradition was continued because colonial administrators realized that it would serve their purposes. Real political power remained in Spanish hands, and native-turned-peasant roles were mostly show. This format strengthened the double-pronged strategy the Spanish favored: The crown (civil) and the church (religious) would guide natives, the latter actively; "the kinship ideology of the calpulli, itself largely fictitious, gave way to a conception of solidarity based on spiritual kinship" (Ingham 1986:189).

Education: A Double Standard

For those who were firmly integrated into the Spanish system, the education and training required for important colonial occupations relegated Indians and mestizos to menial, manual labor. Treated as children, the natives were tutored in ways that were demeaning, and even learning the Spanish language was a guarded process that proceeded slowly, lest it encourage thoughts of freedom (Ricard 1966).

At first, concerned missionaries provided a sound education, especially in mission schools. Frequently, some bright Indian students were given special attention. For these Indians, education meant becoming priests to instruct others in the new faith and doctrine (Haring 1963). However, this approach soon ran counter to the overall Spanish policy, which demanded an unlimited number of illiterate manual workers; and in any case, class and racial barriers prevented total assimilation. For the priests and teachers that were turned out with this education and became Hispanicized, the experience only whetted their appetites for more autonomy and freedom. These select few thus were marginalized in a different way. As part of their thrust toward liberation, they often led fellow natives against the Spanish (Padden 1967).

In the late sixteenth century the Indian education experiment was abandoned (Ruiz 1992). Clerics had unwittingly undermined grander colonial designs and precipitated a clash between church and civil authority. Consequently, around 1570, Jesuit priests and secular clergy more responsive to the crown were brought in to reverse the practice of favoring Indians. The new clerics developed programs that catered to *criollos*, Spaniards born in the New World.

Too much education was considered dangerous, so only a select few were allowed this privilege. Thus, the educational reversal had two purposes: to de-emphasize native intellectual development, focusing instead on craft training, and to concentrate on criollo instruction in order to enhance their leadership skills. Even a moderate assimilationist policy was aborted, as basic understanding of the Spanish language and reading and writing were kept from most Indians. "In the . . . villages only the chiefs or principales understood Castilian or could read and write, and the same may be said of many Indian communities in the Spanish American republics of today" (Haring 1963:209). Except for a few humanist missionaries, the Spaniards made no effort to teach and preserve the many Indian languages. Consequently, an Indian education was eliminated, and Spanish policy kept them from a European education. However, this action had some benefits. Isolated communal Indian villages and dozens of Indian mission towns were left alone and thus were able to preserve aspects of native culture—in many cases even to the present day.

Colonial society was supported by native labor.

The initial successes of clerics wishing to help and convert the native population had a short history. Many socioeconomic benefits resulted from clerical intervention, such as preservation of village land holdings, even though self-interest is what drove the church fathers. Ostensibly, the clerics intended to shield Indians from exploitative and oppressive encomenderos. However, as mentioned previously, these benefits were nullified before the end of the sixteenth century.

Instead of higher education—poetry, rhetoric, history, science, mathematics, and the many calendars—Indians were instructed in elementary, vocational subjects. Already mentioned were the many occupational roles Indians filled and the blending of styles into what was increasingly becoming a Mexican culture. In addition, missionaries taught the Indians masonry, carpentry, blacksmithing, horticulture, pastoralism, and the domestic chores necessary to operate colonial society optimally (Haring 1963). Thus, Indian cultural life was limited because their occupations were basic. High culture was reserved for the Spaniards and their offspring, and all that remained for Indians and mestizos was what Foster (1960) has called the "part-society" of peasant life.

Native Reactions and Resultant Problems

The Indians and mestizos reacted in a variety of ways to the patterns by which Spaniards shaped conditions to their own benefit (Gibson 1964). One generalized type of reaction that arose intermittently was nativist resistance, which stressed self-determination and the survival of Indian culture. This often took the form of a messianic revitalization response, such as the Caste Wars of Yucatan in the nineteenth century (Farriss 1993; Gruzinski 1988). It can easily be generalized that most indigenous peoples, at one time or another, fought and struggled to maintain their independence (Kicza 1993; Spicer 1962). Some chose not to risk failure, inasmuch as the Spaniards maintained military superiority, and instead retreated into wild, unsettled regions (Raat 1992); the Tarahumara and Yaqui of the northwestern Mexico region are most notable in this regard.

On numerous occasions, sporadic, unorganized resistance escalated into large-scale rebellions. One example was the Pueblo Revolt of 1680, which occurred in the northern outposts of the Spanish empire, now the United States Southwest (Weber and Rausch 1994; Bolton 1921). In this case, thirteen years passed before the Spaniards returned, and then only after the Indian coalition had dissolved. Likewise, tribes such as the Apaches and Comanches, and many others, successfully resisted for the duration of the Spanish presence. Recent events indicate that this attitude of resistance still prevails in some areas, as evidenced by events such as the 1994 New Year's Day insurrection of the Zapatista Liberation Army in Chiapas (Collier and Quaratiello 1994). Nativist resistance became a cultural characteristic of many Indians and later, mestizos; one might say that they had a permanent chip on their shoulders. Although resistance was seen by the Spaniards as deviant because it undermined their social order, it could also be interpreted as a highly adaptive human mechanism to correct injustices and deprivations. In other words, deviant behavior may become a norm when it fulfills some socially useful function (Ricard 1966).

The Spaniards, of course, attempted to suppress native resistance:

"the colonists developed new techniques anticipating . . . similar methods to be employed two and a half centuries later on the expanding United States frontier [such as the] covered wagon . . . ; soldiery . . . organized itself into flying detachments for purposes of patrols and escort. The fort or presidio made its appearance alongside the mission . . . and Spaniards established colonies of armed Indian peasants from the urban area as strategic outposts in the hostile countryside" (Wolf 1959:193; see also Gerhard 1993).

An emphasis on male physical strength and prowess was closely associated with native reaction. With roots in Spain and the Mediterranean area, Mexican male dominance evolved into an institutionalized behavior. A *macho* (masculine, virile person) equates physical with social power (Hewes 1954; Ramos 1962); he is a fighter and a hard-working protector of home and family in the mold of a traditional patriarch. Because of the misfortunes that befell the natives at this time, there was a need for this male attitude and behavior, especially to defend the honor of females, many of whom were victims of Spaniards. As one writer states: "The Spanish conquest was also a sexual conquest" (Raat 1992:34). On the other hand, the macho syndrome includes some negative traits, such as a close-minded, masculine tyranny in the home and locality. Both aspects were shaped by political and social oppression.

Another legacy linked to machismo was an increase in drinking and fighting. Before Spanish contact, "the use of *pulque* [liquor from the maguey cactus] had ordinarily been confined to the sick and aged . . . for public ceremonies and religious celebrations. Consistent popular drunkenness had been unknown. But following the conquest the native population rapidly took to drink" (Gibson 1964:150). Although this has been disputed (Lockhart 1992), the Spaniards encouraged drinking by expanding maguey plantations and opening more *pulquerias* (bars and stores). While the Spaniards benefited from this enterprise, the Indians used drinking as an escape from the reality of oppression and an escape valve to allow for the venting of violent and aggressive behavior (Kearney 1986).

As a result, along with the drinking habit, intragroup fighting became the norm. The Indian "chip on the shoulder" became a cumbersome burden that dared any man, usually the closest one and preferably one without the power to retaliate, to knock it off on any pretext (Romanucci-Ross 1986). Fearlessness in the face of death, a positive Indian trait accepting the inevitable end of life, made matters worse, for now they accelerated a confrontation with death by being overly sensitive to imagined insults and quick to fight. Indians released pent-up frustrations on fellow Indians or mestizos who experienced similar conditions of oppression (Wolf 1959).

Social mobility was adversely affected by jealousy. Many foremen of haciendas and owners of small Indian stores, who had become part of the colonial social order, were considered traitors by their people. Mestizos and *Ladinos* (Hispanicized Indians) were particularly targeted. This early atmosphere of competition for the few relatively higher-class positions open to Indians (even though low by Spanish standards) gave rise to an attitude of *envidia* (hate and envy) rather than support and admiration for those who made it (Foster 1990; Wolf 1959). It kept Indians competing against each other for the few available positions, instead of cooperating to create more opportunities. Another consequence, closely related to envidia, is the way in which peons censured those who attempted to become assimilated into the Spanish mainstream. Within the emerging peasant way of life, the juxtaposition of these contradictory and paradoxical attitudes and habits definitely drained human energies and resources. It turned a once proud people into a segmented and diffused society unable to fully reach its potential.

The days of *calmecac* (higher education) were gone; no longer were Indians intellectually and spiritually in control under the new social order. Advanced military training, received in the telpochcalli, was obviated as Indians were forced to assume lower positions as supply carriers and unskilled foot soldiers. Although Indians and mestizos were the backbone of the military, they did not receive the credit for victories or the opportunities to rise to hero status. Except for the tribes that allied themselves with the Spaniards, it was a long time before natives were allowed to participate actively in military affairs.

Color: Roots of Racism and Racial Barriers

Human interactions are always tainted by biases and prejudices that make one person or group feel superior over someone else. Indigenous groups before European arrival certainly showed this by mistreating one another on the basis of cultural or regional differences. However, all of this changed in the European encounter with the New World and other territories worldwide. Race and racism took a new form because of the scale, magnitude, and intensity of the contact experience (Banton 1987). It was a prolonged and deep-rooted affair that soon became permanent. In its permanency, it institutionalized certain practices, among them the self-righteous belief that the European races were better than Indians. To compound matters, the Europeans mixed with the native populations (and later, African slaves) to create shades of races and a "race" problem for many hybrids.

Indians especially experienced these problems in Mexico, and social relations were structured to keep natives and mestizos socially immobile. For this purpose, Spaniards made race, and a host of conditions associated with it, a crucial feature of the social system that became fixed and perpetuated (Morner 1967; Elizondo 1983). Anthropologists today disagree about the utility of the biological concept of race as applied to humans, but it is clear that as a social construct, it has been and remains very important.

Much of the thinking behind these developments revolves around ethnocentrism, the prevalent mindset of each ethnic group to see the world through its own cultural lenses. In doing this, it is common to be insensitive to other groups' ways of doing things. In other words, ethnocentrism is a way of feeling superior to others. Practically all human groups succumb to an ethnocentric attitude, including Indians (Lockhart 1992; Wagley and Harris 1958). In this case, however, the Spaniards (and Europeans generally during the age of expansion and conquest) were responsible for the introduction of a different variant of it. It is one thing to follow a benign type of ethnocentrism, where one feels proud and confident of his or her way of life. It is quite another matter to negatively intensify this attitude, infringing upon and denigrating the rights and privileges of others. This is a malignant ethnocentrism, better termed racism.

Ethnocentrism and Development

The Spaniards used racial criteria to consolidate their ethnocentric program. Racial prejudice and discrimination cemented the economic relationships underway—this was the introduction of an incipient brand of racism (Cox 1970). Race joined with other barriers to perpetuate inequalities and inequities. Since the age of exploration and discovery, racial prejudice has often been an integral aspect of the formation of a class system based on inequality. The designation of social race worked to advance one racial group at the expense of another and neatly meshed with and solidified socioeconomic development/underdevelopment arrangements. Individual differences based on innate intelligence could not make this system work, for the Indians had at least an equal percentage of potentially intelligent members as the Spanish (Brues 1990). Therefore, a simple device was introduced to act as a hindrance to upward mobility: One group was credited with superior qualities to become and remain dominant, while the other was assigned inferior traits to keep them subordinate (Graham 1990; Wolf 1959; Kicza 1993).

Indians were considered dreary, reticent, lazy, and backward by the Spaniards, who generally looked down upon them (Gibson 1966). Cultural habits and customs are often the criteria for a superior/inferior relationship. The Spanish cultural imperialism program, as noted previously, made natives feel culturally inadequate. But what happens when the subordinate group assimilates the dominant culture? This possibility was foiled by introducing racial barriers. Changing one's culture is far easier than changing one's race or face. Simply stated, racial dogma is adopted to prevent the so-called inferior races from attaining their political rights and status as equal competitors.

In establishing the colonial class system, the Spaniards viewed dark-complexioned natives as biologically and physically inferior (Zavala 1943). There was no real basis for this thinking, but the actual social realities dictated that a new belief system was needed. Thus, one's physical appearance determined how high a person would climb on the social-class scale. This attitude, together with the elimination of educational programs for Indians, locked the natives into menial status. Being paternalistic and treating the Indians as children made it easier for the Spaniards (Zavala 1943).

Mestizaje: Racial Mixture

Coming to the New World without Spanish wives or companions, the conquistadores had to work out other arrangements (Skidmore and Smith 1992; van den Berghe 1967; Morner 1967). When Indian nobles presented young women to the Spanish victors, the Spaniards soon recognized a benefit besides satisfaction of their sexual appetites. By accepting this overture, they gained legitimate entrance into Indian society. In future years their sons could claim dual leadership status: by right of conquest and through the line of native aristocratic descent (Gibson 1964). Soon after, they were part of the criollo group who became "rivals of their Spanish parents" (Ruiz 1992:54).

The queen and her court at a town festival.

More often, Spanish males consummated sexual unions by force, adding sexual conquest to the spoils of war (Raat 1992). Many of the first mestizo offspring resulted from incidents of forcible rape (van den Berghe 1967; Padden 1967). "Because formal marriages between Indians and non-Indians were rare, it is safe to say that the great majority of first generation mestizos were the bastard offspring of Spanish men and Indian women" (Gibson 1964:144). With the exception of the offspring of Indian elites, it was rare indeed to find a mestizo who could claim an Indian father and Spanish mother (Cope 1994).

Years later this continued to be true. Bands of mestizo children, fifty or more in number, wandered the countryside seeking sustenance and security, rejected by both Spaniards and Indians. Mestizos were shunned by their Spanish fathers because of their native features and non-Christian, illegitimate birth. Similarly, because they represented a living physical memory of the rape of Indian women and Indian civilization, they were turned out from indigenous communities (Wolf 1959). Illicit unions involving Africans added to the mixed and dispossessed population. As noted, with the sharp decline of the Indian population, more Africans were brought in to maintain the size of the labor force, especially in the tropical lowlands. Blacks joined the mestizaje phenomenon to further diversify the racial heritage of Mexico. Coastal regions today, particularly Vera Cruz, Guerrero, and Oaxaca, strongly reflect this influence in both the physical appearance of the people as well as the culture, food, and music (Aguirre Beltran 1946). As the in-between-people, the "solos" (alone, abandoned) or cholos and castas, were often found in the interstices of society—the back alleys, the taverns, mining camps, and so on—and limited to these social settings, affected unions with similarly dispossessed outcasts. The offspring thus produced in larger number comprised an almost infinite variety of hybrids (Wolf 1959). There was a gradual increase of the mestizo population, and by the end of the colonial period they constituted 11 percent of the people in Mexico (Raat 1992).

Mestizo Mentality

"The growing mestizo element in the population suffered even more than the legally protected Indian communities, and was further stigmatized with being the product of casual liaisons of Spanish men and Indian women" (Hewes 1954:217). Not surprisingly, the mestizos learned to see themselves as alone in the world. The unjust rejection by the original (parental) participants in the New World left the mestizo abandoned and unaccepted by nearly everyone. Included in their exclusion and isolation was an awareness that social privileges and political influences were outside their orbit. This gave rise to the mestizo mentality, an approach to life that was unconventional and sometimes deviant. As survivors, they had to readapt anew each day, improvise on the spot, and accept the shifting nature of their social condition. Through the use of "smoke and mirrors," such a person navigated the hidden passageways of society (Wolf 1959). "Undoubtedly, much of the aggressive, boisterous, and untrusting nature of the early mestizo mentality grew from this experience" (Ramos 1962:57–63).

In the mestizo philosophical framework, fearlessness and a sense of vulnerability shifted according to the situation, both real and imagined. "Where the Indian saw power as an attribute of office and redistributed it with care lest it attach itself to persons, the mestizo would value power as an attribute of the self, as the personal energy that could subjugate and subject people" (Wolf 1959:239).

One could easily affix a mental state based on the racial variety of the mestizos. Coming from Spanish-Indian or Indian-African racial backgrounds, and amalgamation thereof, they were a hybrid race representing a color spectrum from white to black, from European to native or African features. There were also new, heretofore unseen variations of color and physiognomic qualities. Mestizos were referred to as Ladinos, a term that originally meant Hispanicized Indian. Later Ladino became synonymous with those (usually mestizos, but often Indians) who had acculturated and risen above the Indian masses (de la Fuente 1967). Within peasant communities, primarily of native origin but gradually including some mestizos, the residents often claimed Ladino heritage if they wanted to "pass" and be accepted as mestizos. This was a calculated attempt to rid themselves of the stigma of race, even though there was no intermarriage or union with a mestizo or criollo to warrant it.

Mestizos played a significant role in the operation of the socioeconomic class system. Although mestizos were legally ranked below Indians, many appeared European and moved up in the social scale simply because of their white appearance. Furthermore, hybrid bloods, a new breed neither totally Spanish nor Indian, also in time found themselves a niche above the peon Indians. Many mestizos resembled natives or Africans and therefore probably remained peons throughout their lives.

Race and Social Class

Throughout the period, races were kept as separate as possible, in what were essentially castes with different types and degrees of power and privilege (Knight 1990). To insure one's station in life, detailed baptismal records listed racial heritage: pure blood mixed once, mixed twice, and so on. Here is an example of how they were recorded:

1. Spaniard and Indian beget mestizo.
2. Mestizo and Spanish woman beget *castizo* (pure blood).

3. Castizo woman and Spaniard beget Spaniard. [Some liken this to cleaning one's blood! The opposite, a castizo and Indian woman union would be cholo, and would thus be tarnishing one's blood!]
4. Spanish woman and African slave beget mulatto.
5. Spaniard and mulatto woman beget *morisco* (Moorish).
6. Morisco woman and Spaniard beget *albino* (brownish color).
7. Spaniard and albino woman beget *torna atras* (restore to original) and so on (Morner 1967:58).

A complicated racial mixture—a little of this, a little of that—earned the names of *ahi te estas* (there you stay) or *sal si puedes* (get out if you can)! Hybrid racial types were placed on the colonial socioeconomic ladder in this manner (van den Berghe 1967).

Effects of Racism

Aside from its role in class relations, the mestizo phenomenon also produced sociopsychological difficulties. Thus, "the mestizo offers a richer opportunity for psychological interpretation than the phlegmatic, subordinated Indian" (Gibson 1966). Cultural marginality was now joined by racial marginality, a mixture of the Old and New World, and often a strange and exotic combination at that (Helms 1975). In addition to valuing assimilation into Spanish culture, subordinate members of colonial society got ahead by honoring the color and appearance of Spaniards. Indians and mestizos became traitors to themselves (Wagley and Harris 1958). Paradoxically, female mestizos were considered excellent mistresses. As the colonial elite used to say, white women for marriage and home, black women for work, and brown women for amorous adventures.

In addition to these psychological burdens, feelings of racial inferiority further oppressed the majority. Many became ashamed of their racial countenance, thinking it disgusting and unworthy. This inferiority complex hindered the advancement of both natives and mestizos. They were taught to dislike their faces so that their minds would remain troubled and uncertain about their self-identity. Meanwhile, those responsible for this attitude went unchallenged. Although this method of rule is unjust, vicious, and unscientific, it assured dominance over the majority population. Unfortunately, native action to remove that burden was generally disorganized and sporadic, and because of this, efforts to unite with others who suffered a similar condition failed. This proves how crippling its effect really was (Wolf 1959; Ramos 1962; Paz 1961; Hewes 1954).

Racism and Group Conflicts

In their efforts to identify with the powerful "superior" race, both Indians and mestizos competed with each other, even though they shared many problems. Mestizos especially copied Spanish ways to get an edge on the Indians. As a result, whenever the opportunity arose, these mestizos harassed and exploited Indians (Zorita 1963). Prodded by protective clerics, colonial administrators shielded Indian communities. Thus, mestizos were harmed by being excluded from both Spanish and Indian towns (Helms 1975). This maneuvering taught them to survive in a relentlessly stubborn way. Nevertheless, Indians were still worse off because they were regarded by both Spaniards and mestizos as a despicable, inferior race. "They ascribe to Indians inferior traits and scorn many of their customs and beliefs as backward, infantile or gross, befitting primitive or rude people" (de la Fuente 1967).

Thus race and racism worked to sociopsychologically constrain a people's thoughts and actions. Once a sense of inferiority followed and replaced more physical subjugation practices, self-rejection and repression assisted in the dominance of the people. Whenever the lid on this defeated attitude was lifted, any area that rebelled against racist practices and conditions was quelled by harsh military force. If resistance intensified, stronger coercive measures were taken, such as punishment or death for the instigators. Native backwardness and underdevelopment were necessary for the success of the colonial empire, and racism, with the emphasis on color and facial features, supported this arrangement.

Chapter 5

Breakup and Transformation of the Social Order

Contact: Enlightment

While military contact usually receives more attention, it must be remembered that human thoughts shape and move those physical actions. The colonial period that destroyed indigenous Mesoamerican lifeways began with pressure from the Spanish sword, an externally derived force. Yet there were get-rich-quick schemes and other motives behind the sword. In the breakup of the colonial social order, actions and thoughts again intertwine (Skidmore and Smith 1992; Romanell 1967), but it is ideas that dominate because the most crucial forces of change come from within. One writer stated this period was a mix of historical memories (i.e., Indian, Spanish, and Mexican) that made for an incompleteness, fragmentation, and strains and stresses that had to be dealt with someday (Florescano 1994). That someday came in several phases, each step in the direction of a resolution of the contradictions (MacLachlan and Rodriquez O. 1980).

Social action is usually based on conditions that require some type of adjustment. Often the necessary changes bring improvements; in the case of Mexico, another step toward incorporation into a "worldwide trading network" (MacLachlan and Rodriquez O. 1980:292), in effect a larger energy system. Incipient peasants, some still in control of their land and labor, were now subjected to a major macrostructural transformation: "The economy underwent a gradual dissolution of the mercantilist capitalist mode of accumulation and its replacement by more capitalist ones" (Cockcroft 1990:45).

The ideas that sparked and drove these processes were slow to unfold but eventually caught the imagination of every disenchanted person in the New World. This period was known as the Enlightenment in Europe, where it had its most profound influence, but repercussions were to be felt in the New World as progress and reform came to mark this transitional historical period, furthering the development of the modern peasant lifestyle (Wolf 1966, 1982; Fagg 1977).

Background to the Enlightenment

Such writers as Rousseau and Locke questioned European thought, and these and other efforts to redefine the nature of society led to the Age of Enlightenment. According to its philosophy, humankind directly shaped sociohistorical conditions and institutions, and events were not accidental. Whatever humans built they could also dismantle and rearrange according to their whim. Previously, humans were taught from infancy what to do and whom to serve, living and dying without questioning the teachings. The Enlightenment undermined this indoctrination by emphasizing the plasticity and malleability of humankind. A person's concept of self or society depended on what authority figures placed in one's mind. The mind was a *tabula rasa*, or blank slate, that reflected what was written on it.

Europeans who were unhappy with existing social conditions gained inspiration from Enlightenment thought. Monarchical European countries led by the top-heavy aristocratic elite—landed gentry, nobility, and clergy—were challenged. They could no longer rule absolutely as they had for centuries. A new image of society was emerging. European upheavals toppled regimes and stimulated the breakup of colonial territories.

Revolutionary Beginnings

There were many ways that Enlightenment thinking reached the shores of the New World: travelers bringing back information, books and pamphlets, merchants and government officials, and simply, fashionable philosophical discussions (Haring 1963). An idea born in one time and place must undergo a process of revision in a new setting, and this happened in the New World. Latin American criollo intellectuals and dissidents rapidly learned from the revolutions in the Old World and applied the knowledge to their conditions—thus developing finer nuances to the theories (MacLachlan and Rodriquez O. 1980). The rise and spread of literary clubs carried these new doctrines far and wide, and the pen surpassed the sword in its ability to subvert the political regime (Gongora 1975).

This assertive program took time to gain momentum, since ideas are never enough—humans must always implement them. Generally speaking, the revolutionary movements in the United States and France were the catalysts that accelerated the revolutionary ideas that eventually touched and pervaded Mexico and Latin America.

The United States Revolution in 1776, especially as the first successful one in the New World, and the French Revolution in 1789 greatly influenced the Spanish colonial social structure. While strongly affecting Europe, the American experience served as an example and had a significant impact on Latin American independence. The effect of the French Revolution was more indirect. Napoleon's armies spread the doctrine of "liberty, equality, and fraternity" throughout Europe, eventually loosening the hold the aristocrat elite had on their subjects. Almost immediately, the Spanish people felt the impact of the French slogans, especially after Napoleon took control of Spain. The political debate and struggle around socioeconomic issues that began in the mother country necessarily involved the colonies and led to dissolution of the empire (Gongora 1975). "They [Spaniards] had imbibed many of the concepts of the French Revolution and British liberalism, and planned a new and liberal Spain" (Simpson 1967:233). Eager participants began proposing social theories to correct unjust and unequal conditions (Bazant 1977). In the end, Spanish bureaucrats were unable to hold back what they feared most: the collapse of central authority, rebellion, and the fragmentation of the colonial empire into competing regions each with its own economic and political agendas (Stein and Stein 1970). In large part, the mercantile economic system became a liability as criollos reacted to the colonial machine that unevenly spread power and influence (Gongora 1975).

Enlightenment Legacy

These years of Enlightenment ferment set the tone for subsequent world history. For example, the question of left against right (the terms originated in the French National Assembly, where change-oriented representatives were seated to the left and the status quo elements to the right), or Jacobins vs. reactionary conservatives, was formalized by the French. In the New World the process of taking sides—whether to create a new political system or to retain and strengthen the old one—was repeated, though the ideological lines were less sharp. The struggle reached some of the most isolated regions and affected many oppressed Mexican people. Criollo intellectuals and writers, lay and cleric alike, began to look at Spain as a province, and "condemnation of the atrocities committed by the conquistadors became a frequent topic in writings, and praise was reserved for the Indian cultures" (Gongora 1975:184), as the center of their universe shifted to the New World. To accelerate and cement this trend, the Pope declared the "universal sponsorship" (meaning recognition) of the Virgin of Guadalupe over New Spain (1757) and archaeological expeditions, discoveries, and writings began to uncover and promote the grand style and refinement of what once was Indian civilization (Florescano 1994).

Other issues increased the revolutionary momentum of the Enlightenment period. Among them: (1) European nations, particularly England, were interested in breaking the Spanish colonial commercial stranglehold and advocated a freer trade policy; and (2) much like North American colonists, the criollos were tired of oppressive colonial rule and sought independence and home rule. These economic issues, in combination with ideas of social justice and examples of revolutionary activity, made a heavy impact on the New World (Sierra 1969). "It may even be that Spain's inability to defend her place in the world's debate was due in part to her tendency to enjoy it while it lasted" (de Madariaga 1947:319).

The first centuries of the growth of a Mexican peasantry were altered by the Enlightenment, open-door trade, and home rule. Ideas stimulated the movement toward dissolution of the colonies. But this was only the first interval. In a gestation period that lasts three hundred years, it takes a great deal of reflection, discussion, and action to move people into a new era and overcome firmly entrenched practices and beliefs. Many years passed before the ideas took hold and eventually flourished. It took a long time to erase the colonial thumbprint even as new impressions were made. As might be expected, confusion reigned after this contact period, as everything and everyone was in flux. Native and, later, peasant resistance was always a part of the colonial experience, but with the end of this era, even more eruptions and disturbances in different provinces marked the nineteenth century, lasting until the 1910 revolution (Cockcroft 1990).

Conflict: Independence

"The Creole [criollo] never gave up his conviction that the American countries belonged . . . to but one class of Spaniard, to the Creole . . . as an aristocrat, a noble: with famous ancestors and a family tree, he despised the recently arrived Spaniard . . . as an upstart usurping positions that rightfully should belong to the Creole" (Sierra 1969:100–101). Thus, the criollo challenge to gachupine rule ignited a full-scale conflict and brought other smoldering issues out into the open. To help in this effort, a new type of nonelite, hard-working, thrifty immigrant, arriving in large numbers in the late colonial period, joined the resident criollos to push for change (Gongora 1975). Because of disastrous financial conditions in Spain, a result of costly European wars, the colonists were pressured into paying more to the mother country (Cockcroft 1990). This excessive burden further drove criollos to seek home rule. During the first years of the struggle, active participation and dialogue centered on nationalism, because political parties were ill-defined and loosely organized (Turner 1968). Later, after the Spanish expulsion, political definitions and distinctions were made, sides chosen, and political and military battles fought.

Before ideological conflicts take root, there must be a receptive soil to nourish them. Hence, "the colonial elite found natural allies in the mestizos, mulattoes, and castas in general; the Indians they handled gingerly . . . if mobilized intelligently, [Indians] could be controlled to aid in the elimination of the handful of Spanish bureaucrats and merchants" (Stein and Stein 1970:114–15). Mestizo discontent resulted from the Spanish policy that disdained mixed bloods. Consequently, the persisting socioeconomic and racial problems of the mestizos and Indians provided fertile ground for colonial unrest, even though these problems were ignored after liberation. Undoubtedly, the discontent of the majority mestizos and Indians contributed heavily to the mounting revolutionary dissent.

Liberals vs. Conservatives

The independence movement in Mexico was particularly divisive and rending. Two opposite sectors worked toward different objectives. With the separation from Spain, one side wanted to continue the same system apart from the motherland and the other side desired to wipe out the colonial order and establish an entirely new one (Alba 1967). Those criollos who wanted separation and a home-rule type of monarchy were known as conservatives. Liberal criollos followed a more humanist orientation and demanded a more extensive program of political reform. To a degree, they desired to improve socioeconomic conditions, basing their program on a constitutional parliamentary model. Initially, the conservatives were stronger; they held powerful positions in the Catholic Church and the military, groups that were highly supportive of their goals. The criollo liberals, a smaller group, championed reform issues, which included minor concessions to mestizos and Indians. Their objectives, however, also included changes that more directly affected their class interests, such as free labor and private property, all leading Mexico on a path to agrarian capitalism (Cockcroft 1990). This in turn would promote more rapid conversion of the Indian and mestizo population into a peasantry.

A further clarification of this political split must be made. Conservatives were usually members of the urban upper class who had developed a centralist political strategy. They believed that power should remain in the cities, the center of sociocultural life. In contrast, liberals favored a federalist plan that catered to provincial chieftains and the nascent middle class (Cockcroft 1990). Their plan emphasized regional input in decision-making processes (Bazant 1977). The liberals' numbers were swelled by many mestizos, especially those with middle-class positions or aspirations.

During the first years of the independence struggle, both the conservative and liberal ideologies were recast under various proponents. Opportunism characterized the political philosophy of many of these self-serving leaders. Nevertheless, political wrangling over the nation's future direction generally found liberals addressing mestizo and Indian issues. It was necessary to include these groups in the political process, for they constituted the majority of the population whose oppressive conditions commanded attention. With tacit support from mestizos and Indians, the liberals more strongly argued for reform, if only giving it lip service, and sometimes doing so to disguise other, more personal goals (Simpson 1967).

A split in liberal ranks resulted. "Some wanted to 'go quickly,' to fulfill the aspirations of Liberalism at all cost and as soon as possible; others wanted to 'go slowly,' to achieve the same ideals at less cost and without haste. The former were called 'puros' or 'reds' [purists] and the latter 'moderados' [moderates]" (Villegas et al. 1974:104). Although lines were not clearly drawn, the moderados were usually criollos and the puros mostly mestizos. One example of a criollo puro was Lorenzo de Zavala, who advocated a vast program of social revolution under the rubric of Mexican nationalism. However, he is the exception to the majority of upper- and middle-class criollos and mestizos, who protected their own interests, with less concern for the condition of the bulk of the population.

In any event, the Mexican nation-state dates from this period and, even today, reflects the recurring conservative/liberal encounter to redefine and direct the people's future (Cockcroft 1990).

1810: El Grito de Dolores

By 1810, there were four million people in Mexico, and increasingly, more were found in urban areas (Gongora 1975).They were divided into three groups: 10 percent of Spanish lineage, 30 percent of mestizo and mulatto background, and the remaining 60 percent of Indian descent (Alba 1967; Rodriquez O. 1989). Dissident activity was already a pattern throughout Mexico, but the cause celebre of independence was El Grito de Dolores (The Cry of Pain), a proclamation made by Miguel Hidalgo, a parish priest, on September 16, 1810 (Archer 1989). Although a criollo, a Jesuit, and fairly well-off, Father Hidalgo felt concern for less fortunate

*Miguel
Hidalgo.*

members of society. He could be characterized as an activist puro. His goal was the liberation of Mexico, even if gachupines must be slaughtered. When the opportunity arose, he led the first large military forces against the gachupines. Shortly thereafter, he was captured and executed by a firing squad. In the aftermath, however, the gates of revolution remained open.

Following in the footsteps of Hidalgo was another small-village priest, the poor mestizo, Jose Maria Morelos. Interestingly, both based their actions on the teachings of Jesus Christ and repudiated the reactionary position of the church. A farseeing political and military genius, barely five feet tall, Morelos rallied the revolutionary forces until his exe-

Morelos leading his forces.

cution in 1815. He outlined radical propositions aimed toward a true social revolution. "The revolution was justified, Morelos insisted, because the perfidious gachupines were enemies of mankind, who for three centuries had enslaved and subjugated the native population, stifled the natural developments of the kingdom, squandered its wealth and resources, and violated the sacred cult" (Simpson 1967:218–19). Some of his goals were the nullification of internal tariffs, the division of the land, the burning of official archives, the elimination of slavery, and the convocation of a congress (Alba 1967).

By 1820, the people had tired of the struggle, as much of the agricultural and mining enterprises of central Mexico had been devastated (Rodriquez O. 1989). The time was ripe for a compromise, despite the fact that both Hidalgo and Morelos had lost their lives for the radical cause. Augustin de Iturbide, a moderate leader, mediated the ideological conflicts between conservatives and liberals. He made a pact with the liberal rebel Vicente Guerrero. As the inheritor of the Hidalgo-Morelos tradition, Guerrero, along with other liberals, had eventually grown weary of the prolonged anarchy. The agreement between Iturbide and Guerrero was called the Plan of Iguala. Its provisions included setting up Mexico as an independent monarchy, ruled by a king or European prince, in which the Catholic church would maintain its privileges, and criollos and gachupines would be considered equals; these agreements were known as the three guarantees (Skidmore and Smith 1992). The guarantees are symbolized by the colors of the modern Mexican flag: green for the monarchy, white for the Catholic church, and red for the union of gachupines and criollos. Religion was the unifying feature of the plan. "It was necessary to defend the Catholic faith. With this issue, the author of the manifesto—whoever he was—

found the common denominator for Spaniards and Mexicans, for land-owners and landless, for whites, Mestizos, and Indians, for higher and lower clergy" (Bazant 1977:27).

1821: Peace

Liberal-conservative ideological rivalries were temporarily put aside when the compromise was reached in 1821. However, they resurfaced shortly after the constitutional monarch, Iturbide, was overthrown and executed in 1824. In the wake of this event, Guadalupe Victoria, a liberal mestizo, became the first elected president of the Republic of Mexico. However, the liberal-conservative battle continued throughout the first half of the nineteenth century.

Change: Experimentation and Nationalism

Age of the Caudillo

"It is not easy to follow the thread of reason through the generation fol-lowing the Independence of Mexico. The loosely cemented strata of colo-nial society had split apart in the cataclysm of 1810–1821, and their mending is still an uncertain and remote aspiration" (Simpson 1967:230). In the wake of this earth-shattering upheaval, economic and political systems and practices were shaken and remained unsettled for over sixty years (Rodriquez O. 1989). This time is best summarized as the age of the caudillo (strong, charismatic leader).

The setting for the rise of military and political strongmen was pro-vided by the liberal-conservative conflict and by dissension among the liberals. There were so many coups, countercoups, intrigues, and palace-guard incidents that political goals became secondary to personal motives. Regional forces began to dominate, usually in the hands of cau-dillos, who aggressively sought local control and even national power positions to amass personal prestige and status (Helms 1975). General Antonio Lopez de Santa Ana, labeled by Cockcroft (1990:72) as an "unprincipled ideological chameleon," was a fine practitioner of this art. Beginning as a supporter of liberal causes, he repeatedly switched sides to advance his own career. For over thirty years, this comic pattern of usurpation and exile continued, while Mexico suffered under the vogue of personal aggrandizement. "From 1821 to 1850, Mexico was in a state of constant turmoil. In thirty years there were fifty governments, almost all the result of military coups and eleven of them presided over by Gen-eral Santa Ana" (Villegas et al. 1974:97). When institutions were weak-ened and lost their influence, strong individuals seized the leadership and the personal privileges that came with it.

Early Difficulties

Despite this instability, liberals made some sincere efforts to challenge church influence, a power amassed over three hundred years (Galeana de Valades 1983). Anticlericalism rose during this time, and when Benito Juarez, the culturally assimilated Indian, took office in 1857, laws were implemented to curtail vested church power and land ownership. Contrary to some interpretations and perhaps as an unintended outcome, these Juarez-inspired laws also infringed on Indian land tenure practices (Cockcroft 1990; Bazant 1977).

The ingredients for Mexican nationalist aspirations could never quite coalesce prior to independence, despite occasional, spontaneous strivings, but after independence an incipient type of nationalism gradually took shape. At first, efforts revolved around construction of an entirely new governmental model. In time, nationalist sentiment produced a hybrid strategy derived from Spanish and Indian traditions (Romanell 1967). Furthermore, foreign nations coveted Mexican territory, recently won but poorly protected because of the political turmoil, and this also ultimately helped the growth of nationalism (Sierra 1969). Such threats from outsiders helped bring Mexicans together, for xenophobic fears often make bedfellows out of enemies (Turner 1968). However, a cohesive nationalist ideology was still not fully formulated by the end of the nineteenth century. Another revolution in 1910 partially fulfilled this goal.

Events in the North. Within liberal ranks, puros, pushing harder than moderados, became frustrated with the slowness of change. Their activity was a prelude to the 1910 revolution. One of them, Lorenzo de Zavala, migrated north to the borderlands, hoping to institute social experiments unwanted by central Mexican authorities (Alba 1967). He later predicted that this northern region (now the United States Southwest) would separate from the increasingly despotic conservative government. This prophecy would later come true, although under different circumstances than he imagined (Bazant 1977).

Borderland settlement appeared imperative because the sparsely populated region required a more permanent body of residents to fend off foreign land-grabs, a threat that mounted after independence (Gongora 1975). However, Indians controlled most of the area, making settlement difficult, if not impossible. To counter foreign intervention, some Mexican leaders sought to establish a colony in the borderlands, inviting non-Mexicans (usually United States frontiersmen) to join them in an outpost of the new nation. Reasons for this varied. Some Mexicans simply wanted more whites there to offset Indian influence. Others, politically idealistic, wished to have the new society modeled after United States democratic traditions. This goal was only partially attained but nevertheless highlights the discontent and frustration of radical Mexican liberals toward conservative policies. One such liberal Mexican invited the well-known British utopian socialist, Robert Owen, to found a new Mexican social order (Alba 1967). Instead, Owen brought the experiment to the United States, where it failed. These and other incidents reflect the Mexican unhappiness with a government unwilling to chart a new political course. Some, in short, refused to wait for change.

Conflict over Indian Program

On several issues, political ideologies were mixed. For example, a goal of the nationalist program was the granting of citizenship and other rights to all residents of Mexican territory. This primarily meant the Indian population, who traditionally had been kept outside the mainstream of social and political life. The conservatives supported Indian national integration because Indians still were closely allied with the church, one of the conservatives' interest groups. The liberals also agreed with the integration policy, hoping to improve opportunities for mestizos as well, but they alienated the natives through lack of an effective liaison with them. Most significantly, the natives showed lukewarm acceptance of the program. Their well-founded wariness was based on history, because further integration was often associated with more complete native exploitation and oppression; the history of transformation from encomienda to repartimiento to hacienda was one of the most obvious examples of change bringing devolution rather than evolution.

Behaving like their Spanish forefathers, the Mexican nationalists refused to acknowledge the basis of native distrust. In fact, the leaders shaping policy ignored the overriding issue of that time: Members from the privileged classes and the masses of the people had always struggled historically, and it was this problem source that was central to the Mexican experience. Using force and punishment, all with "the good of natives" in mind, Mexican leaders rushed headlong into accommodation programs without assuring the people of their good intentions. For example, liberals broke up Indian communal lands and villages with the idea of helping them. Instead, as noted previously, it created more problems for the Indians, who were made unhappy for their own good.

"In the first twelve years of independence, Mexico had experimented with monarchy, moderate constitutional republic, radical populist regime, conservative government, and liberal government; each in turn failed to produce stability" (Bazant 1977:61). Lacking this foundation, or perhaps because of its tenuousness, the native and mestizo populations remained backward. It did not matter whether the social planners were gachupines, criollos, mestizos, or culturally assimilated

Indians; the majority of the people, mostly Indian in this period, continued as before—on the receiving end. Eventually change took place, but not before much bloodshed had occurred and many years had passed.

References

Aguirre Beltran, G. 1946. *La poblacion negra en Mexico, 1519–1810*. Mexico: Ediciones Fuente Cultural.

Alba, V. 1967. *The Mexicans: The making of a nation*. New York: Praeger Publishers.

Altman, I. 1991. Spanish society in Mexico City after the conquest. *Hispanic American Historical Review* 71(3): 413–45.

Archer, C. I. 1989. Where did all the royalists go? New light on the military collapse of New Spain, 1810–1822. In *The Mexican and Mexican American Experience in the 19th Century*, ed. J. E. Rodriguez O. Tempe, AZ: Bilingual Press/Editorial Bilingue.

Banton, M. 1987. *Racial theories*. Cambridge, England: Cambridge University Press.

Bazant, J. 1977. *A concise history of Mexico: From Hidalgo to Cardenas, 1805–1940*. New York: Cambridge University Press.

Bolton, H. 1921. *The Spanish borderlands*. New Haven: Yale University Press.

Borah, W. and S. F. Cook. 1960. *The population of central Mexico in 1548*. Berkeley: University of California Press.

Brues, A. 1990. *People and races*. Prospect Heights, IL: Waveland Press.

Burkhart, L. M. 1989. *The slippery earth: Nahua-Christian moral dialogue in sixteenth-century Mexico*. Tucson: University of Arizona Press.

Cancian, F. 1967. Political and religious organization. In *Handbook of Middle American Indians*, Vol. 6, ed. R. Wauehope. Austin: University of Texas Press.

Carrasco, P. 1965. The Mesoamerican Indian during the colonial period. In *Indian Mexico: Past and present*, ed. B. Bell. Los Angeles: University of California, Latin American Center.

Carroll, P. J. 1991. Blacks in colonial Veracruz: Race, ethnicity, and regional development. Austin: University of Texas Press.

Chance, J. K. 1978. *Race and class in colonial Oaxaca*. Stanford: Stanford University Press.

Chevalier, F. 1966. *Land and society in colonial Mexico*. Berkeley: University of California Press.

Chinas, B. 1983. *The Isthmus Zapotecs: Women's roles in cultural context*. Prospects Heights, IL: Waveland Press.

Cockcroft, J. D. 1990. *Mexico: Class formation, capital accumulation, and the state*. New York: Monthly Review Press.

Collier, G. and E. L. Quaratiello. 1994. *Basta!: Land and the Zapatista rebellion in Chiapas*. Oakland, CA: Institute for Food and Development Policy.

Cope, R. D. 1994. *The limits of racial domination: Pleabeian society in colonial Mexico City, 1660–1720*. Madison: University of Wisconsin Press.

Cox, O. C. 1970. *Caste, class, and race*. New York: Monthly Review Press.

Deans-Smith, S. 1992. *Bureaucrats, planters and workers: The making of the tobacco monopoly in Bourbon Mexico.* Austin: University of Texas Press.

de la Fuente, J. 1967. Ethnic relationships. In *Handbook of Middle American Indians,* Vol. 6, ed. R. Wauehope. Austin: University of Texas Press.

de Madariaga, S. 1947. *The rise of the Spanish American empire.* New York: Macmillan Inc.

Elizondo, V. 1983. *Galilean journey: The Mexican American promise.* San Diego: Orbis Books.

Elliott, J. H. 1963. *Imperial Spain 1469–1716.* New York: The New American Library, Inc.

Ericson, J. E. and T. G. Baugh. 1993. *The American Southwest and Mesoamerica: Systems of prehistoric exchange.* New York: Plenum Press.

Fagg, J. E. 1977. *Latin America: A general history.* New York: Macmillan, Inc.

Farriss, N. M. 1993. Persistent Maya resistance and cultural retention in Yucatan. In *The Indian in Latin American history: Resistance, resilience and acculturation,* ed. J. E. Kicza. Wilmington, DE: Scholarly Resources, Inc.

Florescano, E. 1984. The formation and economic structure of the hacienda in New Spain. In *The Cambridge history of Latin America,* Vol 2: *Colonial Latin America,* ed. L. Bethell. Cambridge: Cambridge University Press.

_____. 1994. *Memory, myth, and time in Mexico: From the Aztecs to independence.* Austin: University of Texas Press.

Foster, G. 1960. *Culture and conquest.* New York: Quadrangle Books Inc.

_____. 1990. *Tzintzuntzan: Mexican peasants in a changing world.* Prospect Heights, IL: Waveland Press.

Frank, A. G. 1969. *Capitalism and underdevelopment in Latin America.* New York: Monthly Review Press.

Friedrich, P. 1968. *Agrarian revolt in a Mexican village.* Englewood Cliffs, NJ: Prentice-Hall, Inc.

Galeana de Valades, P. 1983. Los Liberales y la Iglesia. In *Down from colonialism: Mexico's nineteenth-century crisis,* ed. J. E. Rodriquez O. Los Angeles: Chicano Studies Research Center Publications, University of California.

Gerhard, P. 1993. *The Southwest frontier of New Spain.* Norman: University of Oklahoma Press.

Gibson, C. 1964. *Aztecs under Spanish rule.* Stanford, CA, 1964, Stanford University Press.

_____. 1966. *Spain in America.* New York: Harper & Row, Publishers.

_____. 1984. Indian societies under Spanish rule. In *The Cambridge History of Latin America, Vol. 2: Colonial Latin America,* ed. L. Bethell, Cambridge: Cambridge University Press.

Gillin, J. 1957. Mestizo America. In *Most of the world: The peoples of Africa, Latin America and the East today,* ed. R. Linton. New York: Columbia University Press.

Gongora, M. 1975. *Studies in the colonial history of Spanish America.* Cambridge: Cambridge University Press.

Gonzales, A. 1997. *Edible Baroque.* New York: Harper Collins.

Gossen, G. H. and M. Leon-Portilla, eds. 1993. *South and Meso-American native spirituality: From the cult of the feathered serpent to the theology of liberation.* New York: Crossroad.

Graham, R., ed. 1990. *The idea of race in Latin America, 1870–1940,* Austin: University of Texas Press.

Gruzinski, S. 1988. The net torn apart: Ethnic identities and Westernization in colonial Mexico, 1600–1900 Centuries. In *Ethnicities and nations,* eds. R. Guidieri, et al. Austin: University of Texas Press.

Gutierrez, R. 1991. *When Jesus came, the Corn Mothers went away.* Stanford: Stanford University Press.

Haring, C. H. 1963. *The Spanish empire in America.* New York: Harcourt Brace Jovanovich, Inc.

Helms, M. W. 1975. *Middle America: A culture history of heartland and frontiers.* Englewood Cliffs, NJ: Prentice-Hall, Inc.

Hewes, G. W. 1954. Mexicans in search of the Mexican: Notes on Mexican national character studies. *American Journal of Economics and Sociology* 13:209.

Hill J. H. and K. C. Hill. 1986. *Speaking Mexicano: Dynamics of syncretic language in central Mexico.* Tucson: University of Arizona Press.

Himmerich y Valencia, R. 1991. *The encomenderos of New Spain, 1521–1555.* Austin: University of Texas Press.

Ingham, J. M. 1986. *Mary, Michael and Lucifer: Folk Catholicism in Central Mexico.* Austin: University of Texas Press.

Israel, J. I. 1975. *Race, class, and politics in colonial Mexico.* London: Oxford University Press.

Kearney, M. 1986. *The winds of Ixtepeji: World view and society in a Zapotec town.* Prospect Heights, IL: Waveland Press.

Kicza, J. E., ed. 1993. *The Indian in Latin American history: Resistance, resilience and acculturation.* Wilmington, DE: Scholarly Resources.

Knight, A. 1990. Racism, revolution, and *indigenismo*: Mexico, 1910–1940. In *The idea of race in Latin America, 1870–1940,* ed. R. Graham. Austin: University of Texas Press.

Leon-Portilla, M. 1963. *Aztec thought and culture.* Norman: University of Oklahoma Press.

Lockhart, J., 1992. *The Nahuas after the conquest: A social and cultural history of central Mexico, sixteenth through eighteenth centuries.* Stanford: Stanford University Press.

———, ed. 1993. *We people here: Nahuatl accounts of the conquest of Mexico.* Berkeley: University of California Press.

MacLachlan, C. and J. E. Rodriquez O. 1980. *The forging of the cosmic race.* Berkeley: University of California Press.

Madsen, W. 1967. Religious syncretism. In *Handbook of Middle American Indians,* Vol. 6, ed. R. Wauehope. Austin: University of Texas Press.

Mallon, F. E. 1995. *Peasant and nation: The making of postcolonial Mexico and Peru.* Berkeley: University of California Press.

McWilliams, C. 1990. *North from Mexico: The Spanish-speaking people of the United States.* Westport, CT: Greenwood Press, Inc.

Morner, M. 1967. *Race mixture in the history of Latin America*. Boston: Little, Brown & Co.

Morse, R. M. 1984. The urban development of colonial Spanish America. In *The Cambridge history of Latin America, Vol. 2: Colonial Latin America*, ed. L. Bethell. Cambridge: Cambridge University Press.

_____. 1989. *New world soundings: Culture and ideology in the Americas*. Baltimore: John Hopkins University Press.

Ortiz de Montellano, B. 1990. *Aztec medicine, health, and nutrition*. New Brunswick, NJ: Rutgers University Press.

Padden, R. C. 1967. *The hummingbird and the hawk: Conquest and sovereignty in the Valley of Mexico, 1503–1541*. Columbus: Ohio State University Press.

Paz, O. 1961. *The labyrinth of solitude*. New York: Grove Press, Inc.

Raat, W. D. 1992. *Mexico and the United States: Ambivalent vistas*. Athens: University of Georgia Press.

Ramos, S. 1962. *Profile of man and culture in Mexico*. Austin: University of Texas Press.

Reck, G. G. 1986. *In the shadow of Tlaloc: Life in a Mexican village*. Prospect Heights, IL: Waveland Press.

Ricard, R. 1966. *The spiritual conquest of Mexico*. Berkeley: University of California Press.

Rodriguez O., J. E., ed. 1983. *Down from colonialism: Mexico's nineteenth-century crisis*. Los Angeles: Chicano Studies Research Center Publications, University of California.

_____, ed. 1989. *Mexican and Mexican American experience in the 19th century*. Tempe, AZ: Bilingual Press/Editorial Bilingue.

Romanell, P. 1967. *Making of the Mexican mind*. Notre Dame, IN: University of Notre Dame Press.

Romanucci-Ross, L. 1986. *Conflict, violence, and morality in a Mexican village*. Chicago: University of Chicago Press.

Ruiz, R. E. 1992. *Triumphs and tragedy: A history of the Mexican people*. New York: W.W. Norton & Co.

Ruiz de Alarcon, H. 1984. *Treatise on the heathen superstitions*, trans. and eds. J. Andrews and R. Hassig. Norman: University of Oklahoma Press.

Sanchez-Albornoz, N. 1984. The population of colonial Spanish America. In *The Cambridge History of Latin America, Vol. 2: Colonial Latin America*, ed. L. Bethell. Cambridge: Cambridge University Press.

_____. 1988. *Espanoles hacia America: La emigracion en masa, 1880–1930*. Madrid: Alianza Editorial.

Sierra, J. 1969. *The political evolution of the Mexican people*. Austin: University of Texas Press.

Simpson, L. B. 1966. *The encomienda in New Spain*. Berkeley: University of California Press.

_____. 1967. *Many Mexicos*. Berkeley: University of California Press.

Skidmore, T. E. and P. H. Smith. 1992. *Modern Latin America*. New York: Oxford University Press.

Sokolov, R. 1991. *Why we eat what we eat: How Columbus changed the way the world eats*. New York: Simon & Schuster.

Spicer, E. 1962. *Cycles of conquest*. Tucson: University of Arizona Press.

Stein, S. and B. Stein. 1970. *The colonial heritage of Latin America*. New York: Oxford University Press.

Turner, F. C. 1968. *The dynamic of Mexican nationalism*. Chapel Hill: University of North Carolina Press.

van den Berghe, P. L. 1967. *Race and racism: A comparative perspective*. New York: John Wiley & Sons, Inc.

Vasconcelos, J. and M. Gamio. 1926. *Aspects of Mexican civilization*. Chicago: University of Chicago Press.

Villegas, D. C., et al. 1974. *A compact history of Mexico*. Los Angeles: University of California, Latin American Center.

Vives, J. V. 1969. *An economic history of Spain*. Princeton: Princeton University Press.

Wagley, C. and M. Harris. 1958. *Minorities in the New World: Six case studies*. New York: Columbia University Press.

Weber, D. J. and J. M. Rausch, eds. 1994. *Where cultures meet: Frontiers in Latin American history*. Wilmington, DE: SR Books.

Whetten, N. L. 1969. *Rural Mexico*. Chicago: University of Chicago Press.

Wills, W. H. and R. D. Leonard, eds. 1994. *The ancient Southwestern community: Models and methods for the study of prehistoric social organization*. Albuquerque: University of New Mexico Press.

Wolf, E. R. 1959. *Sons of the shaking earth*. Chicago: University of Chicago Press.

_____. 1966. *Peasants*. Englewood Cliffs, NJ: Prentice Hall.

_____. 1982. *Europe and the people without history*. Berkeley: University of California Press.

Zavala, S. 1943. *The Spanish colonization of America*. Philadelphia: University of Pennsylvania Press.

Zorita, A. 1963. *Life and labor in ancient Mexico*. New Brunswick, NJ: Rutgers University Press.

Stage III
Mexican Independence and Nationalism, 1821 to 1846

The era of Enlightenment increased autonomy and made natives and the budding mestizo peoples demand still more independence. Gradually, this feeling also led to the use of Mexicano as a source of ethnic identity—one name, one people. This was a stage characterized by bold experimentation, by excursions further and further from earlier influences. Yet it is also a time of great confusion, where the shifting sands of cultural variation have not yet settled. Peasant lifeways were further forged from this time of ferment and flux and began to show signs of permanence in some regions.

Part of the people had one foot in the past and desired to maintain that connection for a sense of security, if not the comforts of that time period. In contrast, others looked only to the future and some vaguely defined goals because the past was so harsh and mean. In addition to these internal sources of ambiguity, the external environment often imposed sharp limits on unbounded innovations and even inflicted sometimes cruel punishment for mishaps and miscalculations.

"Parts" of a nation, of course, are much more concrete than are the competing aspects of economic, social, and political forces and changes. The land, the people, the manner of subsistence, a reliance on the American Trinity, represented a semblance of stability in the midst of ill-defined and poorly conceived strivings for nationhood. In this rather abrupt transition to a broader and more sophisticated social and economic network, peasantry became more of a factor in the lives of the indigenous and mestizo peoples. Storm and stress characterized this time period. At times, reformist leaders attempted to move the country toward major (if ill-defined) social and economic revampments. As often occurs, more conservative elements thwarted such intrusions, turning the society and economy back toward institutional forms established during the colonial period. As these reform and counterreform contests continued, many people left the centers of political strife to colonize the frontier regions of Mexico. In these new locales, they often patterned their social establishments on those that predominated in the land of their origin. Amid this activity, Mexico was also threatened by the expansionist tendencies of powerful foreign nations, the United States and France in particular.

In this flurry of changes, major turning points often emerged in strange and unpredictable ways. The Anglo-American acquisition of Mexico's northern provinces was one of the more severe blows suffered by Mexico in the years between independence in 1821 and the 1910 revolution. For the Chicano people within the territories annexed by the United States, an abrupt and earth-shattering end had come to their strivings to remake themselves. While Chicanos in the United States continued to be affected by events in metropolitan Mexico, other social forces and places became more important in their everyday lives.

In anticipation of that importance, our study of this tumultuous period will focus considerably more attention on events in the Mexican frontier regions than has been the case in previous chapters. Because the era was full of surprises and unpredictable turns and lasted until the 1910 revolution for Mexicans living in Mexico, this stage includes some discussion of late nineteenth-century events in Mexico, such as the role of land tenure under the regimes of Benito Juarez and Porfirio Diaz.

Puros
MODERNAS
gauchpines
Criollos

Chapter 6

Intact and Stable Social Order

Class: Ideological Struggle Between Liberals and Conservatives

Mexico under Criollos

Independence seemed to produce little change for the masses. The gach-upines were removed from the socioeconomic structure, but they were replaced by the criollos. The nature of social relations thus remained the same (Meyer and Sherman 1987) "Mexico still retained many elements of her colonial heritage. Her economy was essentially dependent on for-eign markets, her social structure was defined along racial lines, and colonial institutions such as the Catholic Church and the hacienda con-tinued to function in traditional ways" (Sinkin 1979:11). Peasant society was sharply reordered in this phase. Nevertheless, some opportunities were also allotted to mestizos and culturally assimilated Indians (Cline 1963). Barriers to social mobility still remained after decades of struggle, but isolated breaches of the barriers did occur.

Political confrontations between conservative and liberal leaders and their followers dominated the scene, and even within liberal ranks debate continued. The puros (radicals) were uncompromising in their beliefs, whereas the moderados (moderates) were open to negotiations with the church (Sinkin 1979; Gomez-Quinones 1994a). At the center of this political discord was the issue of how to reconstruct the social and economic sectors to best enhance Mexico's future. Liberals accepted both the event and the spiritual promise of independence, while conservatives only acknowledged that it had happened and believed that no significant social alterations were needed (Hale 1968; Gomez-Quinones 1994a; Nutini 1995).

Minor as well as major issues were intensely debated among the powers competing for leadership. The groups were often unable to come to an understanding. These indecisions had disastrous effects on Mexico for the first fifty years following independence (Cline 1963; Meyer and Sherman 1987; Cockcroft 1990; Gomez-Quinones 1994a). Haciendas, debt peonage, and sharply defined class differences continued during this period of strife. There was a move toward a redefinition of the status and role of the peasant, in part through the incorporation of Indians into a class society as "citizens" in an effort to rid the country of the constraints of a caste system (Frye 1996). This restructuring did little to reduce social and economic inequality. "Instead of achieving a nation of free and equal Mexicans, the country was almost entirely in the hands of a class of white hacendados and of national and foreign investors. . . . The country belonged politically, economically, and culturally to the few" (Lomnitz-Adler 1992:277).

Peasant Conditions

In the political arena, the liberal and conservative viewpoints presented contrasting theoretical perspectives. Yet when the time for policy implementation arrived, liberals also followed self-interest motives. As a result, the majority of Indians and mestizos remained exploited and powerless. Leaders of all persuasions followed the customs of a former age, while the majority, despite changes in their formal legal status, continued to suffer.

From 1820 to 1850, the republicas de indios were still holding on, but from 1850 to 1890, they began to lose out due to liberal reform laws; especially during the Porfiriato (the reign of Porfirio Diaz). The downside of the creation of the Mexican state was the diminution of what little self-rule and autonomy the Indians held. "In accordance with the constitution, states began to force the natives to break up their communal patterns" (Vanderwood 1992:26). Meanwhile, the mercantilist orientation of the colonial economy gradually gave way to a more fully capitalist system, exacerbating the problems of the expanding peasantry (Cockcroft 1990).

Indeed, before the end of the nineteenth century, under the dictatorship of the mestizo Porfirio Diaz, the situation deteriorated. Eleven thousand hacendados managed to gain control over about 57 percent of Mexico's land by dispossessing villagers previously covered by colonial protective legislation. As a result, approximately fifteen million people were left without land, some of them in rural villages once controlled by peasants (Cockcroft 1990; Skidmore and Smith 1992). The liberal Benito Juarez had initiated the sale of Indian communal and mission lands to promote reform and individual ownership by the peasants (Bazant 1977); instead the holdings went straight to wealthy private buyers

(Whetten 1948; Miller 1989). The Indians did not surrender their holdings without protest. Peasant uprisings took place throughout the 1840s and early 1850s in Michoacan, in Oaxaca, in Puebla, and in the state of Mexico (Officer 1987; Cockcroft 1990; Redfield and Villa Rojas 1990; Vanderwood 1992; Hu-DeHart 1993; Taylor 1993).

Modern mural of Benito Juarez in Chapultepec Castle, Mexico City.

Republicas de Indios

Nearly all social entities in Mexico enjoyed the sensation of freedom from colonial powers. Indians and mestizos participated in the struggle for independence but were unable to enjoy its fruits. The Indians did not involve themselves in the public life of the new independent country, and many avoided contact with the white man. They continued to seek out their living in the missions or by working as peons, and carried on living in their republicas de indios (Wolf 1965; Meyer and Sherman 1987; Ruiz 1992).

It has been argued that the republicas were the most tradition-bound units in Mexican society, each maintaining a system of internal government that had undergone very few changes since the early colonial period (Meyer and Sherman 1987). Wolf, however, argues that peas-

The Epic of American Civilization: Anglo-America.

ant communities have always had some contact with the rest of society
through state taxes, church tithes, or through working in local haciendas; "these communities were given organizational form by the colonial
bureaucracy, as integral components of the Hispanic state and its economic system" (Wolf 1982:145)

A white person or mestizo rarely lived in a republica, except for an
occasional parish priest (Meyer and Sherman 1987). The Indian peasant
as "in the past . . . rose before dawn, walked from his pueblo to his fields

The Epic of American Civilization: Hispano-America.

(if he had a parcel of land), and came home at nightfall. At nine in the morning and three in the afternoon, he ate corn tortillas flavored with chili sauce and beans and drank atole, a liquid corn gruel. Once in a lifetime, he ate meat but drank himself into a stupor with pulque or *aguardiente de cana*, a liquor distilled from sugarcane" (Ruiz 1992:197).

An hacendado and his mayordomo.

Haciendas

The expansion of haciendas required more cheap labor, supplied by dispossessed Indians, and further broadened the power of the hacendados (Wolf 1965). These transformations incorporated the peasantry into a larger regional and later a national political economic network.

The hacienda system turned Indian peasants into part-time laborers; their traditional economic means of survival now became dependent upon their wages. Hacendados also frequently ran out of money. This resulted in a policy in which only the best land was farmed and production was reduced to keep wages down and allow the land prices and rents to be raised (Wolf 1965; Wolf 1982). Mexico City and a few other large cities started importing less agricultural products from distant regions and began to rely on local production. Many large haciendas went bankrupt (Rodriguez O. 1989). "Mexicans encouraged foreigners to invest in agriculture. Europeans purchased large estates in the early 1820s, but they also lost money. . . . Agriculture, like the rest of the economy, would not fully recover until the 1880s" (Rodriguez O. 1989:20).

The major innovation of haciendas was in the organization of labor, as technology played a relatively unimportant role in a labor-intensive system. Outside interference with this human apparatus was rigidly opposed (Wolf 1965; Nutini 1995). Thus, the hacienda remained the same internally in the midst of swirling social upheavals and political struggles. Granted citizenship on paper, the Indian was bound to the same lowly status. "The problem was compounded by the fact that the

Mestizo leadership, adhering to the imported European and American models of industrial liberalism, considered them an impediment to the development of the country" (Nutini 1995:285–86).

Within this socioeconomic tangle, the changes from a colonial caste to modern class system were filled with new additions and arrangements. Viewed separately, these alterations meant very little, but as a whole they spelled the beginnings of a major shift to a market system that overlapped with past practices. Cultural lag was reflected in the ways that Indians maintained certain customs and language habits as broader economic networks were being introduced (Cubitt 1988; Nutini 1995).

Peasant Economy and Ideological Changes

The peasant household, in Mexico as elsewhere, is a productive unit that is "horizontally" involved with other households like it and "vertically" involved with superordinate power holders (Wolf 1966). "The peasant's economic activities are related to the larger society of which he is a part. The grain, fruit, meat, wine, pottery, fish, cotton, or flax he produces go not only to feed and clothe his family, but also to maintain the priests, artisans, merchants, bureaucrats, kings, and soldiers who make up the urban population or who are the carriers of the Great Tradition of his society. He is tied into a system of distribution and taxation in which his goods and services become part of a regional and national network of economic exchanges. In many cases he participates in an impersonal market where prices respond to supply and demand" (Diaz 1967:51).

As indicated above, peasant producers during this period were being remade into free wage laborers, adding new variations to the rural masses. "Many became pauperized and survived by begging, engaging in day labor, farming on a tenant or sharecropping basis, or tilling subsistence parcels granted them by *hacendados*, whom they served as debt-peons. Those attaching themselves to the haciendas were sometimes better off than their job-seeking counter-parts. . . . A few peasants managed to succeed as rancheros" (Cockcroft 1990:53).

The Role of Women

Independence for peasant women was not liberating; the "gains of the late eighteenth century, which had opened the doors to women, had fallen largely by the wayside" (Ruiz 1992:196). Economic difficulties during this time drove more and more peasant women into the city in search of work. Revampments in the republicas de indios and haciendas meant that some uprooted peasants had to seek work somewhere else. A third of the labor force of Mexico City was made up of women, 82 percent of who were Indians or mestizas (Ruiz 1992). Jobs available for women were mainly in the line of domestic work, although they also worked as spinners in the textile mills, food preparers, waitresses, and as vendors on the streets and in the marketplaces (Meyer and Sherman 1987). Employment, however, was not an emancipating experience; the working woman was widely stigmatized. Peasant women were forced to accept work that was considered degrading and that questioned their honor. "Domestic service, the greatest source of employment for women in the nineteenth century, was considered humiliating and was usually abandoned as soon as possible" (Arrom 1985:160). One of the few careers that earned women respect and prestige was midwifery (Arrom 1985).

Events in Northern Mexico

Debate on the future of Mexico also occurred in the northern territories. Although the issues took on a different complexion and were discussed within a smaller circle of participants, there appeared to be a clear tendency toward a liberal solution. Some leaders even went so far as to suggest that a Mexican nationalist program should be patterned after the United States. This was particularly true in California and New Mexico, two fully established settlements. California's situation (not

Mexican urban workers at the time of the revolution.

forgetting the importance of New Mexico and, later, Texas) serves to increase our understanding of important social-class patterns, especially in light of the 1846 war, its aftermath, and modern historical developments.

Conditions in the borderlands, especially California, were similar to those in Mexico. A smaller-scale hacienda system prevailed, with land ownership again determining social rank and role. The Colonization Act and the Reglamento of 1828 allowed land to be settled and owned privately (Nava and Barger 1976). Landowners were known as gente de razon (people of reason, and usually all non-Indians), and social life revolved around their privileged circle. Some worked their ranchos, but most preferred the traditional hacendado role. Captain Jose Bandini noted in 1828 that most of the gente de razon preferred to spend their days socializing, gambling, and riding. Indians were relied on to do the work around the hacienda, as many of the owners had neither trade nor profession (Hutchinson 1969; Phillips 1993; Monroy 1990; Swagerty 1984). Mestizo and Indian *pobladores* (settlers) usually worked as vaqueros (cowboys) and foremen, but if independent, often operated *ranchitos* (small ranches) for themselves. Many also served gente de razon as household domestics (Vigil 1974; McWilliams 1990).

It has been argued that the social structure of Spanish California was similar to that of the Deep South, with the gente de razon being the equivalent of the plantation owners; the native California Indians, the slaves; and the Mexicans, the "poor white trash" (McWilliams 1990). Later, mestizo and Indian immigrants became transient, unskilled laborers. They spoke poor Spanish, and their lot was often little better than that of the California Indian, except that they had hopes of future improvement. They were known as cholos (half-breeds; Indians in transition from one culture to another and somewhat marginal to both). In Mexico, they would have occupied the lower level in the social-class hierarchy. However, in California there were others who occupied this rung, allowing the cholos to ascend the social ladder (Borah 1970). The lowest group, of course, was the California Indians. Most of them could not improve their social status, as they were caught in a vicious cycle of poverty, racism, and oppression. City officials of pueblos like Los Angeles even sold Indians. As previously noted, native women were even lower, as sexual conquest and violence often accompanied or followed military and political subjugation under a patriarchal colonial society that shaped gender relations (Castaneda 1993).

Economic Enterprises in the North

Gente de razon, pobladores, cholos, and California Indians comprised the class system. Other borderland regions used different class labels, but essentially the same unequal system obtained. For example, in New Mexico two classes existed: *ricos* (rich) and *pobres* (poor) (McWilliams 1990; Oboler 1995). In contrast to California Indians, New Mexico Indians were much less integrated into Mexican society because they had more effectively resisted total Spanish subjugation. The central government of that era had tried to improve opportunities for all Indians (Hutchinson 1969), but the program that sought to integrate them into the national culture was poorly implemented.

Before Mexico's independence, California Indians were widely dispersed geographically, and the Spanish soldiers had to locate and capture them to force them to work on colonial enterprises and accept Christianity (Jackson and Castillo 1994). According to a British observer of those events: "If . . . any of the captured Indians show a repugnance to conversion, it is the practice to imprison them for a few days . . . and thus they continue to be incarcerated until they declare their readiness to renounce the religion of their forefathers" (Moquin and Van Doren 1971:133). With Indian aid, twenty-one missions had been founded in California, each strategically located one day's ride from another. While the missionary goal was native religious conversion and training, much energy was also expended on making the socioeconomic unit self-sufficient. This scheme mirrored Mexico's hacienda system in thoroughness and severity (Phillips 1993). Over two hundred years, the Spanish in America had perfected the use of the mission as an instrument for binding Indians to the state (Borah 1970).

Housing over thirty thousand Indians and with holdings valued in millions of dollars, the missions flourished as religious-economic centers. The colonists introduced Spanish and Mexican technology and products, making them the mainstays of economic and social life (Samora and Simon 1977). Some of the new subsistence products were cattle, sheep, pigs, grapes (both wine and raisin), citrus fruits, avocados, olives, pomegranates, pears, wheat, flax, alfalfa, beans, and cotton. Indian labor cared for and produced them. Indians were also trained for various occupations, such as vaquero, shepherd, blacksmith, horticulturist, brick and tile maker, irrigator, miner, and church attendant (Hass 1995). As noted previously, Hispanicized Indians were given better jobs, and after the secularization of mission lands, they served the gente de razon.

Breakup of California Missions

After Mexican independence, the anticlerical movement affected colonists in the northern region. Many wealthy Californians, including both long-time criollo settlers and newcomers, sought to weaken church power. Since the seat of religious authority was so far away, making administration nearly impossible, gente de razon stepped in to improve

The Vaquero.

their fortunes. Secularization of the missions took place in 1834 to 1843, resulting in a society where the church and religious beliefs were of little significance in guiding the actions of individuals (Hale 1968; Hutchinson 1969; Moquin and Van Doren 1971; Officer 1987; Gomez-Quinones 1994a). Church land came under civil control and was redistributed by government grants.

Immediately after secularization, nearly five hundred land grants created from the former mission lands were distributed to newcomers. Many of the earlier land-grant residents also benefited by adding more land to their estates. Land grants were of two types: individually owned, and controlled in common by a community of residents, usually as a grazing range for livestock. In California, the primary unit was the individual estate. Within their land-grant boundaries, some patron Californians allotted smaller parcels, ranchitos, to their faithful workers and supporters.

Variations of the System in New Mexico

The New Mexico land system developed along different lines. After 1598, settlers had carved out large land units and often set aside communal landed estates (more here than in California) for settlers engaged in raising sheep or cattle (Sanderson 1986; Gomez-Quinones 1994b). As a result of this early beginning, socioeconomic life flourished, and despite the persistent conflicts with neighboring dissident Indians, some degree of stability (and some racial mixture) had been established by the time Mexico became independent.

In 250 years, the Spanish-speaking population of New Mexico swelled to sixty thousand, the largest colony in the north. A rico/pobre dichotomy prevailed, with Indians in the lowest position, of course, but intense conflict had subsided as the social relations between the groups became established. Within this relatively quiet setting, the large and small rancheros and their workers carried on an independent, self-sufficient life. Many surrounding Indian groups, however, had resisted full Hispanic control and maintained a semblance of autonomy in the region, although there was some diffusion of Hispanic culture.

Independence did not have a great effect on New Mexicans; New Mexico had always been far removed from the centers of power. The greatest effect was the removal of the strict trade embargo placed on Mexico by colonial Spain; this opened up the region to commerce and communication, accelerating the rate of changes that already were taking place and leading to an increased Anglo immigration (Gutierrez 1991; Gomez-Quinones 1994a).

The first Anglos to arrive in New Mexico were merchants selling their wares. They were followed by trappers hunting for pelts in New Mexico's Rockies. Pioneers in search of land came next. Finally, the soldiers came to annex New Mexico. The Anglos continually slandered the Indians and Hispanos of New Mexico, claiming divine rights of conquest and asserting what they viewed to be their own moral and cultural superiority (Gomez-Quinones 1994a). The "nineteenth-century Protestant apostles of American democracy found in New Mexico a depraved people who wallowed in promiscuity, whose devilish fandangos corrupted, and whose addiction to vice had created an indolent and mongrel race" (Gutierrez 1991:338). New Mexicans were now in conflict with Anglos over the very same issues they had been in conflict with when the Spanish arrived—religion, labor, land, and water. It was a clash over America's modernism and Mexico's traditionalism.

Rancho Life

Much of the rancho life in California resembled that of the missions before it, but with some variations and important additions. Almost nation-sized in extent, the ranchos became centers of cattle raising, which soon mushroomed into a lucrative commercial network. All of the activities and paraphernalia associated with this industry surfaced here: rodeos, vaqueros, branding, and so on. Trade with New England merchants developed, in which hides and tallow (used in the manufacture of soap and candles) were exchanged for manufactured products from the eastern seaboard. Cattle hides became popularly known as "California bank notes," and the United States leather industry flourished. Mexicans who carried the balls of tallow to the waiting clipper ships were left with a slick mess of grease on their backs. They came to be known as "greasers," an opprobrious label eventually used toward all things Mexican.

Women were also active participants of the cattle-ranching society. It has been noted that the working woman, "la mujer trabajadora," in actual fact did more manual labor than the ranchero himself. She wove clothing and blankets, made cheese, and bleached beeswax, in addition to performing all her household duties. Before modern capitalist growth, women were actively engaged in agricultural production and related income-producing activities, as well as being property owners (Fowler-Salamini and Vaughan 1994).

Interestingly, the early Yankee settlers (mountain men, traders, seamen, and adventurers) were readily accepted by gente de razon. They did not view the Anglos as enemies, and much intermarriage took place with the Mexicans (Cotera 1976; Officer 1987; Acuna 1988; Blea 1992). Most of the immigrants became Hispanicized and acquired their own land grants. Afterward, as a result of intermarriage, many Yankees inherited large parcels of land that gente de razon had willed to their daughters. General George Patton of World War II fame is a descendant of one such marriage. Assimilated Yankees became the social equals of Californios, with the cholos and Indians remaining in the lowest position (Samora and Simon 1977).

Mexican Texas

For a variety of reasons, Texas was an interesting region of northern Mexico. Initially settled in the early eighteenth century by soldiers and

A family of Californios at the turn of the century pose in their Sunday best in front of their home.

civilians, in addition to a tenuous mission system, the area was one of the hardest environments of the frontier. Particularly noteworthy was how Indians there, armed with weapons that were secured from French sources in Louisiana, were able to fend off Spanish soldiers and colonists. As a result, the Spanish presence was shaky (Weber 1992). As compared to California and New Mexico, the experience of Texas with emigrants from the United States was also different. Anglo settlers first came into Texas in 1821, when the Mexican government granted colonization rights (De Leon 1983; Raat 1992; Gomez-Quinones 1994b). Their ideals were to rescue Texas from a primitive lifestyle; "newcomers saw Tejanos as mongrels, uncivilised, and un-Christian—a part of the wilderness that must be subdued" (De Leon 1983:4). These views carried over into their treatment of Mexicans during the brief period that Texas became a republic: "Texas Mexicans suffered from forced marches, general dispossession, and random violence" (Montejano 1987:27). In what is now east Texas, over a hundred Mexican families were forcibly uprooted, losing their homes and lands (Montejano 1987; Oboler 1995).

Culture: Budding Mexicanismo

First Steps Toward National Unity

With the exception of the trend toward a national Mexican culture, most institutions remained the same during this period. Patterns of language, religion, family structure, and many other traditions persisted. The overriding societal theme was that all citizens should be consolidated into the nationality both spiritually and economically, thus facilitating national unity (Turner 1968). While liberals and conservatives were locked in a power struggle, with the issue in doubt for decades, the liberals sought educational reform for natives. However, the legislation on education was soon repealed by Santa Ana, the "Attila of Mexican Civilization" (Hale 1968:175), who became president of Mexico in 1832 and later gained notoriety in the Texas war of secession from Mexico.

The conservatives adamantly opposed social transformations. Neither political group's policies clearly dominated before 1860, with the exception of the liberal reforms of the mid-1850s. A last-ditch conservative effort to reassert control ended disastrously. By inviting the French archduke Maximillian to establish a Mexican monarchy in 1864, some conservatives incurred the animosity of patriotic Mexicans of all political shades (Bazant 1977). After the foreign intervention failed, liberals took over national leadership. Porfirio Díaz, a liberal mestizo who had been a top general under Juarez in the defense against the French, ruled as dictator of Mexico until 1910. At the beginning of his regime, the liberal reform movement had already waned, as the national mood moved toward peace and away from confrontation and chaos.

If one were to examine the writings of reformers of this period, it would appear that a tremendous social upheaval was taking place. However, these ink-and-paper innovations were never implemented. Indians and mestizos were consistently barred from joining the mainstream. Current practices are surely derived from these earlier conditions. Children of mixed descent and Indians who had become both linguistically and culturally acculturated were placed in the social category of Indian and were not accepted as being Mexican. The only way to counteract this and be called Mexican was to move to another area, where one's history was unknown. Mexican leaders were concerned more with shaping a national identity and establishing an entrepreneurial class than with improving conditions for the masses (Turner 1968).

Repercussions were experienced in other realms of Indian, peasant life, namely, religion. Religious syncretic alterations had retained many Indian practices and beliefs that emphasized the group and community affairs. Rituals and ceremonies still balanced social needs with economic activities in the governance of villages. "While the Indians stress equality, personal relationships and mutual aid, capitalist ideology encourages competition, individuality and the subordination of personal feelings to rational self-interest" (Cubitt 1988:71). A change from the cooperative/communal to the competitive/individual made Indians even more vulnerable. Religion and religious practices had always provided a salve to the aching Indian spirits. In these new times of outside pressures and increased exploitation, religion became even more important.

In this ideological and economic miasma, peasants were integrated into something new that would eventually transform them into proletariat, whose lives were dominated by wage labor (Kearney 1996; de Janvry 1981:95–96; de Rouffignac 1985; Cubitt 1988; Fowler-Salamini and Vaughan 1994).

Psychocultural Aspects of Peasantry

Authors have often described peasants as having a certain "peasant mentality," with the following characteristics: fatalism, passivity, conservatism, distrustfulness, and superstition. However, the view that peasants are conservative and reluctant to change has been challenged (Cubitt 1988). Foster (1979) created the image of the "limited good" to describe the fact that Mexican peasants tend to "see their social, eco-

Nineteenth-century communal Indian village.

nomic, and natural universes—their total environment—as one in which almost all desired things in life such as land, other forms of wealth, health, friendship, love" exist in quantities that are insufficient to even fill their minimal requirements and there would be no direct way for them to increase their available supplies (Foster 1987:124).

Various terms have been used to describe peasant society. "Closed communities" refers to those peasant communities with land ownership and distinctive cultural traits. The harmony and reciprocity of peasant life is often emphasized in these accounts, with little attention being paid to external influences and the hardships of poverty and rural life (see, for example, Foster 1979; Cubitt 1988; Hewitt de Alcantara 1984).

Peasants rely on folk medicines to cure ailments and illnesses. They believe in witchcraft and magic. However, each area within Mexico has a distinct cultural tradition. "Cultural patterns . . . may also be distinctive of particular communities. All the villagers in a region speak the same indigenous language, but they may have their own particular costumes, jewelry, dances or other customs. One community in Mexico is famous for its *voladores*, the flying men who, tied by a strap to a central pole, whirl dangerously around" (Cubitt 1988:67).

Peasants are known for establishing solid social networks with their family and through fictive kin, known as *compadres* or *comadres*. Compadrazgo is "the particular complex of relationships set up between individuals primarily, though not always, through participation in the ritual of Catholic baptism" (Mintz and Wolf 1967:174). It furthers social solidarity both "horizontally," across the same class, and "vertically," across classes (Mintz and Wolf 1967).

As mentioned previously, national reconstruction was blocked by political turmoil. The socioeconomic structure suffered from the lack of concern political leaders showed over the poverty-stricken majority of the population. Class differences were as sharp as they had been one hundred years previously (Cumberland 1968; Lomnitz-Adler 1992).

Decline of Cultural Imperialism

Increasingly concerned with their national image, Mexican leaders sought to build on Enlightenment thinking. They did this by applying European concepts to the nation's evolving cultural style (Hale 1968). Efforts at emulation, however, added to the divergence already prevalent, with each individual or group championing one European attribute or another, all equally detrimental to a nation built on an indigenous base. The comment of one liberal spokesman, Jose Maria Luis Mora, highlights an attitude that ran counter to the needs of the people of that time. He claimed that "the glory of the legislator does not

Unemployed urban nomad.

Street vendor in central Mexico.

Muleteers loading maize in Guanajuato, Mexico.

consist in being an inventor, but in guiding his subjects (*comitentes*) toward happiness" (Hale 1968:155). As it turns out, these "subjects" were the liberal elite. However, a few leaders continued to strive toward shaping a truly national culture.

The outstanding cultural themes of this period were the evolution of a political philosophy and the rise of a nationalist consciousness (Cline 1963). Internal military upheavals affected the direction of these goals, sometimes helping them and other times slowing them or stopping them altogether (Sierra 1969). During the approximately seventy-year period following the break from Spain to the beginning of the Diaz government, Mexico was in a state of disarray in the struggle for national freedom. There was no stable government during this time (Skidmore and Smith 1992; Gomez-Quinones 1994b; Nutini 1995).

Eventually Mexico stopped mimicking other nations and charted a course of its own making (Skidmore and Smith 1992; Gomez-Quinones 1994b), but not without severe difficulties. For example, the weakness shown by a fledgling nation such as Mexico created the opportunity for foreign intervention. The previously mentioned French-imposed monarchy was one example. The Mexican-American war of 1846 was even more disastrous and ended with over half of Mexico's territory lost to the United States. Both affairs, coming at a vulnerable time for Mexico, increased public support for a nationalist path and solution (Turner 1968; Sierra 1969). Furthermore, the growing sense of cultural and racial homogeneity encouraged nationalist awareness (Turner 1968). The 1910 revolution would bring this about much faster.

Cultural Variant in Northern Mexico

Settlers in the northern reaches of Mexico mirrored many of the shifts in attitude in higher social circles. Government and military officials had been sent to rule and maintain order, thus complementing missions in the religious sphere (Pitt 1968). The mission, pueblo (civil rule), and presidio (military defense) affected cultural life. The pueblo and presidio ensured that native laborers would be kept in check and that foreign intruders would be resisted.

Even at this early date, California and other parts of northern Mexico represented a dual heritage. The syncretic experience that shaped Mexico was repeated here, but, as might be expected, with different causes and results. Hispanic culture was brought to California mainly by the Mexicans, rather than the Spaniards (Borah 1970). Also, in the eighteenth century, the Spanish were having difficulties with the Indians in what would now be northern Mexico and the Southwest of the United States. During the late sixteenth and seventeenth centuries, a successful Indian countermovement to the Spanish had surged in the area (Borah

1970; Officer 1987).

A combination of Spanish and Indian vocabulary and names for rivers, mountains, deserts, and other geographical features resulted. The names of the southwestern states are a carry-over from this period. California, New Mexico (a syncretic name), Nevada, and Colorado are from Spanish words, and Arizona, Texas, and Utah are named after Indian tribes. In California, many place names originated from Indian sources, including Lompoc, Malibu, Pacoima, and Pismo.

In colonial California, Indian laborers had built many buildings following a syncretic style, for instance, Indian adobe bricks with Spanish tile roofs (Samora and Simon 1977). "As Anglo-Americans moved into the former Spanish possessions, they found institutional and cultural patterns so well established that it made more sense to adapt to them than to change them" (Weber 1992:333). Much of the terminology identified with the United States Southwest, such as that used in agriculture, livestock raising, and mining, is borrowed from the Spanish and Mexicans.

Economic Influences on Cultural Patterns

The Spanish-Mexican legacy includes more than words alone. Raisin culture, vineyards, wheat, flax, cotton seeds, as well as the many other resources noted previously were introduced by the Spanish. The successful Californian vineyards, with thirty million vines producing over seven million gallons of wine after 1848, were actually planted in or near the original Spanish vineyards (McWilliams 1990). Indian labor contributed greatly to agricultural expansion and maintenance. Spaniards, Mexicans, and later other groups benefited from plentiful, cheap Indian labor, which made labor-saving technology unnecessary. The aim was for the Indians to maintain the missionaries and provide most of the food for the presidios, while also being able to provide for themselves (Borah 1970; Monroy 1990).

As a result of native labor, rancho social life bustled in the postcolonial period, especially for richer criollos and mestizos. In the lucrative livestock industry, for instance, the cattle roundup season involved several weeks of work, followed by a time of feasting and drinking. The work ethic was not oriented to preparing for future needs, but to working hard in the present in expectation of the fun that would come immediately after. This ethic, as well as the good climate, cheap Indian labor, and plentiful supply of land, meant that the ranchos ran smoothly (Sanderson 1986; Pitt 1968).

Even the work was designed for entertainment and included numerous contests of roping and bull-dogging. Fiestas for religious, marital, baptismal, and other important occasions were common and sometimes lasted a week. Often, rancheros throughout California were invited to the

affair. Hired hands, vaqueros, and some domestic servants also participated, though they might celebrate in separate rancho buildings.

Like politics and philosophy, ranchero social habits were patterned
on those of upper-class Mexico City residents. A formal social etiquette
prevailed, which seems pretentious or bizarre in a region far removed
from sophisticated civilization. A rustic environment had generally not
prevented criollos and mestizos from enjoying the social rituals of their
antecedents in spite of the difficult circumstances. This was less true of
New Mexicans, who over two centuries had fashioned a sociocultural life
more suited to their environment (Sanchez 1967).

Color: Mestizaje and Lingering Racism

First Challenges to Racism

Interracial unions were more common in Mexico after independence
than during colonial times. However, although in 1822 legal distinctions
as to race were ended, racial terminology continued to be used in official
documents in many cases, especially regarding marriage statistics, until
1940 (Navarro 1970). The race question became even more important
with the spread of mestizaje (Estava-Fabregat 1987). The racial compo-
sition of Mexico during the nineteenth century began to change greatly
with the increase in numbers of mestizos due to miscegenation, intermarriage between Indians and whites (Turner 1968). According to census figures, mestizos rose from 27 percent of the population in 1824 to 53
percent in 1900, becoming the majority group in Mexico.

In such areas where mestizaje was common and prominent, one
could observe the racial variations from white/mestizo to Indian, which
also corresponded to matters of acculturation and location. Certain
regions and cities were very Spanish culturally and racially and some
mestizos with typically Indian appearances were better able to accommodate to the dominant culture by moving to these places (Knight 1990).
Importantly, this same process of miscegenation was unfolding in northern Mexico, especially among Africans and Native Americans (Forbes
1993).

Criollos and some mestizos who passed for white were the first to
challenge racism. Motives for their actions varied, but racial tolerance
was the primary reason for many; also, enlightened philosophical viewpoints had become fashionable. Equally significant was the fact that criollos linked their egalitarianism with the notion of human progress
(Bazant 1977).

Problems of Redefinition

The hidden motive for the criollos' nondeprecating view of mestizos may have been that they, too, were of mixed racial background. Perhaps they felt guilty about hiding this fact, but more likely they wanted to eliminate the barriers that had kept them from advancement. Unfortunately, they were not motivated enough to nullify the conditioned psychological effects of the colonial past. Even radical liberals such as Lorenzo Zavala continued to support racist practices, as his argument for the expulsion of Indians shows: "he urged them to 'force the barbarians to organize themselves into regular societies or leave the national territory, as the North Americans are doing with their Indians'" (Navarro 1970:147).

Although criollos became more inclined to reevaluate the effects of racism, they were too imbued with the past to break with it completely. While seeking improvements, they still agreed that the lower classes prevented full national development. Latin American elites would state that it was the "apathy, indolence and improvidence" of the masses that led to underdevelopment (Stein and Stein 1970:183).

Role of Mestizos

In addition, despite a national mood bent on curbing racism, mestizos attempted to pass as whites and became repressive fixtures of the social order (Stein and Stein 1970; van den Berghe 1967). This continued to be the case during the Anglo period, when they adopted a "fantasy heritage" (McWilliams 1990) of racial purity, which was more than likely one of their strategies for maintaining their status and power within the Anglo racial hierarchy (Acuna 1988).

In fact, Mexico's "middle class of politicians, professionals, military officers, tradesmen, and assorted urban and rural segments was essentially a Mestizo population" (Nutini 1995:286). As a result, the criollos formed "an unspoken alliance with an essentially Mestizo political leadership; a shaky peace henceforth constituted the cornerstone of the political and economic life of the nation until the Revolution of 1910" (Nutini 1995:280).

Mestizos generally fell in with this attitude, and so with independence, the mestizos became the "Gachupines of the Indians" (Navarro 1970:148). They created even more suspicion among Indians by mistreating them in order to obtain more favorable positions for themselves. As previously noted, social conditions forced mestizos into this path. Casual farmers, middlemen, workers, and others who had no legal position in the colonial regime set up residence on the outskirts of Indian villages and other communities near haciendas, mills, or mines. Their marginality often compelled them to adopt antisocial patterns of behavior (Wolf 1965). Underemployment of the racially mixed contributed to the creation of urban slums, with a poverty-stricken population always welcoming any opportunity to make money (Cumberland 1968). Groups of "guerilla brigands" wreaked havoc in Mexico during Independence and after (Vanderwood 1992; Joseph 1992). "Haciendas were looted and burned; cattle stolen and dispersed. The followers of bandits . . . became infamous for their crimes" (Vanderwood 1992:23–24).

Race and Class Linkages

The abolition of "Indian" as a legal category meant that caste now "became secondary to class as a form of social identification" (Knight 1990:72). However, "the use of the term 'Indian' became synonymous with a combination of material poverty and cultural 'backwardness.' Class distinction was again framed in racial terms, so that poor mestizos—especially peasant mestizos—were called 'Indians' by the upper classes, while rich mestizos were 'whitened'" (Lomnitz-Adler 1992:276). Indianness, however, was "not defined solely or even primarily in somatic terms. A range of other characteristics determined 'racial' . . . identification: language, dress, religion, social organization, culture and consciousness" (Knight 1990:73). Indians, therefore, could move up the social scale if they changed their social habits, which could occur with migration, education, and occupational shifts (Knight 1990; Cubitt 1988; Lomnitz-Adler 1992).

Individuals nevertheless were ranked in the social-class system on the basis of their racial appearance, unless their behavior clearly contradicted such indicators; race and class were tied together. Generally, the darker and more Indian-appearing one was, the lower the social class position, and the whiter, the higher. Furthermore, many leaders, such as Mora (a prominent liberal politician), sought to encourage the immigration of Europeans in order to "whiten" the population, while at the same time restricting the entrance of Asians and Negros. Mora's plan in the mid-nineteenth century was that white foreigners should be given preference over the "colored" races in "everything that did not constitute a 'clear violation of justice'" (Navarro 1970:154). This "provoked a valorization of whiteness . . ." (Lomnitz-Adler 1992:276).

The modifications that occurred were mostly in people's awareness of racism, not in any substantive changes that were made concerning it. Previously, a closed class system existed. "Opaque partitions" kept colonial classes separate, blocking out the vision one class had of another. Very few were publicly aware that the social class system was based on racial differences. With independence, the opaque partitions were exchanged for transparent (or maybe merely translucent) ones. Classes still were separate, but now people realized that the white Europeans were on top, the medium-hued mestizos in the middle, and the dark Indians at the bottom. The people on top or in the middle would not break the partitions, and as a result, racist ideology and practices persisted.

The Latin American elite flourished during this period, while the situation for the working class, mostly the dark-skinned population, worsened (Morner 1967). They still were affected by the social mobility barrier, which emphasized facial features and the color of one's skin. An exception to that centuries-old social rule was rare indeed—although one exception was the presidency of the assimilated Indian Benito Juarez.

Indians in the North

These words of a Franciscan missionary illustrate native conditions in California and generally throughout the northern region: "The Indians of California may be compared to a species of monkey . . . and particularly in copying the ways of the 'razon' or white men, whom they respect as being much superior to themselves; but in so doing, they are careful to select vice, in preference to virtue. This is the result, undoubtedly, of their corrupt, and natural disposition" (Heizer and Almquist 1971:4). Pseudo-scientific racial theories of the time contributed to racist attitudes; it was believed that persons of mixed race inherited not the best characteristics of each race, but the worst (Gutierrez 1991). Taking into account the experiences of the Mexican Indians and mestizos, it is no wonder that those who were racially different became ingrained with an inferiority complex and negative self-image.

Chapter 7

Breakup and Transformation of the Social Order

Contact: Anglo-American Expansionism

Roots of Contact

While Mexico was struggling with internal problems, increased contacts with foreigners, particularly Anglo-Americans, led to further disruptions. Initial contacts with the Anglo-American north introduced to Mexico concepts of democracy and social revolution far different from the Spanish social and ideological heritage. These helped to expand the horizons of emergent Mexico. However, further contacts soon introduced a decidedly less favorable concept: Manifest Destiny, the fated expansion westward of the United States to the Pacific coast and even beyond. This theory first made its appearance in America in the mid-1840s and soon became a popular slogan (Meier and Ribera 1993:55; Merk 1963:24). To Mexico's misfortune, America expanded westard toward Alta California, New Mexico, and Texas; the three insufficiently protected Mexican provinces (Bauer 1974:xix). Driving this expansion was the idea that Anglos (and whites) held superiority over Mexicans as a people and race (Montejano 1987; De Leon 1983)—an attitude embraced by the mostly southern-based American newcomers who held disparaging views toward "darker" people. Manifest Destiny also had an economic component and served as a rationale for why a traditional, agricultural society had to give way to a far superior modern industrial system (and people!) (Montejano 1987; Mirande 1987).

The notion that some superhuman power has ordained imperial expansion is not new; such ideas often motivate those who carry forth the flag of conquest. It is perhaps true that the underlying goal of expansion is to obtain new land and wealth for the victors. Thus, the Moorish and Christian conquests and the spread of Spanish Catholicism to the New World were accompanied by both idealistic motives and material rewards. After World War II, Marxian governments fell into a similar pattern. The expansionism of the United States in the nineteenth century also plainly exhibits a desire for land and resources (Ulibarri 1963:169). Although different from the peasant situation in Mexico, it gives some indication of how landed farmers in some parts of northern Mexico were to be transformed under the United States into wage laborers with nothing but their labor to bargain with; the migration of labor soon became more of a factor in their lives, just as it would later for the Mexican peasants in the early part of the next century.

Expansionist Tradition in the United States

The United States had barely come into being when the doctrine of Manifest Destiny was formulated. Americans felt an obligation to spread from the Atlantic coast to the Pacific coast (Bauer 1974:2). Thomas Jefferson moved American boundaries toward Mexico by maintaining that the 1803 Louisiana Purchase included territory extending to the Rio Grande (Griswold Del Castillo 1990:11; Ulibarri 1963:9). Even before Mexican independence, Americans had settled in Texas and, in some cases, had participated in attempts to seize control of the region (Meier and Ribera 1993:37; Hollon 1961:96). One observer stated that racialism "was planted in the unique psychohistorical experience of the white Texas pioneers and settlers" (De Leon 1983:12). As noted in chapter 6, American merchants in the same time period had established a major commercial presence in California. Many had settled there, intermarried with the local aristocracy, and added their own antipathy to Mexican control to the Californios' desires for greater autonomy (Meier and Ribera 1993:64; Pitt 1968:4).

Background to American Takeover

The years following Mexico's independence from Spain were marked by increased American immigration into the Mexican frontier provinces. Many—perhaps most—of the immigrants carried with them the conviction that their new homes would eventually become part of the United States, and their activities helped to promote that idea. Americans in Texas and New Mexico chafed under Mexican government policies and spread their discontent among the local aristocracy (Weber 1973:83–84, 125–31). Communications from Hispanicized Yankees in California further whetted the Eastern entrepreneurs' desire for good seaports and expanded trade and also—whether intentionally or unwittingly—provided important strategic military information (Pitt 1968:12; Bauer 1974:12).

Mexican authorities attempted to secure the northern provinces by developing land-grant policies to encourage Mexican citizens to settle in the frontier regions. American immigrants were also given land and citizenship rights in an effort to win their loyalty to the Mexican government. While these policies led to prosperity for many settlers, some Americans viewed them as an expression of the government's weakness, and they continued their efforts to subvert Mexican rule. Mexican leaders were working from a position of weakness and freely accepted all grantees, but the end result found that "we made a present of Texas to the Americans of the North" (Castaneda 1976:310) and thus hastened the transition from a traditional to a modern society, with far-reaching consequences for the mass of the Mexican people.

Officials of the American government encouraged intrusions into Mexican territory and sought, both openly and surreptitiously, to promote American incorporation of Texas, New Mexico, and California. With the exception of the displacement of the American Indians, it was the first major imperial adventure by the United States and the beginnings of a militarization of American society (Raat 1992:76). As early as 1825, the government sent Joel Poinsett (whose name is now remembered for the Mexican flower he brought back) to Mexico to attempt to purchase Texas (Price 1967:16; Rippy 1926:5). A later envoy from President Andrew Jackson offered Mexico five million dollars for the territory (Acuna 1988:12). In California the United States consul, Thomas Larkin, worked on persuading Californians to reject Mexican government, both in name and in practice (Rosenbaum 1981:32). As a respected and influential figure, he was confident that California would become American territory through peaceful means (Pitt 1968:21). Some observers have likened these events to American dealings with the North American Indians and, as noted above, with African slaves (De Leon 1983). Price, for example, argues that the American belief that there was little difference between Indians and Mexicans was reflected in their views on diplomatic relations: serious diplomacy with Mexico was difficult (Price 1967:17).

Repercussions of Annexation

In time, these developments led to open warfare despite fierce, if disorganized, resistance by Mexico and forceful opposition in the United States Congress to American annexation of the territories that comprise the present southwestern states (Gomez-Quinones 1994a:182–85). In Mexico, these losses set the stage for further instability, another major foreign intrusion, continuing hostilities along the northern border, and still-prevalent bitterness and suspicion toward the American government (see Gutierrez Ibarra 1987 and Martinez C. 1991 for the Mexican version of the account in the Spanish language). For Chicanos living in the newly American territories, the annexation brought a new layer of oppression, but with a decidedly different macrostructural arrangement. What one author has said of early American immigrants to Texas proved to be true throughout the Southwest: "many of the new arrivals were aggressive, opinionated, domineering, and intolerant. They made little effort to disguise their feeling of racial superiority and their belief that their democratic institutions were God's bequest to a select few. The frontier spirit of equality was admirable, but it applied only to the white race" (Hollon 1961:107; see also De Leon 1983; Montejano 1987).

Conflict: End of the Mexican-American War, Continuation of Strife

Texas as Prelude

Texas was the first battleground in the Mexican-Anglo conflict. Although it was the American government that endorsed the policy of westward expansionism, Mexico, in fact, contributed to its execution by allowing Anglo-Americans to own Mexican territory (Griswold Del Castillo 1990; Castaneda 1976). Anglo settlers had no intention of listening to a Mexican authority, whom they considered inferior. Moreover, Mexican control was tenuous; the center of power was hundreds of miles from this outpost, which made political and military directives nearly inoperative. When Mexico sent in troops to stop the generous Anglo colonization program, it was too late. The clamor for a free and independent nation was led by influential Anglo leaders and dissident Mexicans. After a major, if bloody, Mexican victory in 1835 in which General Santa Ana demolished the Alamo defenders, an army led by Sam Houston caught Santa Ana napping at San Jacinto. The defeat of Santa Ana's forces necessitated his acceptance of Texas independence (Meier and Ribera 1993), and the Lone Star Republic was born in 1836.

The loss of Texas led almost directly to Mexican military conflicts with the United States (Fuller 1936:38). From 1836 to 1846 there were constant battles, forays, and skirmishes between the rebel Texans and the Mexicans, most ending in a stalemate. To the advantage of the Texans, the Mexican government was too greatly occupied by domestic affairs, so that troops were only sent to the border several years after the defeat of Santa Ana at San Jacinto. The policy of some Texan leaders was to create a constant war at the frontier until Mexico would be ready to negotiate (Webb 1935:48). The Mexican congress never legally ratified a treaty to give Texas an independent status. Although the United States remained publicly neutral to avoid domestic political enmity, Texas was admitted to the union as soon as approval could be secured. This annexation occurred despite congressional opposition based on fears for trade relations with Mexico and on northern antislavery sentiment (for Texas was admitted as a slave state).

Texas Annexation and Intrigue

By annexing Texas, the United States was now faced with a state where conflicts persisted. In fact, the Mexican government regarded the annexation as a declaration of war. By following the 1844 Democratic Party platform, which advocated western expansion and Texas annexation, the newly elected President James K. Polk placed the United States on a collision course with Mexico (Hollon 1961:154–57; Price 1967:114–15). However, a new dimension was added to the acquisition of Texas: Polk's emissaries were instructed to offer anywhere from fifteen to forty million dollars for the territories of New Mexico and California! In the eyes of the Mexicans, this overture added insult to injury. The Mexicans considered the American annexation of Texas illegal because Mexico had never ratified Texas independence. Moreover, the annexation of Texas was in violation of the terms of the 1819 Adams-Onis American treaty with Spain, which specified that the western boundary of the United States was to be the Sabine River, the present-day border of Louisiana. This line was clearly outside the area of Mexican Texas (Horgan 1954:475; Livermore 1969:24). To complicate matters further, the United States government accepted the Texas claim of the Rio Grande as the boundary between the alleged independent Texas and Mexico proper. Polk, in fact, in order to encourage Texan leaders to accept annexation, promised them that the American government would support their claim to the Rio Grande. This was a risky step, as the recognized border of Texas was the Nueces River, about 150 miles to the north (Griswold Del Castillo 1990). The American offer to purchase additional territory, without negotiating the status of Texas, was viewed as a subterfuge for it seemed plain that the United States intended to take it anyway. Anglo-Americans often managed to expand westward by provoking wars with Mexico (Acuna 1988:19; Cockcroft 1990:71).

Declaration of War

Polk was prepared for war in any event. An engagement involving the American and Mexican armies that took place between the two rivers was the excuse he needed. His May 11, 1846, declaration of war message to

Congress stressed that "American blood was shed on American soil" (Merk 1963:88). This stands out as one of the most duplicitous phrases ever spoken by a president. War was declared—even though Mexican soldiers had lawfully defended Mexican territory from foreign aggression.

The Mexican-American War was speedily brought to a conclusion. By 1848, the United States had forced its version of the disputed Texas boundary on Mexico and had seized additional Mexican lands extending beyond the Rocky Mountains. With each Yankee victory, expansionist enthusiasm flourished. What Castaneda (1976:307) has described as American "plans to acquire what belongs to their neighbors" and Livermore (1969:13) labels "this lust for territory" was publicly proclaimed in many circles. The annexation of Mexican territory was justified in terms of extending civil and religious liberty, and industrial and commercial enterprises (Livermore 1969:12). A popular idea, at the time, was that the Mexicans were therefore being "rescued" by the Americans (Fuller 1936:81). Northern congressional opposition—whose ranks included the young politician, Abraham Lincoln—could not reduce this fervor.

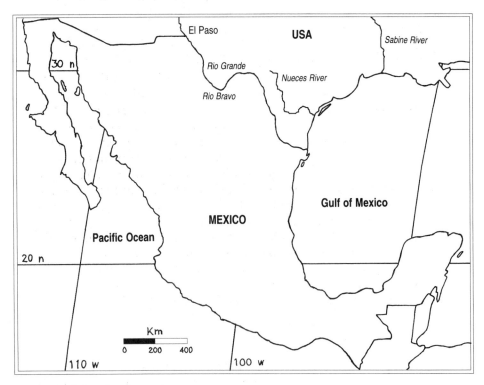

Area of river border controversy.

Skirmishes and Resistance

In spite of the seeming rapidity of the war, much Mexican resistance was encountered in both Mexico and the borderlands; over fifty thousand Mexicans, most of whom were peasants, lost their lives in this affair (Cockcroft 1990:72). Several incidents in California show that the Mexicans fought bravely and successfully (Pitt 1968:34). The revolt in Los Angeles, a skirmish at Chino (just south of Los Angeles), and the Battle of San Pasqual (near San Diego) are three examples of well-organized, well-executed victories over American forces. The affair at San Pasqual was a humiliating defeat for United States forces, who lost over twenty men, with more wounded, particularly since it involved the General of Western Operations, Steven Kearney, and his scout, the famous Kit Carson. Furthermore, there was not one Mexican casualty (Bancroft 1888:344–45). In New Mexico, the revolt of 1847 by disgruntled pobres (peons and Indians) further underscores native resistance (Zeleny 1974:105–8; Weber 1973:125). However, Anglo numerical and technological superiority won out in the end.

The battle was lost, the war formally ended, but fighting raged on. Conflict was in fact present in this area since 1846 and continued long after the Treaty of Guadalupe Hidalgo was signed (McWilliams 1990:98). The Mexican elite, gente de razon and ricos, who believed they would benefit from the new rule, were surprised when in only a few years their land was taken from them (Montejano 1987:47). Subsequent political struggles in the United States Congess over what to do with this land brought another, bigger war: "In the immediate aftermath, internal tensions were exacerbated to the point that the Civil War became more probable" (Gomez-Quinones 1994b:182).

Unfortunately, those who caught the initial onslaught were the poorer Mexicans, the pobres, peons, and cholos. Since they were on the first line of defense, they were brought into contact and conflict much sooner. The few ranchitos they possessed were occupied immediately. Unlike the more affluent members of Mexican society, the owners of large ranchos whose land was stripped away piecemeal, the poorer classes were the first to react against these transgressions.

Outlaws or "Social Bandits"?

Although the actions taken by these Mexicans were sporadic and disorganized, the conflict sometimes reached a revolutionary level. Instead of fighting against soldiers in full military uniform, the rebels battled law enforcement officers such as Texas Rangers and sheriffs in the towns and hinterland (Montejano 1987; De Leon 1983; Webb 1935:177). Antagonism generally characterizes the contact between two very different

American marines storming the Chapultepec Castle.

Mexico City under attack.

cultures, which is reflected in the fact that historically, borderlands between different peoples are zones of conflict (Mirande 1987; Clendenen 1969:1). In addition to this, there was the frontier violence that marked the period, in which outlaws of all races made life miserable for settlers and entrepreneurs. One writer referred to them as "prairie pirates, seizing any property that comes in their way, murdering travellers, and making descents upon trains and border villages" (Taylor 1934:31). Such conditions only worsened Mexican-Anglo relations.

Mexican guerrilla or resistance activity persisted through the nineteenth century; similar repercussions and ripple effects occurred in Mexico proper in various regions where peasant unrest and disturbances challenged the government (Raat 1992:75; Cockcroft 1990). Anglos vehemently maintained that the Mexican rebels were nothing but common, ordinary bandits (Acuna 1975:43; Webb 1935:178). However, many became folk heroes to the oppressed Mexicans, and some observers maintain that this social banditry was revolutionary in character (Hobsbawn 1959; Vigil 1974; Gomez-Quinones 1994b). Social bandits usually flourish after a war, when their group has been subjugated. Native resistance mounts because the whole social order is changed in favor of the victor (Pitt 1968:75). It is noteworthy, however, that in the theater of agrarian unrest that central Mexico became at this time, the rebellious laborers and peasants who attacked haciendas also were labeled criminals.

There were dozens of social bandits in the border regions (Rosenbaum 1981:51–63). Joaquin Murietta and Tiburcio Vasquez in California, Sostenes L'Archeveque in New Mexico, and Cheno Cortina in Texas are only a few of the more famous ones. Murietta's career apparently began because of the abuse he and his family received (Vigil 1974:34–37). Furthermore, he had resisted the discriminatory treatment meted out to Mexicans in the mining region of California, where gold had recently been discovered (Ridge 1969). His spree of antisocial acts lasted from 1851 to 1853. Accounts as to his death (or escape?) vary.

Another social bandit was Tiburcio Vasquez. Some accounts have him riding with Murietta, but it is certain that by 1854 he was branded an outlaw by Anglo justice (Greenwood 1960). Before he was captured and hanged in 1876, he said: "Given $60,000.00 I would be abⁱ ᵉ to recruit enough arms and men to revolutionize Southern California" (L₁eenwood 1960:13).

The situation in New Mexico was somewhat different because many Indians joined the Mexican resistance (Swadesh 1974:64). It was under the influence of Anglo-Americans, rather than Mexican-Americans, that lawlessness took place. The Anglo-Americans were fortune-seekers who profited from the fact that American law and order were not yet effective in the area (Gonzalez 1993; Zeleny 1974:150–51). The career

Joaquin Murietta.

Tiburcio Vasquez.

Juan "Cheno" Cortina.

of Sostenes L'Archeveque, one among many who resisted, is illustrative. "After his father was shot down by Anglo-Americans in . . . eastern New Mexico, the young man lost little time in acquiring twenty-three 'gringo' notches on his gun" (McWilliams 1990:120–21). Later, a group known as Las Gorras Blancas (the White Caps) (Acuna 1988) became famous when they stood up against land barons, particularly since they escaped capture and punishment (Rosenbaum 1981:112; Weber 1973:234).

Juan "Cheno" Cortina, the Tejano (Texan), was another Mexican who fought injustice and inequality (Montejano 1987:32). His life exemplifies the widespread resistance of the period and also the continued ties of Chicanos in the United States with Mexico. Cortina has been both praised (Paredes 1958) and condemned (Webb 1935; Clendenen 1969). His career was an unusual one. He survived all attempts to stop him, finally ending up as a top official in the northern Mexican state of Tamaulipas (Acuna 1988:49; Vigil 1974:41). Early in his life, Americans labeled him the "Red Robber of the Rio Grande"; later, fellow government officials in Mexico distrusted him, and it was alleged that he plotted conspiracies (Bazant 1977). He even fought on the Union side during the Civil War, clearly an instance of political expediency. "Throughout his life he betrayed, changed sides without hesitation, murdered and stole . . . and his lack of any moral foundation made it impossible for him ever to be more than a glorified bandit" (Clendenen 1969:42). So went the pattern of conflict—some claimed that resistance was pure and simple criminality, while others argued that it was based on a just cause (Rosenbaum 1981). As De Leon has maintained, however, it was the most violent era in Texas history, reflecting the "ingrained contempt Anglos had for 'greasers'" (De Leon 1983:88).

Conflict as Pattern

The Mexican people generally supported the individual acts of social bandits. In all the regions where Vazquez and Murietta operated, they were aided both morally and physically by their countrymen. Frequent crowd protests occurred in which accusations were made about the dual system of law enforcement—Mexicans were punished and Anglos went free. The solidarity of the Mexican people was reflected in countless incidents during the 1850s and 1860s (Vigil 1974:41–42; McWilliams 1990:129–32). After 1848, opposition to the courts mounted when a similar double standard was practiced: The gente de razon found their titles at risk, losing both in the courts and to their American lawyers (Paredes 1958:31). Furthermore, Anglo reactions often involved the creation of a special corp of law enforcers, sometimes amounting to a private army. None were more formidable in seeking out and persecuting Mexicans than the Texas Rangers (Raat 1992:74; Webb 1935).

In the former Mexican territory, there were many adventurers, mostly Anglos but some Mexicans, who planned and carried out filibustering missions against Mexico (Rippy 1926:90). Some even attempted to conquer Central American republics (Rippy 1926:93, 177). An undeclared war pervaded the entire border region, along the two-thousand-mile line now technically separating the two countries, and this state of affairs continued until well into the twentieth century (Montejano 1987:33; Clendenen 1969:xv). The chaos and conflict associated with cattle raids and filibustering in the first decades has continued to the present, manifested now as problems regarding immigration and drug trafficking.

These and other notable events increased Mexican awareness of their station in society. One avowed champion of the people in Los Angeles was Francisco P. Ramirez, the editor of the newspaper *El Clamor Publico* (The Public Outcry). His coverage of events and personalities of the 1850s attests to a tension-filled climate (Pitt 1968:189–93; Vigil 1974:42–48). While the newspaper carried the usual fare, it also took up the cultural, economic, and political problems of the Mexican people. An especially newsworthy item on September 16, 1856, concerned the United States government's refusal or reluctance to live up to the Treaty of 1848, a document that was clearly intended to protect Mexican rights (Vigil 1974:23).

Change: New System for Mexican-Americans

Treaty of 1848

Mexicans and Indians are the only minority groups in the United States who were conquered and whose rights were protected by treaty provisions (Mirande 1987:9; McWilliams 1990:103; Chavez 1984). The Treaty of Guadalupe Hidalgo (1848) resolved several issues and established a political boundary. Through it, a huge region that was formerly the northern-most province of Mexico became the Southwestern province of the United States. The most noteworthy articles concerned the protection of land grants and cultural rights, especially the protocol added later, which referred to the Louisiana Purchase stipulation of 1803 (Griswold Del Castillo 1990:53; Ross 1928:22–23). According to this treaty, some Mexican practices would be protected. Land grants and tenure rights established during the Mexican period would be respected on the basis of international law (Ross 1928:22). On paper, the treaty serves as a guarantee for legitimate land grants in Texas, New Mexico, Arizona, and California, but it never was seriously embraced by the United States government (Griswold Del Castillo 1990:54–55). "It joined the ranks of hundreds of other treaties that the United States made with Native

American tribes in the nineteenth century that have been almost totally ignored since then" (Griswold Del Castillo 1990:173; see also Weber 1973:165–66).

Furthermore, Mexican cultural customs and patterns were to be given equal consideration with Anglo culture; this meant recognition and accommodation of the Spanish language and Catholic religion (Cockcroft 1990:73). For example, in California the first state constitution was written in Spanish and English (Pitt 1968:46). In other regions there was a definite trend, at least initially, toward respect for the Spanish language (Zeleny 1974:274). This policy came to an end somewhat abruptly when a backlash occurred on several fronts. In addition to the conflict conditions already noted, the Mexican-Americans began to be subjected to prejudice and discrimination on the basis of their cultural customs and language (Moquin and Van Doren 1971:181).

Ethnic Rivalry and Hostility

It was not mere coincidence that land rights and cultural accommodation declined sharply at the same time. There is clear evidence of Anglo encroachments and eventual absorption of both small and large parcels of Mexican property (Zeleny 1974:147–48; McWilliams 1990:120). One observer of Texas says: "But it is certain that the traditional belief in unfair deprivation of private property in land remains an element in the

Mexican cession.

background of Mexican emotional hostility to Americans. Both Mexicans and Americans told me their versions of what happened, the Americans often corroborating the Mexicans" (Taylor 1934:188). After the Mexican-American War of 1846, a dual economy with a dual wage system evolved (Blea 1988). "Chicanos were excluded from education, or their education was inferior. Political participation was impossible, and they lost the land (the basis of their wealth). Chicanos suffered religious discrimination, shootings, hangings, and general violence. Many women were raped and otherwise violated . . . Women, men, and children resisted the hated and feared Texas Rangers" (Blea 1992:46–47).

All in all, after the Mexican-American War and up to 1880, U.S. citizens of Mexican descent lost some 20 million acres (Cockcroft 1990).

Moreover, the dominant Anglos became increasingly convinced that socioeconomic and cultural privileges should not belong to a "culturally and racially inferior" people; they were a "mongel race that not only incorporated the genes of the 'redskin' but also those of the 'nigger'" (De Leon 1983:15). For example, Anglos complained that the large ranchos were poorly developed by the Mexicans (Moquin and Van Doren 1971:190; Ross 1928:48). They also believed that Mexican customs retarded the full use of land and natural resources; that is, too many fiestas hindered large-scale development. The new leaders maintained that the cause of civilization would advance with land control in Anglo-American hands, and that "if Mexicans could not keep pace with Yankee progress, or improve their standard of living, it was their own fault" (De Leon 1983:26–27).

In this era of Anglo-Mexican relations, Manifest Destiny provided a cultural reason to expropriate land and continue the growth and development of the United States, as "territory lost by Mexico to superior arms was used by the United States to launch its own industrial revolution" (Raat 1992:55–56). During the war, hostile attitudes were sown and nurtured by each ethnic group (Acuna 1988:19). When competition over land intensified, there was an increase in invective on both sides. During the war, Anglo soldiers, many of them rowdy backwoodsmen, took special joy in killing "greasers," desecrating Mexican churches, and raping the women; Mexican women were also stereotyped as sluts who would willingly sleep with any man (De Leon 1983). The word "greaser" became a commonly used derogatory term for Mexicans. According to one writer, it referred to their greasy food (Paredes 1978:69). To Jeremiah Clemens, an 1840s observer, the ethnic label described the whole Mexican group: "The people look greasy, their clothes are greasy, their dogs are greasy, their houses are greasy—everywhere grease and filth hold divided dominion" (Dobie 1969:179). Not to be outmatched, Mexicans referred to Anglos as gringos, a corruption of the Spanish word *griego*, meaning one who speaks Greek (gibberish) (McWilliams 1990). Thus attitudes were set, epithets were invented, and the behavior that followed was a vicious demonstration of how territorial conflict can set human against human.

Roots of Friction: Economic Competition

The first target was land, which was gradually taken over by the Anglos. Soon after, Mexican labor was sought, secured, and exploited. With land and labor under Anglo control, it obviously followed that wealth (capital) would also fall into their hands (Samora and Simon 1977:177–78). As a result, the Mexican people were left largely without resources, almost destitute. It is now fairly clear that these initial changes paved the way for a more capitalistic system where the cattle and agriculture industries became commercialized for export, with Mexican labor dominated by entrepreneurs (Montejano 1987; Cockcroft 1990:53; Raat 1992). "This transition took longer in New Mexico than in California or Texas, but the result was the same" (Raat 1992:73).

As noted previously, the friction between the two groups, which revolved around racial and cultural issues, obscured the real problem source—economic competition. Racial and cultural practices that establish a dominant/subordinate relationship are often obvious, but there is a reason why one group discriminates against another racially or culturally (Price 1967:18; Acuna 1988:7). The Anglo discrimination only added to the previous burden of racial and cultural oppression experienced by the Mexican people. As Wolf states, it reflected the effects of "North American Capitalism," a juggernaut that demolished "unproductive" societies, burying traditional commercial and social practices and replacing them with new ones (Wolf 1969:288).

Variance in Treatment of Mexicans

A complex situation arose. Those Mexicans who could not look and act the part of Europeans were accorded a subordinate status. Generally speaking, some gente de razon had a somewhat easier time because of their Latin background; but in Texas the distinction between Castilian and Mexican soon lost its usefulness (Montejano 1987). It was the poor, darker individuals unassimilated to the European model who suffered more abuse. In the words of a modern writer: "One cannot understand the discrimination that has been visited upon Mexican-Americans without taking into account the color of their skin and the fact that they look like Native Americans or part Native Americans" (Forbes 1964:4). The treatment received by the socially immobile, dark, and Indian-acting Mexicans further emphasized the Anglo attitude that "the only good Indian is a dead Indian" (Price 1967:17). Many of the lighter-hued, Spanish types felt superior to the other Mexicans. The descendants of gente

Mexicanized Apache warriors led by Geronimo.

de razon still, to this day, deny their Mestizo heritage and the fact that their ancestors acquired Mexican, rather than Spanish, land grants (Pitt 1968:290).

A Mexican intragroup split resulted. Because the more oppressed elements suffered considerably, they tended to group together against those who were above them on the social scale (Montejano 1987). To protect their interests (McWilliams 1990:121–22), many gente de razon joined Anglos in opposing the resistance acts of the Mexican masses (*Evening Free Lance* 1927:Preface). Despite this uneasy alliance, they, too, lost out in the end, becoming bankrupt and poverty-stricken in some instances. They continued to be viewed by Anglo-Americans as being Mexicans, except in ceremonial occasions when certain traits become "Spanish" (McWilliams 1990:209).

New Dimension to a Sense of Inferiority

The Mexicans' racial makeup was the primary obstacle placed in the path of socioeconomic mobility. If that barrier was not enough, then cultural criteria were used to undermine their advancement. For many, it was truly a perplexing situation, since they were only beginning to master the Spanish language when a new dominant one was substituted for it. However, the new social structure was not so new after all, since it generally resembled the old colonial one in at least one respect: Native Mexicans were on the bottom. Where it differed is in the nature of the macrostructural revampments. How they were situated on the bottom was new, especially in the ways they were being stripped of their traditional lifeways piecemeal and relegated to a different role in an industrial economy.

Basis of New Cultural Blending

The native cultural style was being replaced by a new one. There was some trepidation among natives concerning this "time is money" and "cold materialism" ethic (Pitt 1968:23–24). Although some features of the Anglo social structure contrasted sharply with earlier systems, enough remained to remind natives of past experiences and adjustments. For example, natives were introduced to a new language, customs, beliefs, and values. Regional subcultures within Mexico now formed part of the United States (Paredes 1978:73), especially in the border area where there were constant interactions and exchanges (Alvarez 1995). Many Mexican traditions, such as Catholicism, were altered, and this further added to the confusion and growing sense of powerlessness. The Anglo-Americans took over all the administrative, trade, and cultural activities. This meant that the newly conquered Mexicans in the area had little say in government policy (Campa 1993). Obviously, certain beliefs concerning the family, work, child-rearing, and the nature of individual and group life had to change if the Mexicans were to survive. But as noted in earlier chapters, the changes from an indigenous to peasant way of life were beginning to take root and become routinized as traditional culture. This syncretic process covering several hundred years was now subjected to another interruption and alteration. It both complicated and aggravated cultural evolution for the Chicano people.

An example of this mixed, uneven change is how Spanish and Mexican society underwent transformations in the area of patriarchy and command and control of the household, especially the subordination of women as an ideal. Spanish customs under the Catholic church definitely granted power and authority to the patriarch, but interestingly, the legal system gave women a number of rights and privileges, such as the ability to inherit property and titles, sign contracts, and so on. With the settlement of northern Mexico, where a harsh environment required new roles and responsibilities for everyone, women found themselves doing things that heretofore were the prerogative of men (Gonzalez 1993). Farming, ranching, and household chores were arranged quite differently as the circumstances of everyday life dictated. These adaptations became particularly acute during the 1821–1848 period, in part because of the trade and relations between Mexico and the United States and in larger order because of the egalitarian currents of the time. Matriarchal households and an increase in female employment were a sign of the times. In short, "family life increasingly became a mixture of the old and the new values regarding paternal authority and the proper sphere for women" (Griswold Del Castillo 1989:99; see also Gomez-Quinones 1994b). Late in the century, women also played a role in some of the progressive and radical politics of the labor movement (Gomez-Quinones 1994b:287).

Unfortunately, aside from concessions made to the "Spanish" elite, some of whom had participated in the development of the new society, and these only of short duration, most of the natives fared poorly because the Anglos made few efforts at cultural accommodation. Mexican culture in the Southwest was crushed by the American socioeconomic belief system. Mexicans felt morally defeated during these early years of subordination (Robinson 1963:296). Over time, positive cultural reintegration finally took place (Robinson 1963:300–301). As noted before, many Anglo-Americans were Hispanicized or mestizacized, thus taking the lead in cultural integration.

Cultural Accommodation or Disintegration

For most natives, a successful life was based on their adoption of new norms; refusal to do so often meant failure. In some respects, the earlier Spanish experience had prepared them for such choices. Perhaps it is universally true that subjugated native peoples must shift and readjust to changing sociocultural conditions. In this prevailing Anglo world, numerous types of native reactions were possible, and most occurred. It must also not be forgotten that "All minorities must cope with the fact of Anglo domination; that is what being a minority in the United States means" (Rosenbaum 1981:151). Notwithstanding this truism, Gomez-Quinones suggests that ". . . the people's sense of identity led them to consider themselves as Mexicans regardless of citizenship or of the boundary line between countries . . ." (1994a:194).

More and more Anglo-Americans and European immigrants poured into the Southwest, especially California. This was particularly true after the gold rush (1850s) in the north and the completion of the railroads (1870s and after) in the south. Almost immediately the Mexicans, finding themselves in the way, began to establish their own communities. Since they played such an important role in the growing economy, they remained close to fertile land, jobs, and the homes of the wealthy. This choice was made in order to survive (McWilliams 1990:217–18). But also, "Throughout this period, Mexicans north of the imposed border continued to maintain their ties, contacts, and mutual influences in many aspects of socioeconomic life with Mexicans south of the border" (Gomez-Quinones 1994b:207).

It was necessary for Mexicans to integrate themselves somehow into United States society, even if only partially. All-out resistance was futile. Some reasoned that if this route were selected and held to, they would surely suffer the fate of the American Indians. One avenue eventually taken, the era of social bandit activity notwithstanding, was for Mexicans to group together for defense. Many Mexicans were still being abused without provocation. Suspicion and distrust characterized the

Anglo attitude, for Mexicans were perceived as deceitful, treacherous people. Therefore, staying within their own spatial and social boundaries, both groups became isolated from each other (Grebler, Moore, and Guzman 1970; Camarillo 1979).

Growth of Economy

During this time the Anglos built a great economic empire. As mentioned previously, many Indian-Spanish-Mexican practices were borrowed by Anglo entrepreneurs. These traditions, readapted by the Anglos, became the mainstays of the Southwest—mining, irrigation and riparian rights, ranching and cattle raising, and so on (McWilliams 1990). Moreover, "by 1900, the mineral output alone of the lost territories amounted to more than the national income of the Mexican Republic" (Raat 1992:78).

In keeping with the dominant/subordinate system of economic relations, the Mexicans were employed in and contributed to many enterprises (Forbes 1964:80–86). Often they did not receive equal pay for equal work (Taylor 1934). Economic competition between the two groups generated conflict and violence, and initially, Mexicans were driven out of the mining region to stem the turmoil. When Anglos eventually gained control, they began to enlist Mexican workers, not as equals but as subordinates. This was only the first of many occupational adjustments. If gente de razon were having difficulties adjusting to the changes, Mexicans were doubly suffering. The occupations they had been trained for were being taken away from them. They were then reappearing on the job market as farm laborers and livery-stable hands (McWilliams 1990:93). Since Mexicans had to eat, they worked at any job, which usually meant the lowest. In Texas, the transition was a classic example of how traditional farmers are challenged and overrun by the cattle industry and commerical agriculture. The end result was a social system that devalued them as a people but welcomed their labor in the buildup of "a farm society based on contract wage labor and business rationality" (Montejano 1987:104).

Farm work as fieldhand peons was not new to Mexicans; it was similar in some respects to the Spanish colonial pattern. And as noted for Texas, the difference here was that *campesinos* (fieldhands) participated in the building of an agricultural empire; in California, it later became unequaled in the world. In addition, when railroads and mining industries spread throughout the Southwest, section laborers were needed to lay and care for the tracks and miners were needed to dig up and process the ore. For this purpose, towns owned and supervised by the railroads and mining companies sprang up, inhabited mostly by Mexicans. So as traditional culture gave way to modern technology and occupations, a new cultural orientation was in the offing.

Decaying rancho in the late nineteenth century.

Fieldhands at an old mission in the 1880s.

Adobe brick makers.

Adaptation Strategies

As noted before, there were several types of reactions to these changes: Some were assimilated into American culture; others were assimilated into the Mexican community; and some resisted through crime (Pitt 1968:262). Many variations of these reactions were possible (Montejano 1987; Stewart and De Leon 1994). For example, some followed a separatist route and escaped into the hinterland. Eventually, though, the Anglo-Americans settled there, making the respite short-lived. Those who wished to protect and maintain ethnic traditions founded town *barrios* (ethnic enclaves) or rural *colonias* (colonies). The colonias evolved from small ranchito settlements. When hostilities ran high, Mexican resisters or social outlaws found sanctuary in such places.

Many of the elite Mexicans, especially in places like New Mexico and California, sought and maintained a semblance of power under the new Anglo political order (Gomez-Quinones 1994a:209–43). Holding elective offices such as mayors, supervisors, sheriffs, and city councilmen, they generally defended the constitutional rights and properties of their compatriots; some even pushed for bilingual education and the accommodation of cultural differences between the two groups. Oftentimes these individuals were in the middle of some rather volatile political situations, such as the Santa Fe Ring in New Mexico, where elite Mexicans and Anglos forged a machine that lasted until well into the next century.

Although assimilation was difficult, especially for Indian-appearing Mexicans, many selected that approach. In large measure, the lighter the skin and the better the English, the smoother the change. However, conflict between the two cultures did not always occur; cooperation was needed for daily life (Paredes 1978:72). Recognizing the benefits of the dominant culture, many Mexicans learned the English language and Anglo customs. And yet, particularly in border regions such as Texas, they also retained important Mexican language and sociocultural traits. Unlike assimilationists, they adopted a nativist type of acculturation—learning the dominant culture but not unlearning the native one. For some the adjustment was shaky, especially since dominant group institutions worked against cultural accommodation. In many instances, the result was a sense of marginality to both cultures. This was a repetition of the native experience in the colonial period, which sometimes had a positive result (a new hybrid culture) and sometimes ended in confusion.

Thus, some rejected separatism, assimilation, and acculturation— or were forced out of these patterns by poor treatment—and continued a life of resistance. Obviously, there were serious problems for those who took this militant path: Resisters faced death or jail. All of these reactions to change became integrated into the already broadly based Mexican sociocultural character. But "the fact remains that most Mexicanos in the United States lost the freedom to live in the way they wanted to live in during the nineteenth century" (Rosenbaum 1981:157). As the years passed, a new cultural synthesis developed.

References

Acuna, R. 1975. Mexican American history: A reply. In *The Chicano*, ed. N. Hundley. Santa Barbara, CA: ABC-CLIO, Inc.

Acuna, R. 1988. *Occupied America: A history of Chicanos*. New York: Harper and Row.

Alvarez, R. R., Jr. 1995. The Mexican-US border: The making of an anthropology of borderlands. In *Annual Review of Anthropology*. V. 24. Stanford University.

Arrom, S. M. 1985. *The women of Mexico City, 1790–1857*. Stanford: Stanford University Press.

Bancroft, H. H. 1888. *California pastoral*. Vol. 34. San Francisco: The History Co.

Bauer, K. J. 1974. *The Mexican War, 1846–1848*. New York: Macmillan, Inc.

Bazant, J. 1977. *A concise history of Mexico: From Hidalgo to Cardenas, 1805–1940*. New York: Cambridge University Press.

Blea, I. 1988. *Toward a Chicano social science*. New York: Praeger.

———. 1992. *La Chicana and the intersection of race, class, and gender*. New York: Praeger.

Borah, W. 1970. The California mission. In *Ethnic conflict in California history*, ed. C. Wollenberg. Los Angeles: Tinnon-Brown, Inc.

Camarillo, A. 1979. *Chicanos in a changing society: From Mexican pueblos to American barrios in Santa Barbara and Southern California, 1848–1930*. Cambridge: Harvard University Press.

Campa, A. 1993. *Hispanic culture in the Southwest*. Norman: University of Oklahoma Press.

Castaneda, A. 1993. Sexual violence in the politics and policies of conquest: Amerindian women and the Spanish conquest of Alta California. In *Building with our hands*, eds. A. De La Torre and B. M. Pesquera. Berkeley: University of California Press.

Castaneda, C. E. 1976. *The Mexican side of the Texan revolution (1836) by the chief Mexican participants*. New York: Arno Press, Inc.

Chance, J. K. 1994. Indian elites in late colonial Mesoamerica. In *Caciques and their people: A volume in honor of Ronald Spores*, eds. J. Marcus and J. F. Zeitlin. Ann Arbor: Museum of Anthropology, University of Michigan, Anthropological Papers no. 89.

Chavez, J. R. 1984. *The lost land: The Chicano image of the Southwest*. Albuquerque: University of New Mexico Press.

Chinas, B. L. 1983. *The Isthmus Zapotecs: Women's roles in cultural context*. Prospect Heights, IL: Waveland Press.

Clendenen, C. C. 1969. *Blood on the border: The United States Army and the Mexican irregulars*. New York: Macmillan, Inc.

Cline, H. F. 1963. *Mexico: Revolution to evolution, 1940–1960*. New York: Oxford University Press.

Cockcroft, J. D. 1990. *Mexico: Class formation, capital accumulation, and the state*. New York: Monthly Review Press.

Cotera, M. P. 1976. *Diosa y hembra: The history and heritage of Chicanas in the U.S.* Austin, TX: Information Systems Development.

Cubitt, T. 1988. *Latin American society*. Harlow, England: Longman Group UK Limited.

Cumberland, C. C. 1968. *Mexico: The struggle for modernity*. New York: Oxford University Press.

de Janvry, A. 1981. *The agrarian question and reformism in Latin America.* Baltimore; London: Johns Hopkins University Press.

De Leon, A. 1983. *They called them greasers: Anglo attitudes towards Mexicans in Texas, 1821–1900.* Austin: University of Texas Press.

de Rouffignac, A. L. 1985. *The contemporary peasantry in Mexico: A class analysis.* New York: Praeger.

Diaz, M. N. 1967. Introduction: Economic relations in peasant society. In *Peasant society: A reader*, eds. J. M. Potter, M. N. Diaz, and G. M. Foster. Boston: Little, Brown and Company.

Dobie, F. J. 1969. *Guide to life and literature of the Southwest.* Dallas: Southern Methodist University Press.

Dow, J. 1977. Religion in the organization of a Mexican peasant economy. In *Peasant livelihood: Studies in economic anthropology and cultural ecology*, eds. R. Halperin and J. Dow. New York: St. Martin's Press.

Estava-Fabregat, C. 1987. *Mestizaje in Iberio-America.* Albuquerque: University of New Mexico Press.

Evening Free Lance. 1927. Crimes and career of Tiburcio Vasquez: The bandit of San Benito County and notorious early California outlaws. Hollister, CA.

Forbes, J. D. 1964. The Indian in America's past. Englewood Cliffs, NJ: Prentice-Hall, Inc.

_____. 1993. *Africa and Native Americans: The language of race and the evolution of red-black peoples.* Norman: University of Oklahoma Press.

Foster, G. M. 1987. *Tzintzuntzan: Mexican peasants in a changing world.* New York; Oxford: Elsevier.

Fowler-Salamini, H. and M. K. Vaughan, eds. 1994. *Women of the Mexican countryside, 1850–1990: Creating spaces, shaping transitions.* Tucson; London: University of Arizona Press.

Frye, D. 1996. *Indians into Mexicans.* Austin: University of Texas Press.

Fuller, J. D. P. 1936. *The movement for the acquisition of all Mexico, 1846–1848.* Baltimore: Johns Hopkins University Press.

Gomez-Quinones, J. 1994a. *Mexican American labor: 1790–1990.* Albuquerque: University of New Mexico Press.

_____. 1994b. *Roots of Chicano politics, 1600–1940.* Albuquerque: University of New Mexico Press.

Gonzalez, D. 1993. La Tules of image and reality: Euro-American attitudes and legend formation on a Spanish-Mexican frontier. In *Building with our hands: New directions in Chicana research*, eds. A. De La Torre and B. M. Pesquera. Berkeley: University of California Press.

Gonzalez y Gonzalez, L. 1974. *San Jose de Gracia: Mexican village in transition.* Austin: University of Texas Press.

Grebler, L., J. Moore, and R. Guzman. 1970. *The Mexican American people.* New York: The Free Press.

Greenwood, R. 1960. *The California outlaw: Tiburcio Vasquez.* Los Gatos, CA: Talisman Press.

Griswold Del Castillo, R. 1989. Patriarchy and the status of women in the late nineteenth century Southwest. In *The Mexican and Mexican American experience in the 19th century*, ed. J. E. Rodriguez O. Tempe, AZ: Bilingual Press.

_____. 1990. *The treaty of Guadalupe Hidalgo: A legacy of conflict*. Norman: University of Oklahoma Press.

Gutierrez, R. A. 1991. *When Jesus came the Corn Mothers went away: Marriage, sexuality and power in New Mexico, 1500–1846*. Stanford: Stanford University Press.

Gutierrez Ibarra, C. 1987. *Como Mexico perdio Texas*. Mexico D.F.: Instituto Nacional de Antropologia E Historia.

Hale, C. A. 1968. *Mexican liberalism in the age of Mora*. New Haven: Yale University Press.

Hass, L. 1995. *Conquest and historical identities in California, 1769–1938*. Berkeley: University of California Press.

Heizer, R. T. and A. J. Almquist. 1971. *The other Californians: Prejudice and discrimination under Spain, Mexico, and the United States to 1920*. Berkeley: University of California Press.

Hewitt de Alcantara, C. 1984. *Anthropological perspectives on rural Mexico*. London: Routledge and Kegan Paul.

Hobsbawn, E. J. 1959. *Primitive rebels*. New York: W.W. Norton & Co., Inc.

Hollon, W. E. 1961. *The Southwest: Old and new*. Lincoln: University of Nebraska Press.

Horgan, P. 1954. *Great river: The Rio Grande in North American history*. New York: Lippincott & Crowell.

Hu-DeHart, E. 1993. Yaqui resistance to Mexican expansion. In *The Indian in Latin American history: Resistance, resilience, and acculturation*, ed. J. E. Kicza. Wilmington, DE: Scholarly Resources Inc.

Hutchinson, C. A. 1969. *Frontier settlement in Mexican California*. New Haven: Yale University Press.

Jackson, R. H. and E. Castillo, eds. 1994. *Indians, Franciscans, and Spanish colonization*. Albuquerque: University of New Mexico Press.

Joseph, G. M. 1992. On the trail of Latin American bandits: A reexamination of peasant resistance. In *Patterns of contention in Mexican history*, ed. J. E. Rodriguez O. Wilmington, DE: Scholarly Resources, Inc.

Kearney, M. 1996. *Reconceptualizing the peasantry*. Boulder, CO: Westview Press.

Knight, A. 1990. Racism, revolution, and *indigenismo*: Mexico, 1910–1949. In *The idea of race in Latin America, 1870–1940*, ed. R. Graham. Austin: University of Texas Press.

Livermore, A. A. 1969. *The war with Mexico*. New York: Arno Press, Inc.

Lomnitz-Adler, C. 1992. *Exits from the labyrinth: Culture and ideology in the Mexican natonal space*. Berkeley; Oxford: University of California Press.

Mallon, F. E. 1995. *Peasant and nation: The making of postcolonial Mexico and Peru*. Berkeley: University of California Press.

Martinez C., Leopoldo. 1991. La intervencion Norteamericana en Mexico. Mexico D.F.: Panorama Editorial.

McWilliams, C. 1990. *North from Mexico: The Spanish speaking people of the United States*. New York: Praeger.

Meier, M. S. and F. Ribera. 1993. *The Chicanos: A history of Mexican Americans*. New York: Hill & Wang.

Merk, F. 1963. *Manifest Destiny and mission in American history*. New York: Random House, Inc.

Meyer, M. C. and W. L. Sherman. 1987. *The course of Mexican history*. New York: Oxford University Press.

Miller, S. 1989. Social dislocation and bourgeois production on the Mexican *hacienda*: Queretaro and Jalisco. In *Region, state and capitalism in Mexico, nineteenth and twentieth centuries*, eds. W. Pansters and A. Ouweneel. Amsterdam: Center for Latin American Research and Documentation (CEDLA).

Mintz, S. W. and E. R. Wolf. 1967. An analysis of ritual co-parenthood (compadrazgo). In *Peasant society: A reader*, eds. J. M. Potter, M. N. Diaz, and G. M. Foster. Boston: Little, Brown and Company.

Mirande, A. 1987. *Gringo justice*. Notre Dame, IN: University of Notre Dame Press.

Monroy, D. 1990. *Thrown among strangers: The making of Mexican culture in frontier California*. Berkeley; Los Angeles; London: University of California Press.

Montejano, D. 1987. *Anglos and Mexicans in the making of Texas, 1836–1986*. Austin: University of Texas Press.

Moquin, W. and C. Van Doren, eds. 1971. *A documentary history of the Mexican American*. New York: Praeger Publishers.

Morner, M. 1967. *Race mixture in the history of Latin America*. Boston: Little, Brown & Co.

Nava, J., and B. Berger. 1976. *California: Five centuries of cultural contrasts*. Encino, CA: Glencoe Publishing Co.

Navarro, M. G. 1970. Mestizaje in Mexico during the national period. In *Race and class in Latin America*, ed. M. Morner. New York: Columbia University Press.

Nutini, H. G. 1995. *The wages of conquest: The Mexican aristocracy in the context of Western aristocracies*. Ann Arbor: University of Michigan Press.

Oboler, S. 1995. *Ethnic labels, Latino lives: Identity and the politics of (re)presentation in the United States*. Minneapolis: University of Minnesota Press.

Officer, J. E. 1987. *Hispanic Arizona, 1536–1856*. Tucson: University of Arizona Press.

Paredes, A. 1958. *With his pistol in his hand: A border ballad and its hero*. Austin: University of Texas Press.

_____. 1978. The problem of identity in a changing culture: Popular expressions of culture conflict along the lower Rio Grande border. In *Views across the border: The United States and Mexico*, ed. R. S. Ross. Albuquerque: University of New Mexico Press.

Phillips, G. H. 1993. *Indians and intruders in central California, 1769–1849*. Norman: University of Oklahoma Press.

Pitt, L. 1968. *The decline of the Californios: A social history of the Spanish-speaking Californios: 1846–1890*. Berkeley: University of California Press.

Potter, J. M. et al. 1967. *Peasant society: A reader*. Boston: Little Brown and Company.

Price, G. W. 1967. *Origins of the war with Mexico: The Polk-Stockton intrigue*. Austin: University of Texas Press.

Raat, W. D. 1992. *Mexico and the United States: Ambivalent vistas*. Athens: University of Georgia Press.

Redfield, R. and A. Villa Rojas. 1990. *Chan Kom: A Maya village*. Prospect Heights, IL: Waveland Press.

Ridge, J. R. 1969. *The life and adventures of Joaquin Murrieta*. Norman: University of Oklahoma Press.

Rippy, J. F. 1926. *The United States and Mexico*. New York: Alfred A. Knopf, Inc.

Robinson, C. 1963. *With the ears of strangers: The Mexican in American literature*. Tucson: University of Arizona Press.

Rodriguez O., J. E. 1989. Down from colonialism: Mexico's nineteenth-century crisis. In *Mexicans and Mexican-Americans in the nineteenth century*, ed. J. E. Rodriguez O. Tempe, AZ: Bilingual Press.

Romanucci-Ross, L. 1986. *Conflict, violence, and morality in a Mexican village*. Chicago; London: University of Chicago Press.

Rosenbaum, R. J. 1981. *Mexicano resistance in the Southwest*. Austin: University of Texas Press.

Ross, I. B. 1928. *The confirmation of Spanish and Mexican land grants in California*. Berkeley: University of California Press.

Ruiz, R. E. 1992. *Triumphs and tragedy: A history of the Mexican people*. New York; London: W.W. Norton and Company.

Saluucci, R. J. 1987. *Textiles and capitalism in Mexico: An economic history of the Obrajes, 1539–1840*. Princeton: Princeton University Press.

Samora, J. and P. V. Simon. 1977. *A history of the Mexican American people*. Notre Dame, IN: University of Notre Dame Press.

Sanchez, G. I. 1967. *Forgotten people: A study of New Mexicans*. Albuquerque: Calvin Horn Pub., Inc.

Sanderson, S. E. 1986. *The transformation of Mexican agriculture: International structure and the politics of rural change*. Princeton: Princeton University Press.

Sandstrom, A. R. 1991. *Corn is our blood*. Norman: University of Oklahoma Press.

Sierra, J. 1969. *The political evolution of the Mexican people*. Austin: University of Texas Press.

Sinkin, R. N. 1979. *The Mexican reform, 1855–1876: A study in liberal nation-building*. Austin: University of Texas at Austin, Institute of Latin American Studies.

Skidmore, T. E. and P. H. Smith. 1992. *Modern Latin America*. New York; Oxford: Oxford University Press.

Stein, S. and B. Stein. 1970. *The colonial heritage of Latin America*. New York: Oxford University Press.

Stewart, K. L. and A. De Leon. 1994. *Not room enough: Mexicans, Anglos, and socioeconomic change in Texas, 1850–1900*. Albuquerque: University of New Mexico Press.

Swadesh, F. L. 1974. *Los primeros pobladores: Hispanic Americans of the Ute frontier*. Notre Dame, IN: University of Notre Dame Press.

Swagerty, W. R. 1984. Spanish-Indian relations, 1513–1821. In *Scholars and the Indian experience: Critical reviews of recent writing in the social sciences*, ed. W. R. Swagerty. Bloomington: Indiana University Press.

Taylor, P. S. 1934. *An American Mexican frontier*. Chapel Hill: University of North Carolina Press.

Taylor, W. B. 1993. Patterns and variety in Mexican village uprisings. In *The Indian in Latin American history: Resistance, resilience, and acculturation*, ed. J. E. Kicza. Wilmington, DE: Scholarly Resources, Inc.

Turner, F. C. 1968. *The dynamics of Mexican nationalism*. Chapel Hill: University of North Carolina Press.

Ulibarri, R. O. 1963. *American interest in the Spanish-Mexican Southwest, 1803–1848*. Ph.D. dissertation. University of Utah.

Vanderwood, P. J. 1992. *Disorder and progress: Bandits, police, and Mexican development*. Wilmington, DE: Scholarly Resources, Inc.

Vigil, D. 1974. *Early Chicano guerrilla fighters*. La Mirada, CA: Advanced Graphics.

Webb, W. P. 1935. *The Texas Rangers: A century of frontier defense*. Austin: University of Texas Press.

Weber, D. J. 1973. *Foreigners in their native land*. Albuquerque: University of New Mexico Press.

_____. 1992. *The Spanish frontier in North America*. New Haven; London: Yale University Press.

Whetten, N. L. 1948. *Rural Mexico*. Chicago: University of Chicago Press.

Wolf, E. R. 1965. Aspects of group relations in a complex society: Mexico. In *Contemporary cultures and societies of Latin America*, eds. D. B. Heath and R. N. Adams. New York: Random House, Inc.

_____. 1966. *Peasants*. Englewood Cliffs, NJ: Prentice-Hall, Inc.

_____. 1969. *Peasant wars of the twentieth century*. New York: Harper and Row.

_____. 1982. *Europe and the people without history*. Berkeley: University of California Press.

Zeleny, C. 1974. *Relations between the Spanish-Americans and Anglo-Americans in New Mexico*. New York: Arno Press, Inc.

Stage IV
Anglo-American Period
1846 to 1960s

The complex historical developments of rural society and peasantry in Mexico reached a new crisis with the civil war of the twentieth century; the remaining fragments of an indigenous past were about to change again. For those Mexicans living in the northern territories annexed by the United States, it came much earlier, and with equal force, at the end of the Mexican-American War. It was a highly variable process in each place and in both time periods. In the United States, the resident Chicano population confronted and participated in a society that passed through a major civil war, abrupt and strife-ridden industrialization and urbanization, two world wars and several lesser wars, and periods of capitalistic expansion and depression. Chicanos in the United States made a transition to the new industrial order and settled primarily in cities. With their uprooting from the land and the subsequent civil war upheavals and other disruptions in Mexico, migration and immigration marked the lives of a people buffeted about by the economic and political forces of the time. Urbanization and modernization were processes that characterized the migrant and immigrant experience, and considerations of time and place are integral elements in understanding developments in this historical phase.

The civil war in Mexico impelled thousands of rural inhabitants northward into the United States. The transition from peasant life to immigrant status is filled with strains and stresses. Human movement on such a massive scale brought many uncertainties for the future. Caution and foreboding became everyday concerns for the people as they struggled to find a place in a rapidly changing world. False starts and missteps occurred with regularity, but with trial and error, most learned from the experience. Nevertheless, a sense of familiarity and control over the new situation came about very unevenly for Mexicans in both the United States and in Mexico.

In the United States, the transformations set in motion by Mexico's independence were abruptly moved in new directions. Imposition of a new Anglo-American order made Mexicans aware of other groups and other social systems, especially in regard to important human links to the environment—jobs, homes, and health. However, earlier struggles and successes had given Mexicans a sense of confidence and awareness. As a result, the momentum to make decisions, learn from mistakes, and plan a new life course, within limits, was definitely under way.

The factors affecting human migration show how economic systems and networks transcend nation-state boundaries, incorporating more resources and more people in their expansion. After the 1910 Mexican revolution, and continuing to the present, immigration has been a major contributor of human resources to support this "globalization" of the economy.

The Mexican people grew and evolved from this experience to take their place among modern populations. Showing autonomy to win independence put them in good stead to make the shift to a modern, urban lifestyle. For some Mexicans the event took place after 1848, and for many more it occurred after the 1910 civil war and throughout various ebbs and flows of the middle and late twentieth century. The Mexican people were dedicated to taking control of their destiny. Too much blood had been spilled, too many lives had been lost, and too many centuries had passed for them to passively accept the tumultuous changes and new and different symbols of authority. Freedom whets the appetite for more of the same and encourages defiance of anyone who threatens to take away what has already been gained. In spite of the numerous setbacks that occurred during this period, the Mexican people continued to move ahead.

Chapter **8**

Intact and Stable Social Order

Class: Industrialism and Urbanization

Background to Capitalism, Roots of Inequality

As the Chicano people entered the twentieth century, the economies of the United States and Western Europe were becoming full-blown capitalist systems. Capitalism is a system in which the means of production and distribution (that is, land, factories, mines, railroads, and so on) are privately owned and operated—more or less competitively—for profit. Capitalism is the culmination of previous systems such as mercantilism, colonialism, and racial/cultural imperialism, and in its short history, has undergone its own internal changes—e.g., laissez faire, monopoly, mixed, and global. The contemporary social-class structure was formed in response to changes in the structure of capitalism, creating opportunities for some and hindrances for others.

Soon after 1860, when intense Mexican ethnic resistance was subsiding, the United States moved into this new age of commerce, investment, and speculation (Cockcroft 1990). Mexico, too, was caught in the web of late nineteenth-century economic expansion, as important United States capitalists, also known as captains of industry or robber barons, invested hundreds of millions of dollars in railroads, mines, oil-wells, and agricultural enterprises (Meier and Ribera 1993; Cockcroft 1990). Thus Mexicans on both sides of the recently established border were incorporated and anchored in these transformations with the effects occurring a little earlier and in a slightly different way for those Mexicans on the northern side of the border. Ultimately, the revampments resulted in a rather profound shift, making both populations subject to shifts in the availability of jobs, thus triggering spatial mobility as migrants moved in search of employment (Meier and Ribera 1993).

It was an age characterized by intense class conflict in both the

179

industrial and agricultural sectors of the United States. Strikes, bombings, arrests, and intervention by government troops regularly appeared on the front page of newspapers. These developments were closely linked to the rise of industrialism and the increasing urbanization of the population. Under these conditions, different types of laborers were employed in varying settings. For a few, the economic expansion, industrialization, and growth of cities brought great wealth; for others, a comfortable living; and for many, poverty. The Chicanos, along with other minorities, were more often found in the last category. As a result of this system, by the mid-twentieth century, 20 percent of America's families controlled 76 percent of the wealth, which means that the remaining 80 percent of the people were left with 24 percent of the wealth (Spencer 1977). Put another way, the top 1 percent of the population owns 48 percent of the nation's wealth, and the bottom 80 percent have just 6 percent (Wolff 1996). Obviously, this method of resource acquisition and distribution causes problems.

One result was that thirty or forty million United States citizens in the 1950s were poor, or below the poverty line of a $3,200 income for a family of four (Harrington 1962:177). Within this category, the percentage of Chicanos was disproportionate to their total population. Nearly a third of the Chicano population in the Southwest, a total of 1,082,000 people, were officially classified as being below the poverty line in 1960 (Briggs 1973). The figure was really higher because many individuals were uncounted, especially unmarried immigrant males.

Still, the largest number of poor people in the United States have always been white: at that time, whites comprised over half of the poor, or more than twelve million people (Harrington 1962). Despite the significance of ethnic connotations, as verified by the high incidence of poverty among Chicanos, the fact that white people also experience inequality and deprivation emphasizes the importance of the class factor. This fact cannot be overstated. As noted previously, the wealthiest families are comparatively few, but commensurate with their resources they have a considerable influence on social and political sectors of American life. However, positions of privilege and power have evaded most citizens, including millions of whites. Inequality—lack of wealth and thus limited social and political resources—is a fact of life for many citizens and especially for minorities such as Chicanos (Meier and Ribera 1993).

The national class structure that evolved in this period can be divided into three main categories, each one having two subcategories: upper (upper-upper, lower-upper), middle (upper-middle, lower-middle), and lower (upper-lower, lower-lower) (Gordon 1964). These strata were based on income, occupation, housing, and various other factors. One's location within the system determined power, esteem, and prestige—or

Foreign-owned oil field in late nineteenth-century Mexico.

lack of them, in the lower levels. Most people were somewhere in the middle sectors.

It is this middle sector, following the lead of earlier bourgeois conventions, that set the pattern for national thought and action. Cultural membership notwithstanding, Mexican Americans followed this style once they became white- and blue-collar workers, resembling other Anglo Americans rather than Mexican newcomers (Penalosa 1973a; Sanchez 1993). It is this lifestyle that many lower-class, socially mobile people strive to emulate. However, because of their typically lower-class standing, Chicanos have had to reach higher to attain that level. One statistical study of selected workers, which controlled for education and occupation, found that the total income difference in 1959 between Anglo and Mexican male workers was $2,050. Of this total difference, $1,141 was attributable to the differing educational and occupational distributions of Anglos and Mexican Americans. The remaining portion of the difference could be mainly attributed to discrimination against Mexican Americans as a minority group (Poston and Alvirez 1976).

Chicano Role in the Economy

The foundation for Chicano poverty was set in the last century (Romo 1983). Chicanos in several regions played a major role in building up the capitalist economy (Montejano 1987). When mining enterprises dwindled, for example, many mineworkers joined farm laborers toiling in the fields. Besides the labor contributions made in the cattle and railroad industries, there were many other unskilled occupations filled by Chicanos (Gomez-Quinones 1994a). According to one writer of the 1920s: "Today we are as a nation building a great empire in our Southwest, and we are building it, to a large extent, out of stones quarried from the human quarries of Old Mexico" (Stowell 1974:122). The same author notes that at that time, millions of dollars of investment capital were "dependent for their productiveness upon Mexican labor" (Stowell 1974:40). Once again, the Chicano masses, Indians, mestizos, and other lower-echelon ranchers, who in earlier stages of their history had participated in building up other empires, did not appreciably benefit from the new wealth.

As these conditions were emerging in the United States, significant events were occurring in Mexico during the regime of Porfirio Diaz. Nowhere were these changes more dramatic than in the role of women. Under a peasant economy, females had shared many of the productive activities of the household. As noted previously, the migration to cities undermined these patterns. City life in an industrial economy introduced a more dependent relationship to the male household head. Later, when women, too, joined the factory labor force, they were subjected to lower wages and worse working conditions than the males. In time, these role and working-condition experiences led to a more assertive posture as women became involved in efforts to improve and advance their cause (Vallens 1978; Macias 1982; Soto 1979).

Further, the Indians and mestizos, mostly peons and low-paid urban workers, remained in a postcolonial state even though a degree of liberation had occurred. Both hacendados and the peons (found mostly in southeastern Mexico), tenants, and sharecroppers (found in Central and Northern Mexico) took social inequality for granted (Bazant 1977). The *porfiriato*, as this era was called, emphasized "unequal economic growth . . . based on increasing exports and a dramatic opening to foreign investment . . ." (Hinojosa-Ojeda 1994:111; see also Cockcroft 1990). In addition, the hacendados, comprising approximately one thousand families, controlled 90 percent of the land, while 85 percent of the rural population was landless (Cumberland 1968). The peasants felt that their

Farm worker in the United States and peon in Mexico.

land had been stolen from them by the hacendados and that it was only just to demand that their means of production be restored to them (Bazant 1977). Thus, conditions were ripe for revolt. While Diaz had appeased the ideological conservatives and liberals, the peasants, Indians, and city laborers were far from content (Tannenbaum 1933; see Katz 1988 for a review of peasant movements and rebellions).

The 1910 Mexican revolution, then, had the earmarks of a common people's revolt. Before the civil war erupted, however, there were recurring attempts by opposition leaders to unseat Diaz. The sentiment against him mounted, and eventually a coalition overthrew his rule. One member of the opposition, Diaz Soto y Gama, had this to say in 1910: "Mexico was ruled by a narrow, unpatriotic, dictatorial clique, which catered to the interests of foreigners and especially the Catholic Church,

Porfirio Diaz.

[and] were conspiring to take over the nation and destroy every last remnant of earlier revolutionary reforms. . . . The ultimate target of . . . the attack was Porfirio Diaz: the Caudillo who betrayed democracy" (Cockcroft 1968:98). In terms of the larger picture, one modern Mexican historian has observed that in Mexico's transition to capitalism, "with its violent upheavals in 1810, the 1850s to 1860s, and 1911–17 . . . the mobilization of peasant participation in these conflicts had long-lasting effects on social, economic, and political development" (Coatsworth 1988:62).

The Mexican civil war lasted throughout the decade and even into the 1920s. Agrarian reform was a key issue for the masses. The military leaders—Pancho Villa, Obregon, Zapata, Calles, Amaro, and others like them—were all unknown children of peasants and Indians. The revolution made them famous (Tannenbaum 1933), as it did many women, who both fought alongside the men and led contingents of their own (Cockcroft 1990; see Salas 1990 for a full review). Many of the demands of the masses were granted totally, others only partially, and still others not at all. Like most revolutions, the Mexican revolution broke the bondage of earlier ages. But, again like many revolutions, unresolved questions remain to this day (Tabler 1988).

Few would disagree that the Mexican masses generally benefited from the upheaval. Although other observers have used different frameworks in discussing postrevolutionary Mexico, the following summary will suffice here. The Institutional Revolutionary Party (PRI) has been the ruling party of contemporary Mexico, and its spokesmen maintain that every presidential regime—each one lasting six years—is part of a "continuing, permanent revolution." After the PRI was instituted in the 1920s, political turmoil quieted. During the 1930s, President Lazaro Cardenas led the nation toward improving social conditions. From 1940 to 1960, the Mexican government emphasized economic and technological development. But after 1960, there was a turn to a "balanced revolution": a pragmatic mix of political, social, and economic reforms as needed, according to the leaders (Cline 1963:191). The revolutionary sloganeering was all rhetoric, however, as the communal landholding system (i.e., *ejidos*) suffered from 1940 onward. Accordingly, the state moved in new directions, undermining *ejidatarios* as a new "agroindustrialism" (or neolatifundismo!) took over. Peasants first became migrants in their own land, moving from region to region to gain a livelihood. Increasingly, however, they soon had to migrate to another nation, the United States, especially after the 1970s (Sanderson 1988). Mexico had been brought into the capitalist network, but in a special way. There was a "dependence on foreign capital, [and] domestic capital's reliance on cheap labor . . . contributed to the great divisions between rich and poor that characterize Mexico today" (Cockcroft 1990:139).

Effects of the 1910 Revolution on the United States: The Push-Pull Factor

The 1910 revolution that profoundly transformed Mexico also had a significant impact on the United States. For one thing, social unrest in Mexico and the destruction of human ties to the land brought internal and external migration. Many adult Chicanos presently living in the United States have a grandparent or older relative who migrated to the United States during that time. It must be underscored, however, that this process of "U.S. employers . . . seeking inexpensive labor" began in the late nineteenth century and accelerated in the aftermath of 1910 (Cockcroft

Pancho Villa.

Emiliano Zapata.

Soldaderas.

General Romero.

1986:36). The presence of immigrants reinvigorated the Mexican culture in the United States and added a more determined, militant element to the labor struggle. Here we will focus on immigration, however.

Along with the "push" factor stemming from the strife in Mexico, an economic "pull" force was simultaneously operating in the United States (Hinojosa-Ojeda 1994). The economic development of the American Southwest drew many Mexican workers to the United States (Reisler 1976). This push/pull reciprocity in large part explains why Mexicans immigrated, some with permission papers and others without them, but always with the aid of intermediaries, both formal and informal. But there are also other reasons. The United States had closed the door to Asian immigration and soon after, in 1924, placed immigration quotas on southern and eastern Europeans, who had served as the United States labor reservoir for over fifty years. As a result, a new pool of workers was needed, and the Mexicans filled this need. Because of previous problems with Mexicans (conflict, resistance, hostility, economic competition, and so on), there was a general reluctance to admit this new "brown horde." There was even a movement to include them in the 1924 quotas, and in the meantime, the Border Patrol was created to monitor them (Weaver 1994). Mexican labor was desired, but the permanent settlement of Mexicans was not. A migration policy that allowed the temporary use of Mexican labor was advocated (Cardenas 1977). However, economic motives won out over social attitudes, and the farmers and ranchers of the American Southwest welcomed Mexican laborers regardless of whether they were legal or not (Stowell 1974). Nevertheless, rampant racism resulted in lower pay and unfair treatment by police; border conflict reerupted in this time period, and in El Paso, 391 Mexicans were killed between 1911 and 1919 (Cardoso 1980). The developing industrial order required "a mass of unskilled workers who could be hired cheaply and dismissed freely . . ." (Hinojosa-Ojeda 1994:111). In time, this initiative would encompass the western hemisphere in an expansionary mode that later incorporated large portions of the globe (Portes and Bach 1985).

The ebb and flow of immigration continued for decades; it actually increased when it became clear that the Mexican government had little interest (acting as a further "push") in assisting the peasants/Indians with communal land development (Hinojosa-Ojeda 1994). Immigration policy has also been greatly affected by the influence of agribusiness on state and federal legislation (Chavez 1991). Immigration restrictions on Mexicans have been periodically relaxed; for example: during World War I and the Bracero (literally "arm" or fieldhand) Program, initiated during World War II (Samora 1971). An additional burden was placed on women in peasant communities during these peak immigration periods, as males typically left the household behind to find work, leaving matters entirely under the supervision and care of their wives, even to the point of making them responsible for the food on the table (Stephen 1991).

Living conditions for these workers were poor, with no appreciable changes forthcoming for many years. Even when the situation was brought to public attention, few forceful efforts at improvement were made. Mexican immigrants were paid lower wages than other local labor; their income was barely at the subsistence level (Cockcroft 1986; Galarza 1964; Reisler 1976). They were subjected to substandard housing and hygienic conditions, and constant job insecurity. Often, settlement patterns resembled a separate village or appendage to towns and ranches (Gonzalez 1994). Agricultural communities varied in their social reality, some more complex than others, especially with the rise of agribusiness (Gonzalez 1994).

Life in an Urban Environment

The influx of immigration occurred during the United States' rise to industrial prominence. A concomitant development was the gathering of more workers in urban areas. Mexicans were a part of this process. Some businessmen went so far as to state "that were immigration to cease, or be cut much below the present average by a quota, they would be left on the verge of bankruptcy" (Gamio 1969:30; see also Alvarez 1976). As Mexicans became increasingly urbanized, they were additionally affected by the problems of urban life, especially pockets of poverty plagued by health problems and crime (Vigil 1988; Moore and Vigil 1993). Even here, they appeared as appendages, urban villages, and struck an obvious chord of distinctiveness as spatially separate and visually blighted communities (Vigil 1988; Gonzalez 1994). Either as barrios (urban) or colonias (rural colonies), such settlement patterns were noted early in the century (Romo 1983; Taylor 1934).

Participation in this transition affected Mexicans in several ways. In California, in 1931, eleven percent of wage earners in manufacturing industries were Mexicans. Today the proportion of Mexicans in various industries ranges from 2.4 to 66.3 percent (Sanchez 1993). The work environment provided a range of new experiences: the new technology of the day, the machines, office equipment and new modes of transportation, affected how time was organized and whether one joined other peoples and groups in new organizations, such as unions and the like. Urban life and routines are an entirely new experience for many newcomers to the United States, not always an easy task of adjustment (Samora and Simon 1977). While a rural-urban transformation is in itself portentous, the Chicano case must be viewed in a magnified form because it also involved a shift across national and cultural lines; an ecological and cultural switch that was ironic for a people who once claimed the same area. In any event, the Chicano

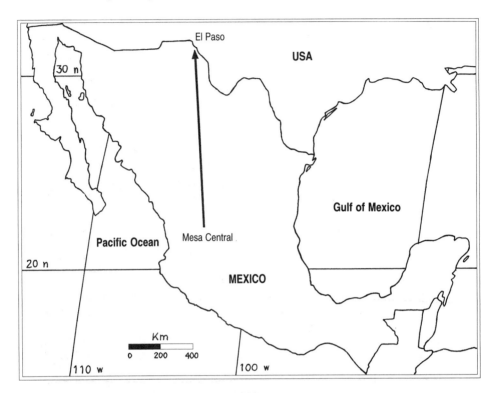

Major immigration route in the 1920s.

tendency to establish ethnic neighborhoods (colonias and barrios, which were similar to other immigrants' housing patterns) was continued and even enlarged.

As previously mentioned, this settlement pattern functioned in two basic ways: it insulated and preserved cultural lifeways, and it helped temper the social abuse and discrimination that were everyday realities. Many social problems that originated with the first groups were, in turn, transmitted to the new arrivals. A group of recent Mexican immigrants either meant a new settlement or an old one enlarged, and since the majority of Mexican immigrants were very poor, various social problems emerged in each of the settlements (Bogardus 1934; Stowell 1974; Samora 1971). In short, it seemed that unskilled, low-paying jobs translated into inferior places to live and raise families. Besides suffering from an oppressive labor position, Mexicans became victims to serious social ills that further undermined their development and well-being. For example, what began as a *palomilla* (cohorting) adolescent tradition of male bonding, mostly for mischief and adventure, was transformed under the pressures of urban life and the social isolation and neglect of several decades, so that barrio youth groups became formalized into street gangs (Bogardus 1934; Moore 1978; Vigil 1990). Other problems with crime, alcohol and drugs similarly intensified during this period.

Additional problems arose with attempts by dominant Anglo institutions to thoroughly reenculturate the Chicano populace. These efforts, known as "Americanization" programs (Gonzalez 1990), were similar to those directed toward Native Americans. Anglo values are taught by the educational system, through regular contact with members of the dominant culture and by those Chicanos who have already been acculturated. However, remnants of the Mexican way of life were kept alive in the home. This process significantly affected class placement.

Internal Colonialism

Economic and social problems have existed internationally as well as nationally. For example, 35 percent of the world's population earns 93 percent of the total income, leaving the remaining 7 percent of the wealth for 65 percent of the population, figures shockingly similar to the national proportions (Starr 1978). These inequities, in large part, stem from European expansionism and the harnessing and control of resources, both natural and human, and how the products of human labor are distributed. While Chicanos have their own unique role in this world drama, struggling against domination and manipulation of various sorts, it is striking to note how similar their situation and experience is to other colonized peoples (Bustamante 1978). Significantly, many of the wars of liberation, independence, revolution, and other social movements worldwide can be traced to these oppressive and unequal conditions.

Indigenous peoples were subjected to this treatment by the United States, as land, labor, and wealth arrangements were revamped. The Chicano variant of this experience has sometimes been called "internal colonialism" (Barrera, Munoz, and Ornelas 1974). This characterization must be applied carefully to each time period, place, and people. For instance, south Texas has had an especially destructive and subjugative history—characterized by, for example, the Alamo, border conflict and filibustering, and social and political ostracism of Mexicans. For some elites in both New Mexico and California, for example New Mexico's Santa Fe Ring, the experience was more one of cooptation and collaboration with Anglos over the Indians and peasants of the area. Nevertheless, Acuna's guarded summarization (1988) of this dominant/subordinate system highlights economic, cultural, and racial inequalities and injustices that occur after a war of conquest in which the victors thoroughly subjugate the vanquished. This model can be applied to Chicanos and other national ethnic minorities (primarily blacks and Indians) in several ways (1) isolation in separate ethnic communities

El Hoyo in east Los Angeles (Fickett's Hollow).

The courts near Los Angeles' Olvera Street

Sonoratown Mexican street rail workers.

Farmworkers' "mobile" house.

(barrios, ghettos, reservations); (2) poor educational preparation; (3) lack of political power; and (4) as a function of the first three, inability to improve their social and economic conditions.

Early in their American experience, Chicanos had begun to exercise their rights as workers. "The discrimination which they encountered . . . had the effect of stimulating them to organize in self-protection" (McWilliams 1990:190; see also Valdes 1991; Gomez-Quinones 1994a). Many strikes occurred because Chicanos were unhappy with receiving a lower wage than whites for similar work. However, Mexican trade-union activities were fraught with difficulties: for example, language discrimination in union proceedings. During the early twentieth century, with the expansion of industrial capitalism, there was an increasing trend toward the participation of Mexican laborers in radical and organized labor movements (Gomez-Quinones 1994b; Sanchez 1994).

Chicanos led a series of farm-worker strikes beginning in the early twentieth century. Throughout this century, they have repeatedly challenged agribusinessmen because of the large proportion of Chicanos in agriculture. In most cases, they were the majority of the workers. Indeed, some rural towns with an agricultural base were comprised primarily of Mexicans (Menchaca 1995; Gonzalez 1994). Overall, Mexicans constituted a major part of the migratory agricultural labor between 1900 and 1940 (Weaver 1994). In 1960, 586,000 Spanish-speaking Americans were part of the labor force in the United States; nearly half were in agriculture (Glick 1966). Improvements were slow in coming, however, for in some areas Chicanos were held in low esteem. For example, in Texas, "Many expressed the views that Mexicanos were a poor, simple, childlike group that needed guidance and close supervision. . . . Both patron and worker accepted the belief that the natural order of things was the superior-subordinate relationships of the rancho" (Foley et al. 1977:15). Similar attitudes prevailed in California, despite the union activity. Growers always desired permanent and reliable Mexican workers, even if they had to tolerate occasional social discontent and periodic rumblings (Gonzalez 1994; Menchaca 1995).

Strike activity spread to other occupations along with increasing urbanization of the Chicano people (Gomez-Quinones 1994b). The issues debated were based mainly on class interests: better wages, improved housing and sanitary conditions, a decent education for children, and many other improvements. This stance aroused the ire of Anglo employers and the general public and in many instances brought even more repressive counterattacks.

The inherent difficulties of a Mexican-Anglo cultural transformation were increased by the effects of urbanization (Penalosa 1973a). White workers in Western Europe and the United States had already experienced or were experiencing this endemic feature of the capitalist system. They suffered similar hardships and met repression when they sought to alleviate or eliminate such conditions. ~~There were~~ important differences for the Chicanos, however, because of their racial and cultural distinctiveness. In the Midwest, Mexicans and blacks were generally charged higher rents than European immigrants for similar or even inferior housing (Valdes 1991; Reisler 1976). Other problems resulting from urbanization and severe economic inequality were poor sanitation and housing conditions, inadequate health services, crime and juvenile delinquency, breakup of the family structure, unemployment, and an overwhelming dependence on the capitalist elite for the means of livelihood (Moore 1978; Moore and Pachon 1985).

Depression, Repatriation, and Post-World War II Mobility

Workers gradually left agricultural occupations for those in the city (Galarza 1964). During this transition, however, the United States was hit by one of its periodic economic crises: the 1930s depression. The Great Depression led to large numbers of Mexicans being deported (Weaver 1994). The public recognized the need for reform, but Mexicans were excluded from the widespread demands to improve living conditions. One irritant to the public stemmed from the Chicano migrant worker organizations and demonstrations against the usual poor working and living conditions. This was particularly true in the highly productive San Joaquin, Coachella, and Imperial Valleys of California.

By 1940, a New Deal compromise had been worked out with the Anglo majority workers. In contrast, Chicanos were deported wholesale. This deportation program, known by the less offensive word "repatriation," was originally initiated against dissident farm workers (Weaver 1994; McWilliams 1990). Eventually, "pressure mounted to remove aliens from the relief rolls and, almost paradoxically, from the jobs they were said to hold at the expense of American citizens. In the Southwest, immigration service officers searched for Mexican immigrants, while local welfare agencies sought to lighten their relief load by urging Mexican indigents to volunteer for repatriation" (Hoffman 1974:2). Under this program, several hundred thousand Chicanos, including thousands born in the United States, were "repatriated" to Mexico.

The government's failure to respond to the needs of agricultural workers only served to stiffen Chicano opposition. "The Mexican nationalism of immigrants often intensified in the United States. 'I would rather cut my throat before changing my Mexican nationality,' declared a laborer who had resided in the United States for twenty-five years. 'I prefer to lose with Mexico than win with the United States'" (Reisler 1976:114; see also Monto 1994).

Even though the Chicano population suffered great setbacks, increasing numbers of them were able to move out of the barrios and into the middle-class bracket (Moore and Pachon 1985). Social mobility was aided by industrial productivity and urban growth in the United States after World War II (Gomez-Quinones 1994b; Alvarez 1976). In this "boom" period, many Chicanos moved to the suburbs, with a few attaining higher socioeconomic levels after pursuing educational and professional career goals (Sanchez 1993). In proportion to the total number, these individuals were few, but they reflect how aspirations of social mobility are joined with strategies of assimilation and acculturation. Chicanos, despite many obstacles, are steadily moving away from lower-class traditional Mexican culture toward middle-class Anglo-American culture, even syncretically recombining traditional lifeways with the better material resources available in the United States. This transformation came in stages, starting with the first generations of Mexicans, as early as the nineteenth century (Sanchez 1993), and continued in an accelerated fashion after World War II when a larger, more determined population pushed for change. In most instances, these developments combined social mobility aspirations with increased adoption of the dominant Anglo culture (Penalosa 1973a).

However, improvements during the post-World War II period can be easily exaggerated; since the previous immigrant generation started with nothing, any upward shift in the subsequent generation appears to be progress (Alvarez 1976). Chicano socioeconomic mobility had taken place, but the average family income in the Southwest was only $4,164 in 1960. When contrasted with the average Anglo income of $6,448, there was still a considerable gap. In addition, the figure of $4,164 includes wages earned by all family members, not just the household head. It was very common for youth to leave school early in order to seek gainful employment and contribute to the household income, even handing their check over to the household head (Knouse, Rosenfeld, and Culbertson 1992; Grebler, Moore, and Guzman 1970). This has appeared to be a pattern with each wave of immigrants since the nineteenth century, as peasant society valued family and group solidarity and reciprocity, particularly under the adverse circumstances dictated by urban life and the demands of an industrial economy.

Trade unionism also benefited the urban working class, including some Chicanos. While many unions have practiced overt discrimination, as well as more subtle forms of exclusion, especially with the better paying, more prestigious blue-collar occupations, Chicanos have still made inroads and taken their place alongside other workers (Gomez-Quinones 1994b; Romero 1979). Because of continuing Mexican immigration, however, there has been an increase in the proportion of Spanish-speaking male workers' "service" and "operative" job categories. Service occupations tend to be low paying, low in prestige (Grebler, Moore, and Guzman 1970), and without fringe benefits and career advancements.

Failure of the Political System

Since shortly after the 1848 War, Chicanos have usually been nearly powerless in the political arena (Meier and Ribera 1993). Constant immigration contributes to this, as new immigrants must familiarize themselves with the American political system. However, it is equally true that the two-party system historically failed to provide adequate representation. This, in turn, created and perpetuated a sense of discouragement and apathy among Chicanos. Since the Roosevelt New Deal, Democrats have been popularly perceived as supporters of Chicano interests, although since World War II, they have appeared to direct attention to the group only during election time. Programs to benefit Chicanos have typically failed to materialize and emerge only as empty promises.

Over the years, several methods were employed to effectively bar or limit Chicano political participation. One was the lack of a proper education, specifically in regard to political awareness and paths of action. Basic education was lacking and specific training and awareness programs, such as widespread voter registration efforts, were sporadic. The college-trained leadership so necessary for political participation was almost nonexistent (Garcia and de la Garza 1977), and much of the political activity sprung from street protests and worker strikes. Although there were sporadic and courageous organizational efforts on the part of certain individuals and groups (Marquez 1993; Gomez-Quinones 1990), the political landscape was almost barren.

Gerrymandering was used to redraw state and national legislative district boundary lines in order to favor one interest group, usually one of the two major political parties (Gomez-Quinones 1991). The Chicano ethnic interest group was sliced, trimmed, and snipped into political oblivion. Greater East Los Angeles, with several hundred thousand Chicanos in 1960, provided a clear example of gerrymandering. The region was deliberately divided to ensure that no state assemblyman or senator would have to rely on a majority Chicano vote to win. Chicanos were a minority in every district; only recently has this situation changed. Because the Chicanos were unable to elect leaders who reflected their interests, their voice went unheeded. The U.S. Commission on Civil Rights finally came to the conclusion that Chicanos in California had been gerrymandered out of opportunities to elect their own representatives to the State legislature or the United States Congress in a proportion that came near to their percentage of the state population (Gomez-Quinones 1991; Garcia and de la Garza 1977).

In districts that were mostly Chicano, other political methods became necessary. For example, in Corpus Christi, Texas, in 1915, there are indications that Mexicans were directed to vote in certain ways by Americans who paid their poll taxes (Taylor 1934). In addition, where Chicanos comprised a clear majority (sometimes close to 90 percent of the populace), Anglo leaders would handpick Spanish-surnamed candidates, "ringers," to run in the election. When such candidates won, they followed Anglo instructions during their tenure. But even in their defeat, the Anglos won, for their candidate took votes away from other Chicanos, who perhaps were running with the intention of serving the community.

Chicanos in Texas took steps to change this state of affairs, even if only on a small scale. In the early 1960s, PASO (Political Association of Spanish-speaking Organizations), together with some non-Mexican groups (the Teamsters and the Catholic Bishops Committee for the Spanish Speaking), successfully managed to depose the Anglo political structure in Crystal City, Texas. This is a classic example of the reintroduction of democracy to the people, who in this case were 90 percent of the electorate. Other political activities in the Southwest during the 1960s finally led to the election of three Spanish-speaking congressmen and one U.S. Senator.

In short, lack of political education and awareness—especially because of the "generational lag" stemming from permanent immigration—undemocratic political districting, and "rigged" elections all led to political disempowerment. Organizational efforts in the aftermath of the civil rights movement have somewhat altered this situation. However, it is no secret that the outcome of many United States elections is almost directly dependent on the amount of money spent. Money is typically a requisite for political power, and abundant money is not usually one of the Chicanos' possessions. Jesse Unruh, a California Democratic leader, stated, "Money is the mother's milk of politics." Chicanos, however, "will enjoy very little political success if they must depend upon economic power to promote their political objectives" (Garcia and de la Garza 1977:67).

In summary, Chicanos have historically been members of the exploited laboring population, kept in a dependent, underdeveloped, and disadvantaged state. In the years between the 1848 Mexican-American War and 1960, those relatively few Chicanos who managed to escape such conditions usually had to abandon much of their cultural heritage to do so. With the large-scale immigration beginning in 1910 and continuing to this very day, the situation has become more complicated and difficult. For both Chicano natives and Mexican immigrants, the adoption of Anglo-American patterns of success often entailed their giving up Mexican ways. Many denied their heritage—claiming instead a Spanish background—to escape from economic and social disadvantages (Weaver

1994; Moore and Pachon 1985). Personal and group problems abound in this context of intense culture conflict, where economic survival is wedded to cultural adjustments and revampments. An awareness of Chicano acculturation and even assimilation to the dominant mode of thought and action is crucial in understanding this period. Was a cultural transformation a precondition to socioeconomic advancement? Did such a transition ensure material betterment? If so, has this changed? The answers have significant implications for the continuing Chicano struggle (Vigil 1997; Moore and Pachon 1985).

Culture: Assimilation vs. Nativist Acculturation

The Shifts and Pulls of Middle-Class American Culture and the Ebbs and Tides of Mexican Immigration

Well over 130 years since the incorporation of the Chicano into the United States, American cultural life has undergone major transformation. Industrialization and urbanization shifted a primarily agrarian society into an international military and political power. Conflicts engendered by these processes led to the development of cultural differences among socioeconomic classes, and especially ethnic minorities. Moreover, the prosperity born of industrialization also brought about a numerically and culturally dominant middle class, alongside a working class that tended to mimic it. The core values of the middle class became widely accepted as typical of American culture—i.e., what you are or what you should become—and the unfolding of mass communications strengthened that predominance.

One element of this value system was the ethnocentric notion that American culture was superior to any other, and the frequent corollary that American people were superior to any other. While values can be simply defined as the "ought-tos" of society and the norms the "blueprints for action," the stage was set for newcomers from different, contrasting cultural traditions to undergo miscues and react in unsteady but also creative ways.

As wave upon wave of immigrants poured into the country to farm the frontiers, man the factories, and build the railroads, the average American greeted them with disdain, at least until they learned the values and norms of the dominant group. Although the immigrant groups contributed greatly to the enrichment of American language, arts, philosophy, and cuisine, the "100 percent American"—as Linton (1975) noted satirically—refused to recognize that his daily life included the use of behavior, beliefs, and materials derived from hundreds of different cultural traditions. Each new wave of different ethnicities in succeeding eras helped change American culture, some even contributing their own values and norms as a subset of the dominant ones.

Social and economic sanctions were therefore fashioned to impede ethnically and culturally "different" people from entering into and participaing fully in the mainstream of American society. To complicate matters, this was in the context of a rapidly changing society. Such contending developments created pressures on the newcomers to assimilate—to discard the "different" traditions of their countries of origin and accept the values and beliefs of the American middle class, including discrimination toward subsequent arrivals who insisted on clinging to old lifeways (Castaneda 1974). Such barriers and restrictions, especially discrimination in employment and housing, contributed to the creation of distinct ethnic enclaves and the maintenance of ethnic pride through nativist revivals and practices. While the common message to immigrants was to assimilate, the external barriers effectively undermined their efforts; it was a mixed message that seriously hindered their integration into American society.

The decline of massive immigration from Europe and Asia after World War I was a watershed in American immigration history. Ethnic enclaves of these groups gradually faded away as they acculturated and assimilated American patterns through subsequent generations. For a complex of reasons, a distinctively Mexican tradition continued to flourish in the United States. The original imprint of Mexican culture before the conquest of 1846–1848, and more significantly the continued immigration of large numbers of Mexicans, led to a different ethnic minority experience. More obvious racial differences between the majority of Mexican immigrants and most Americans also contributed to the perseverance of Mexican culture. Unlike the sons and daughters of European immigrants, who learned American ways at school, the children of most Mexican immigrants, with Indian or mestizo heritages, were noticeably different in appearance from the white majority and were less freely accepted by its members. Similar constraints also operated with regard to Asians, American Indians, and blacks.

Although retaining a distinctly Mexican flavor, the culture that developed among Mexican-Americans nevertheless was affected by somewhat the same processes at work in other cultural minorities. The result was a hybrid culture mirroring a wide range of elements from both Mexican and American backgrounds (each of which is itself a complex of various origins), as well as unique patterns created through a fusion of elements from both traditions. Language usage is one example. "Such a complex continuum has given rise to four types of cultural-linguistic personalities: the monolingual in Spanish, the monolingual in English, the bilingual, and then . . . there is the child who speaks a patois" (de Leon 1970:36; see also Valencia 1991).

The strength of Mexican-American culture lay in the fact that it could draw from these two rich cultural traditions, the mestizaje style of Indian and Spanish motifs and the entrepreneurial industrialism of modern life in the United States. Yet that opportunity also gave rise to grave problems, for important aspects of the two traditions were in conflict, and many Chicanos found themselves unable to sort the valuable from the harmful traits successfully (Weber 1992); ". . . we see the historic southwestern borderlands as a complex mestizo frontier" (Weber 1992:358). In that setting, the cultural syncretisms have generated a whole range of ethnic identities (Bernal and Knight 1993).When cultural moorings were loosened, however, a kind of cultural impoverishment sometimes resulted, an empty marginality, with young people in particular turning to self-destructive values and behavior (Vigil 1988).

The culture of the dominant majority in the United States was modeled from many themes, partly because of the large size of American society (Dinnerstein and Reimers 1988). Nevertheless, certain core values, rooted in what has been labeled a "white Anglo-Saxon Protestant ethic" (giving rise to the acronym "WASP" or, less commonly, "McWASP" to emphasize its middle-class identity), have been of particular importance (Gordon 1964). Individualism, a work ethic, competition, an achievement orientation, and a sense of communalism are some of the central tenets of this pattern (Bellah et al. 1985).

Not least significant in this context was the value placed on physical distinctions: Irish, eastern European, and southern European immigrants were all once considered racially inferior by the average American, and that superior attitude persisted much longer toward people who were more racially distinct (Menchaca 1993). From the first large waves of immigrants to the present continuing flow from Mexico, Central America, and Asia, this association of cultural adaptation being mediated by racial appearance has played a primary role in the remaking of American culture.

In keeping with the rewards that the industrial state has produced, American middle-class society focuses much of its culture on work and competition for achievement and on visible symbols of the value of work. Work also plays a significant role in Chicano culture. However, Chicano culture features other characteristics that cross social-class categories (Romero 1979), and combined with habits based on the way work was structured in a colonial economy built on indigenous labor and traditions, the adjustment to the American situation was quite different.

Nevertheless, cultural life was heavily influenced by class status and the new industrial economy. The organization of the productive labor of a society is one of the most significant aspects of culture (Fernandez 1977). In this atmosphere of material consumption, people demanded a certain type of food, clothing, or shelter that they could select from a seemingly endless array. The necessary cultural accouterments that accompany these possessions—words to describe them, values to guide human energy in obtaining them, customs and rituals involving them, and so on—provided cultural divisions to augment those based on class criteria. These standards motivated United States citizens, including Mexican Americans.

Contrast Between American and Mexican Culture

Not all people had the same attitudes toward motivations for success. The middle-class American ethic was an industrial society's reworking of western and northern European cultural traits that arrived with the early English-speaking immigrants to America. Besides the cultural customs, northwestern Europe contributed Protestantism, a tradition that subsequently evolved from a collection of religious beliefs and practices into a general philosophy of life emphasizing hard work, individualism, and frugality (Gamio 1969; Marger 1994). Implicit in that philosophy and explicitly stated by some of its proponents is the concept that material success is a sign of God's blessing, and failure a sign of his displeasure.

Several other points highlighted the culture. First, values emphasized a universe in which humankind had full mastery. Every person in society had an equal opportunity in all matters. If inequalities existed, it was because some people did not strive to reach their potential. In other words, it was one's own fault if he or she failed to achieve success. Furthermore, by work and achievement, one could gain control over natural forces. Because of this optimistic opportunism, societal members conformed to a standard that would bring material advancement for each individual (Diaz-Guerrero 1975). If everyone adhered to this pattern, group success would be enhanced (Inkeles 1977; Diaz-Guerrero 1978; Kluckholm and Strodtbeck 1961). While individual effort and achievement were extolled, it was also understood that there were many problems associated with them: unbridled personal aggrandizement interfered with the common good, and so on (Bellah et al. 1985).

One can perceive the technological orientation of this worldview. The age of industrialism proved that machines could master previously unheard-of tasks. This achievement infected the human spirit, causing humans to strive to make nature bend to their wishes. The Protestant ethic complemented this goal, for it stems from the deeply held belief that God will reward those who work hard, struggle against any obstacle, and thus receive earthly success and, most importantly, spiritual salvation (Bellah et al. 1985; Foley et al. 1977). This is how new tools and techniques shaped and cultivated a new way of thinking and became part of the legacy of the industrial revolution.

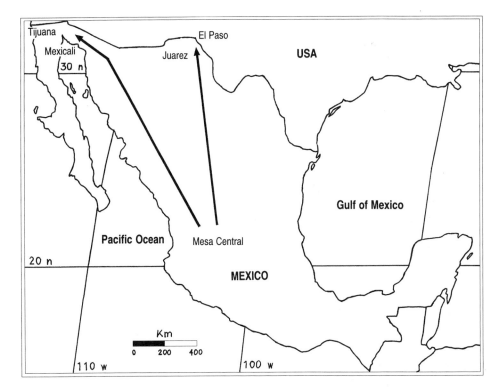

Immigration routes in the 1940s.

Traditional Mexican cultural characteristics contrast with those just cited in major respects, some sharply and others only slightly. The cultural contrasts between Mexico proper and its northern settlements in the nineteenth century were previously mentioned. This has continued to be true throughout this century (Moore and Pachon 1985). Mexican culture has been extremely heterogeneous because of mestizaje, and the waves of immigrants varied in the cultural style each brought to the United States (Cockcroft 1986; Portes and Bach 1985). They come from different regions of Mexico, and recent immigrants are a more urbanized group in contrast to those from rural areas in earlier times. Also, of course, one must take into account the cultural changes that Mexicans underwent after several generations of exposure to United States customs. Thus, in over fifty years of immigration, numerous Mexican "cultures" were placed in the context of United States society (Weaver 1994; Vigil 1997).

Nonetheless, there are still some broad major features of Mexican culture worthy of consideration, at least to establish a basis for discussion (Weaver 1994; Zavella 1987; Menchaca 1995; Sanchez 1993). The family was of central importance, and there was a strong tendency toward stressing work and the production of goods for the group rather than the individual. This fact deserves special mention because Mexicans also valued the work ethic, but not for its own sake (Briggs 1973; Kluckholm and Strodtbeck 1961). Their past and present performance in agriculture and light industry has underscored this fact, despite former California Senator George Murphy's pejorative remark in the 1960s that "Mexicans are good farm workers because they are short and built low to the ground" (Servin 1970:140).

Generally, work organization and group cooperation were aimed toward fulfilling basic needs, with an emphasis on material gain for survival (Weaver 1994). The present was valued more than future savings, and people were admired for who they were, rather than what they did (Kluckholm and Strodtbeck 1961). Females were subordinate to males, and there was a clear preference for a patriarchal family head. While accepting the everyday struggles of life, people had learned to assuage disappointment and look beyond defeat and failure (McWilliams 1990). Coming from a peasant background with these traditions to a modern urban one is a major change, but when this is coupled with the strife and strain associated with immigration conditions and barriers, the adjustment is momentous (Kearney 1996). A clash of values is a predictable outcome, for how can a rural, almost communal outlook mesh with a fast-paced industrial style?

These sketches of American middle-class and traditional Mexican cultures are of course incomplete, but they provide some indication of the major styles that influenced Mexican-American culture and point to some of the syncretisms and conflicts within that culture. To fully describe Mexican-American culture is a difficult chore (Velez 1996), and some observers (e.g., Romano-V. 1973) have raised important questions challenging such an endeavor. The assessment of personal values would vary with each individual, whether middle-class, white, Mexican, or a mixture (Keefe and Padilla 1987). However, the basic values of future goals versus present needs and doing rather than being are clear contrasts; gender inequalities and patriarchial fixtures are somewhat similar but are arranged in different ways for varying purposes between the two groups (Mirande and Enriquez 1979). For example, Mexican culture has formalized terms to reflect gender roles and attitudes, such as *machismo* (manliness, social and sexual dominance, and so on), *hembrismo* (subordination of females), and *marianismo* (motherhood, sacred spiritual superiority associated with the Virgin Mary). Machismo is a very controversial and debated issue among Mexicans, especially among women who feel that this belief system has worked to suppress and demean them (Macias 1982).

In these and other beliefs and patterns, what is unusual in the case of Mexican Americans (a people who blend several cultures) is that these contrasts were present within one person (Ramirez 1985; Arvizu 1974). Many individuals had independently fashioned a cultural style that combined values, giving them "situational" consideration as the time and place warranted (Vigil 1997).

George Sanchez, a Mexican-American educator, spoke to the issue of cultural openness or accommodation and championed the contribution Mexican culture could make. Other writers have supported this position, with one suggesting that the "psychology of the Americas" facilitates this orientation (Ramirez 1985). Along with the more obvious material cultural items and practices such as language, music, folklore, architecture, foods, crafts, and customs, there are deeper attributes to consider. Some of these would include the formal respect accorded a person, the sense of loyalty to family and nation, the profound spiritualism that undergirds religious beliefs, and particularly, the kind of quiet strength that assists in overcoming burdens and obstacles (Sanchez 1967). In some areas of the Southwest and border regions, this cultural accommodation is happening (or has already happened) and is in direct contrast with the sometimes negative appraisal some critics have given to Mexican culture (Kluckholm and Strodtbeck 1961).

A few Mexican Americans, and even some Anglos, were able to syncretize aspects of both cultures; they learned to plan for the future and live the present fully. They enjoyed work for its own sake, remembering that work was only a means, not an end, and therefore they could benefit from the fruits of their labor immediately. Increasingly, more observers and writers are touting this reflexive, more cosmopolitan cultural style, and in part, have added support to the still growing awareness of cultural pluralism and multicultural education (Spindler and Spindler 1990; Gibson and Ogbu 1991; Vigil 1997).

Strategies and Problems of Adaptation

In this time period, acceptance of aspects of both cultures was a positive response to the problem of culture conflict and the potential for maladaptation. The fact that it was a hit-or-miss occurrence made it difficult and frustrating for many people. As noted, acculturation was a broad process of change taking place in one or both cultures, and this varied with time and place conditions and the ethnic makeup of the population. In addition, there was considerable variation in the types of reaction. Compounding matters during phases of rapid change were class and gender transformations, where opportunities for upward mobility often entailed extreme cultural adjustments (Chavira 1994).

Many Mexicans took the route of assimilation (Kluckholm and Strodtbeck 1961; Hass 1995). This strategy began after the American

Pecan shellers in Texas.

Making parachutes in San Diego, California, for the World War II effort.

annexation, when Mexicans lost their land rights and began to familiarize themselves with the new cultural standards in order to maintain or
improve their economic conditions (Monroy 1993; Zeleny 1974). Assimilation usually occurred after long exposure to the dominant culture, but
there were some who decided to accelerate the process. If they had
lighter complexions, for example, they might first prefer to be called
American, but if forced to commit themselves, they would claim a Spanish descent (Menchaca 1993). Although there were many mestizos
among them, the Hispanos in New Mexico and California, in the early
twentieth century, started calling themselves Spanish Americans or
Californios in order to differentiate themselves from other Mexicans
(Almaquer 1994; Alvarez 1976). Within the intracultural variation
among people from Mexico, there also were European oriented individuals whose racial appearance and cultural bearings were closer to the
Anglo (Kluckholm and Strodtbeck 1961). Minimally, they were certainly
accustomed to dominating those below them.

In some instances, this assimilation reached extremes in which
people became flag-waving superpatriots and worked to master perfect
English. They socialized their offspring to this end. In their efforts to rid
themselves of Mexican culture, however, they often aroused the wrath of
fellow Mexicans. "No Mexican is so despised as he who denies his race"
(Gamio 1969:93).

(1)   Assimilation entails the complete transformation from one culture
to another (Gordon 1964; Bernal and Knight 1993; Castaneda 1974).
There was no mistaking what assimilated Mexicans did politically, economically, religiously, and socially, even seeking marriage partners from
the dominant group. Interestingly, in New Mexico the Hispanos were
able to effect a coalition with the Anglos because of Mexican willingness
to accept the new culture (Gomez-Quinones 1994a). This alliance, known
as the Santa Fe Ring and somewhat patterned after East Coast political
machines, dominated the state up to the present generation. In this case,
assimilation meant retention of political and economic power.

For many Mexican Americans, however, assimilation was a sad
experience because dominant Anglo society was so exclusionary. Mexican elites were obviously of a higher status and thus had a somewhat
easier time of it, but even they suffered instances of blatant rejection.
Thus, the assimilated Mexicans often were in limbo; they had changed,
but no one cared to find a place for them in middle-class white society.
Many even changed their telltale Spanish surname: Martinez to Martin,
Ramirez to Raymer, and Barajas (meaning cards) to Cards.

(2)   Another adaptive alternative for Mexicans was to change their secondary social allegiances while maintaining the primary ones; this
occurred in the initial phases of contact with Anglos. This meant functioning in all the important secondary Anglo areas to improve life's oppor-

tunities but keeping a primary Mexican ethnic identity, social relations, and cultural traditions (Gordon 1964; Spindler and Spindler 1991). Such people would take the path of acculturation—i.e., a bilingual/bicultural stance (Vigil 1997)—but maintain a primary, private life by speaking Spanish to their families and following Mexican customs. During work hours, at school, or in any place outside the primary area, they would adopt an appropriate English-speaking, Anglo-acting posture. According to a lifelong advocate of this strategy, "Cultural buffer areas do exist and people living within their boundaries belong to both civilizations cultur- ally" (de Leon 1970:43). Phelan and Davidson (1993) have referred to these people as "border crossers." Acculturation of this sort means living one's private life one way and public life another—or because of whim or need, mixing them up with almost equal dexterity. Of course, there were already people who had managed to assimilate some of the positive func- tional aspects of both cultures. In the modern period, such a strategy entailed a reversal of the assimilation process, with many reconnecting with their parents' and grandparents' roots. This dual process has been referred to as nativist acculturation (Vigil and Long 1981), or additive rather than subtractive acculturation (Gibson and Ogbu 1991): learning a new culture but not discarding the old one (Vigil 1997).

Ethnic identification processes and ethnic identity labels involve birthplace, language usage, and customs and practices, among other fac- ets. For this reason, they are controversial, and there are as many schools of thought and theories about labeling as there are labels. What- ever labels people apply to themselves, or others use to designate them, it is important to underscore the dynamic nature of acculturation since it often involves constant reshufflings and revampments (Sanchez 1993). Individuals who took this nativist acculturation approach could refer to themselves as Mexicans if they wished; or, to reflect the bilingual and bicultural nature of their existence, as Mexican Americans; or, to empha- size their secondary participatory rights, as Americans of Mexican descent. Whatever their choice of label, they still were reasonably ade- quate in both cultural standards. As many other ethnic minorities in dif- ferent times and places have discovered, however, there are psychological hazards for anyone who functions in both worlds (Suarez- Orozco and Suarez-Orozco 1994).

What occurred in this regard was a continuation of the Chicano marginal syndrome that dated from colonial times, with the conquest of indigenous groups and the transformation of much of the population into peasants. Especially hard hit were the cultural moorings of the people (Sanchez 1976). In the early colonial period, cholo became a pejorative label that characterized an Indian who was only partly (marginally) acculturated to the Spanish way of life. (This word has survived to the present and is currently used to describe street youth, especially those who belong to gangs [Vigil 1988]). Thus, over time a person often found him- or herself in a state of flux. For example, one southern Texas Chicano noted: "I think like an Anglo and I act like an Anglo but I'll never look like an Anglo. Just looking at me, no one could tell if I am an American or one of those blasted Mexicans from across the river. It's hell to look like a foreigner in your own country" (Madsen 1964:8).

Drinking, fighting, anomie (normlessness), drugs, and other forms of cultural disorientation were often exhibited by individuals who were unable to fashion a stable bilingual and bicultural world and who were not securely rooted in either Mexican or Anglo culture (Suarez-Orozco and Suarez-Orozco 1994; Bernal and Knight 1993; Saldana 1995). This phenomenon sometimes involved cultural conflict between generations (Sanchez 1993; Alvarez 1987; Vigil 1997; Gamio 1969).

This dilemma had several sources. For some it was a personal choice resulting from the pressures of cultural conformity and discrimination. One of my former students once expressed it in this way:

> "I didn't know you were Mexican." "I'm not, I'm Italian." I can actually remember saying this to my friends in school yards, dances and anywhere else the dreaded question would pop up. I tried as hard as possible not to be a Mexican, for that was the only way I thought I could be happy. Due to my light color and height I could easily pass for a white with the right clothes on. When the "surfer" craze was on I was right in there, wearing the latest surfer get-up I could find; but the funny thing was that I always felt so self-conscious, the fun was gone from acting this way. You must understand that at that age I never thought about who I really was, but just what I wanted to be, which changed from white fad to fad. In history class I remember being totally embarrassed when we studied Mexico. They would show films of old adobe huts with the mother patting tortillas and the father working in the fields. Everyone thought this was funny and I remember wishing that Mexico was all skyscrapers to show the others how great we really were.

Perhaps the most forceful factor stemmed from socioeconomic issues. Investigations on ethnic identity often stress the telling effects of environmental forces and socioeconomic pressures on the psychological well-being of individuals undergoing cultural change (Suarez-Orozco and Suarez-Orozco 1994; Padilla 1995; Melville 1994). Frustration and discouragement often resulted when someone learned all he or she could about his or her occupation but was paid lower wages than the others doing the same work or was passed over when the time for promotion arrived. Chicanos increasingly began to feel alienated as a result of the antagonism toward Mexican culture and the racial discrimination expressed by Anglos (Weaver 1994; Moore and Pachon 1985; Briggs, Fogel, and Schmidt 1977).

The combination of forces interfered with the attainment of middle-class status for many. Worse yet, self-racism was exacerbated when members of the subservient culture accepted and internalized the cultural superiority views of the dominant group and began to believe that they were incapable of any meaningful action (Almaquer 1994; Melville 1994; Menchaca 1995). This accounted for much of the intragroup ethnic "sensitivity" to imagined and real slights, whether from language differences, surname changes, or a contrast in cultural lifestyles and customs (Bernal and Knight 1993; Rubel 1966). One novel, titled *Pocho*, a term for a Mexican American with Anglo mannerisms, emphasizes the concern with resisting self-hate when a father tells his son: "Promise me—that you will be true unto yourself, unto what you honestly believe is right. And, if it does not stand in your way, do not ever forget that you are Mexican" (Villarreal 1970:169).

As mentioned before, a strong contributor to this self-hate was the social snubbing one received because of racial appearance. It was particularly offensive to those who had learned the new culture and were prepared to contribute but were unable to change their race or appearance. Of course, some elements within American society challenged such ethnocentric practices. For example, anthropologists were among those who advocated "cultural relativity," that is, a belief that each world culture is intrinsically worthy of respect and appreciation. Also, many humanitarian people and organizations accepted those who were ethnically different and sometimes offered aid in their defense.

Besides the negative individual experiences, discrimination against Mexican Americans as a group also contributed to and exacerbated the situation. Law enforcement personnel, for instance, often mistreated and physically abused Mexican Americans because they lived in the barrio or colonia community (Escobar 1998). It was fairly common for the police to stop any Mexican for questioning, without cause or provocation (Vigil 1988; U.S. Commission on Civil Rights 1970). Residence in an area considered to have a high crime rate meant the increased possibility of police questioning and perhaps harassment. One former Los Angeles police chief was frank about it: "Police deployment is heaviest in minority sections of the city because, based on statistical reasons [the police chief] believes it to be a fact that racial minority groups commit more crime" (Morales 1972:48). While this occurred mainly in the low-income areas, it also frequently occurred in "better" sections of the city, especially if someone appeared out of place in an upscale neighborhood.

New Syncretism: Pachucos

Mexican Americans knew they were not accepted in many parts of town and so created their own world and tried to make it as self-sufficient as possible (McWilliams 1990). Thus was born a unique, defensive, and creative reaction to marginality. A new culture was invented to curb the confusion. No doubt this syncretic process began earlier, and the most easily recognizable example is with cattle ranching, which was a blend of Northern Mexican ranchero culture with Anglo-American innovations (Paredes 1993; Paredes 1978). However, the syncretic variant that sprang up in the 1930s and 1940s following large-scale Mexican immigration was especially significant. It was a step, perhaps an unsteady one, toward what later became known as Chicano culture (Barker 1972).

   Pachucos was the name given to this generation of Mexicans who attended Anglo schools in large numbers. (*Pachucas* were the females of this generation and lifestyle.) Their lifestyle was innovative. Some observers criticized this pattern as an ostentatious variant of the zoot-suit style of that time, but with a decidedly Mexican turn. Unjustly perceiving the pachucos as rebels and outlaws, many observers neglected to consider the cultural-conflict aspects of their predicament. Pachucos wanted neither to integrate into American culture nor to become Mexican again. It has been said that a pachuco's "whole being is sheer negative impulse, a tangle of contradictions, an enigma. Even his very name is enigmatic" (Paz 1961:14). Others, while not championing the pachucos' cause, expressed a more sympathetic view: It was racial segregation, economic exploitation, and cultural insensitivity that thwarted Mexican integration into American society. Pachuco youth were forged out of this tense, uneven cultural experience (Ruiz 1993; Sanchez 1993; Sanchez 1974).

   Much of what became recognized as *pachuquismos* (pachuco inventions) was in many instances *pochismos*—chopped up English or Spanish, or simple word mixing (Galarza 1971). Still, the style became widespread, because pachucas and pachucos strove to make something good out of a bad situation. The style seemed to resonate with youth who identified with the feeling and attitude then emerging, as it eventually spread to different regions of the Southwest. Tensions between home and school were the inspiration for these developments. The young student was caught in a cultural squeeze between school measures to induce students to adopt Anglo traits and home instruction to retain Mexican customs (Barker 1972). Rather than accept this state of confusion, many drew from both cultures to form a new one. Pachuco language symbolizes this trend. English was Hispanicized and Spanish was Anglicized, as these words attest: *Ay te watcho* (I'll be seeing you), *chante* (shanty), *daime* (dime), *brecas* (brakes), *bote* (jail, "can" translated into Spanish), and *ganga* (gang) (Griffith 1948). In Texas a Tex-Mex argot has evolved, which often is created by adding a Spanish sound at the beginning or end of an English word (*cookiar, watchiar, parkiar, marketa,* and so on); Anglos in close contact with Mexicans along the border region have adopted some of this style (Alvarez 1995). Occasionally it is the other way around, but Spanish-speakers are usually more pressured to adapt to English.

Other pachuco characteristics involved dress, manners, and social attitudes, for they took pride in their creations. For example, the zoot suit (a suit that the hip urban crowd wore in the 1940s) became the pachuco uniform, with male and female versions. It is interesting that the modern version of the pachuco, the low-riding cholo, has also developed a peculiar lifestyle, much of which is borrowed from the pachuco innovators. However, the cholos' situation is noticeably different from that of the 1940s generation. Some have fashioned or adopted debilitating cultural patterns, including much more frequent drug use and gang killings that became widespread in the 1960s and 1970s.

The pachuco adaptation was an attempt to resolve the implicit contradictions of two cultural worlds. When a "critical mass" of second-generation Mexican Americans emerged in the 1940s, a presence was established to carry culture change and acculturation to another level. Many of the pachuco generation escaped the worst effects of marginality and, as a result, became fairly stable bilinguals. Furthermore, there was a long history behind the pachuco. The pachuco dialect, for example, although it included Hispanicized English, Anglicized Spanish, and invented words in Nahuatl and Archaic Spanish, was mainly made up of Calo—Spanish gypsy slang, supposedly popularized by bullfighters. Although the pachucos and their creations were castigated for their behavior—for they conformed neither to Mexican nor Anglo-American cultural standards—a generation later, many observers have changed their opinion and now point out the significance of this generation (Sanchez 1993; Garcia 1989).

Separatism

There were other cultural adaptive responses. Except in isolated areas such as certain northern reaches of New Mexico or south Texas, there has always been a tendency for some to defiantly challenge the U.S. presence in the Southwest. Thus, in a decidedly self-conscious manner, some Mexican Americans took a separatist approach, turning their backs on assimilation, acculturation, marginality, and syncretism, especially if they could not handle the pressure or refused to accept strains of cultural conflict. Separatism entailed either returning to Mexico (Vigil 1974) or promoting the reconquest of the Southwest. Separatist initiatives have been used throughout the twentieth century by those who advocated an aggressive, militant stand against the Anglo system. To the south, in Mexico, peasants were fighting for justice in the 1910 revolution. Struggles for justice, however, were not confined to Mexico, as the Southwest was perking with political activity (Gomez-Quinones 1994a). During

World War I a group of Mexican Americans, led by a barber, formulated the San Diego Plan (named for a small town in Texas) (Gomez-Quinones 1994a; Webb 1935). This plan, albeit grandiose, aimed for the overthrow of the United States government and advocated the return of all territories once belonging to Mexico and freedom and land for similarly oppressed Indians, blacks, and Asians.

Another separatist scheme, the Sinarquista movement, was more widespread, especially in California. During World War II the group supported an Axis victory, with the goal of regaining sovereignty over the Southwest. There were two thousand members in the United States by 1942. Active groups existed in Southern California communities such as San Fernando, San Bernardino, Ontario, El Monte, and Oxnard; and in Texas at El McAllen, Mission, and Laredo (McWilliams 1990). Despite the "falangist" (Spanish fascist party), right-wing orientation of the Sinarquistas, Mexican Americans of various political factions rallied behind this "nationalist" program; again, the organizational efforts involved more "talk" than plans, but it, too, reflected the hidden resentment some Mexicans had toward the United States. The party was based in Mexico. A further reminder of this historical memory is that until 1943, the maps used in some Mexican schools had the words "Territory temporarily in the hands of the United States" printed over the United States Southwest. It was no coincidence that these two thrusts transpired during WW I and WW II, when the United States was most vulnerable.

Mexican Background: Effect of Time and Place on Culture and Identity

Time and place issues make understanding Mexican Americans a very complicated task. As natives overwhelmed by American forces, there was the aftermath where many antagonisms and resentments festered and set the future tone of Mexican-American relations. Large-scale and continuing immigration followed in the twentieth century, and the effects of this experience have been previously outlined (Cardoso 1980; Portes and Bach 1985; Briggs 1973). As noted, the transition from indigenous to peasant to immigrant charts a macrohistorical evolution and transformation of nearly five hundred years to create different cultural currents. According to a 1930 study, three basic cultural traditions were prevalent in Mexico at that time: modern European, indigenous, and mestizo (a mixture of the first two). The indigenous and especially the mestizo traditions accompanied most Mexican immigrants to the United States (Weaver 1994; Gamio 1969). As a result, the changeover from an indigenous or culturally mixed background to a "modern" way of living was very abrupt and of multiple dimensions (Gamio 1969); tantamount to a horizontal (moving to the United States) and vertical (facing urban life) adjustment simultaneously. The profound problems for cultural adaptation thus created were softened somewhat as early immigrants usually settled in rural areas, but by 1930, 57.5 percent of the total number of immigrants were living in urban areas (Romo 1983; Sanchez 1993). This trend continued and strengthened throughout the 1940s (Alvarez 1973).

Time and place factors figure very prominently in an examination of these processes (N. L. Gonzales 1967; Moore and Pachon 1985; Vigil n.d.). Mexican immigrants brought a culture that reflected their time (historical or cultural tradition) and place (regional variations). Their new cultural life was strongly influenced by where they settled—what state in the Southwest, or in a rural or urban area—and how long they lived in the United States—generational distance from Mexico. It is also fair to state that amount of time in the United States affected and usually improved their occupational mobility (Knouse, Rosenfeld, and Culbertson 1992; Sanchez 1993; Gomez-Quinones 1994b; Alvarez 1973). Similarly, aspirations of social mobility and amount of income would operate to alter the cultural adaptation strategy.

One way to determine the changing strategies is by looking at cultural habits of the past and perhaps examining the motives behind a person's chosen ethnic label (Melville 1994; Menchaca 1995; Bernal and Knight 1993). For example, two important Mexican cultural traditions are compadrazgo and, to a lesser degree, machismo, a topic of extreme importance in considering questions of gender (Chavira-Prado 1994). Machismo has been discussed already, so a brief comment will suffice. The changing work pattern caused by industrialization and urbanization has revised this cultural trait, as it has gender patterns in general. Women have played significant roles under these technological and lifestyle changes, doing factory work as well as excelling in other occupations created by the industrial economy. In addition, urban problems have added to the disintegration of the positive aspects of machismo. In former times the patriarch, for good or bad, dominated and maintained stability in the family. In the city, where unemployment and street crime often undermined the male role, many women took over as household heads (Moore 1991; Briggs, Fogel, and Schmidt 1977). Thus, for both positive and negative reasons, gender expectations and roles were changed (Chavira-Prado 1994; Ruiz 1993; Del Castillo 1990).

Likewise, compadrazgo—an intense bond of cooperation and friendship among parents and godparents—was affected by cultural changes. It has been suggested that as Mexican Americans have become more fully integrated into urban middle-class culture, the internal family structure has been reordered (Grebler, Moore, and Guzman 1970; Moore and Pachon 1985; Foley et al. 1977). Compadrazgo has been both denigrated as a hindrance to coping in the context of the United States

(Briggs, Fogel, and Schmidt 1977), especially in an industrial economy that values individualism and personal achievement, and extolled as an aid for collective survival (Grebler, Moore, and Guzman 1970). Nevertheless, even as time and place as well as generation have altered this extended family orientation (Alvarez 1994), it appears that it has remained an important part of Chicano lifeways (Keefe and Padilla 1987). In this context, an open, fluid family network works as social capital where respect and devotion are enhanced for a person who is dutiful and helpful.

Cultural alterations became the common lot of Mexicans, sometimes a painless affair and in other moments a traumatic occasion, depending on the circumstances. The factors of time and place were operating here. Investigators have found that the amount of time spent in the United States has a definite effect on cultural adaptation, especially because of discriminatory experiences (Almaquer 1994; Weaver 1994). Studies on self-image find that Mexican immigrants often have a more positive perception of themselves than do Mexican Americans (Suarez-Orozco and Suarez-Orozco 1994; Vigil 1997); this may be true despite the low self-image they might have in Mexico if they are dark mestizo or Indian. In regard to compadrazgo and machismo, it is safe to state that after one or more generations, a cultural value shift, or at least a type of modified readaptation, would occur (De Anda 1996; Vigil 1997; Moore and Pachon 1985; Grebler, Moore, and Guzman 1970). Acculturation is often a means for an individual to escape a situation of domination. However, it also reflects status inequalities and what should be marveled at is how Chicanos were able to retain or maintain a semblance of their past culture as they learned the new one.

It must be noted that not only is time in the United States a factor, but the time element in Mexico is also instrumental. Today, Mexican compadrazgo, machismo, and other aspects of Mexican culture generally are different from what they were even twenty years ago. In part, this has been a product of evolutionary change, but it is also a by-product of the globalization of the economy. In short, economic exchanges and networks have preceeded cultural ones. Mexicans, especially at the middle-class level, have been increasingly abandoning their old traditions in favor of new ones created by their desire to become more like Americans (Weaver 1994; Penalosa 1973a).

Acculturated Mexican Americans showed a range of cultural responses in this time period (Vigil 1997; Trueba 1991). The ethnic label they selected is often indicative of their cultural style and orientation, as noted earlier, although generation, language usage, and so on are also important components of cultural style. Time and place obviously play a role here, but Anglicization tends to occur when there is the predisposition to change and a lack of barriers to prevent it. Thus, some "Spanish-appearing" individuals might identify more with white people, as the latter might be more receptive and open to them. Other motivations to assimilate might include shame of culture, avoidance of extended family members, and desire to get ahead. It has also been noted that growing up outside a Mexican neighborhood can aid access, exposure, and identification with Anglo culture (Vigil 1997; Penalosa 1973a). In other words, when Mexicans moved geographically closer to the Anglos, they tended to select a more Anglo ethnic identity. Thus, it is reasonable to assume that ethnic identification has been tied to cultural practices (Bernal and Knight 1993; Romanucci-Ross and De Vos 1995).

In the case of marginal individuals, the variance is much more unpredictable. This is the case particularly during the cultural transitional phase of familiarity with and integration into Anglo culture, which typically occurs sometime between the first and second generations. Some people never quite anchor themselves in the dominant culture nor do they totally extricate themselves from the native culture. Without a set pattern, these people might at times be extremely Mexican and at other times very Anglo. A constant battle appears to have developed in their minds: sometimes Mexican, then Anglo, then a fleeting mixture of the two, and finally perhaps neither one. Choloization is what the author has called it elsewhere (Vigil 1988, 1997), and a whole range of ethnic labels reflect it.

Strengths and Weaknesses of Mexican Culture

In spite of the inherent pitfalls in cultural transformations or the overall materially poor life of Mexican Americans, there remain some outstanding cultural features. It has been suggested that Americans could learn many things from Mexicans, especially "to do with the business of how to live life better" and also, perhaps, how to live life better with death in the offing (Diaz-Guerrero 1978:306). In general, Anglos tend to avoid thoughts of death, knowing that it is there waiting but not wanting to think about it. In contrast, Mexican Americans have long accepted the presence of death and, as a result, have lived each day as if it were their last; *Dia de los Muertos* is just one of the celebratory events associated with this belief. This could be a legacy from the Indian belief in the dual nature of life whereby one extreme cannot be understood, much less lived, unless its opposite is also embraced. A contributing factor most certainly is the life of poverty that many live, inclining them to live their lives more fully and enjoy the small things.

The ways work and recreation are thought of and conducted are worthy of examination. It has been said that "Anglos work full time and enjoy life part time, and Mexican Americans work part time and enjoy life full time." As noted, Mexicans have a strong work ethic (Briggs 1973); in contrast to the Puritan ethic, however, Mexicans view work as a means of survival rather than as a value in itself. Material objects are also viewed as necessities rather than as ends in themselves (Murillo 1976).

Many observers have remarked on the frequency of parties in Chicano life, but few have noted the religious nature of many such affairs, with an almost "complete form of communication with the spiritual world and with others involv[ing] the mind, body, and soul" (Najera-Ramirez 1994:328; see also Weaver 1994). This might be an inheritance from pre-Columbian times or from religious fiestas of the Spanish colonial period (Kluckholm and Strodtbeck 1961). In any case, when someone arranges a baptism, birthday party, wedding, or funeral wake, a great deal of effort goes into ensuring that the guests can drink and eat to their heart's content. Although this custom has been criticized as too ostentatious for "poor people," it continues in a somewhat altered form. Similar customs are practiced among working-class people in other parts of the world. The various elements and symbols in the *Fiestas Patrias* (patriotic fiestas), such as food, folk costumes, music, dances, the Cura Hidalgo, the Virgen de Guadalupe, the Grito de Dolores, and *charreadas* (vaquero rodeos) serve to reinforce and affirm Mexican cultural identity (Melville 1978; Najera-Ramirez 1994; Sands 1993; Pena 1985).

Besides the symbolic significance, such events have a sound economic and historical basis. The habit of sharing material resources helps other family members and friends even if it might take away from the already meager belongings of the family (Murillo 1976). At the same time, however, it reinforces bonds with others and builds up what is sometimes called "social capital," i.e., an assurance that others will try to assist you when you need help. Mesoamerican peasant Indians still practice economic redistribution through civil-religious ceremonies (Foster 1987). An affluent person extends an open invitation to the community to share in his good fortune as a demonstration of community involvement and dedication. This is more a sharing than a showing off of wealth, and a different way to attain status. Great pleasure is derived from providing guests with an enjoyable relief from their daily, arduous work.

The above are examples of positive traits, despite the criticism and stereotyping some have directed at them. In contrast, a long history of oppression and domination by separate forces has generated many destructive Chicano cultural features. Poverty especially has helped to produce generations of poorly educated, low-skilled, unemployed, and marginal elements. Cultural imperialism on the part of white America is primarily responsible for their plight (Paredes 1978).

Aspects of Cultural Imperialism

Barriers to the acquisition of American culture were nowhere more rigid and detrimental than in the schools and the whole educational apparatus (Valencia 1991). Schools are next in importance to the family as a socializing agent, and for newcomers from a peasant, rural background, schools are *the* gateway to the dominant culture. How the children of these immigrants were received, integrated, accommodated, and cultivated educationally remains a dark page in American history. Separate schooling for Mexicans and Americans, although not legally institutionalized, has long been the custom in many southern California cities (see Alvarez 1987, on which the film *The Lemon Grove Incident* is based). The fact that these "Mexicans" are American citizens does not seem to be of importance (Gonzales 1990). This historical pattern is true for most of the Southwest (Valencia 1991; Grebler, Moore, and Guzman, 1970; U.S. Commission on Civil Rights 1971). Mexican Americans have for many years completed less schooling than any ethnic group of Americans except American Indians. In 1960, Anglos averaged twelve years of school; blacks, ten years; and Mexican Americans, eight years (Grebler, Moore, and Guzman 1970). Furthermore, it is clear that many more Mexican Americans start school than finish it, which means that parents send their children, but the schools cause them to drop out, or worse, push or kick them out (Valencia 1991). Mexican Americans themselves have often been blamed for their learning deficiencies, under the "cultural deficiency" rationale (Buriel 1984). Some researchers have suggested that Mexican-American children are mentally inferior to American children of the same age (Sanchez 1967). However, these early "scientific" reports failed to factor in how racial barriers and attitudes and socioeconomic realities were related to educational performance (Valencia 1991; Gamio 1969).

In conjunction with other factors, cultural imperialist programs have hindered Chicano educational advancement; the Anglo's sense of cultural superiority was a factor in the post-1848 period, but accelerated and reigned supreme during the first decades of immigration in the twentieth century. For example, after arriving at school, a young child's first lessons were in English, and if he spoke Spanish inside or outside the classroom, he was typically scolded (Briggs 1973). Often, a student who spoke Spanish was threatened with having his or her mouth washed out with soap; many stopped talking to avoid such treatment. Schools continually refuse to recognize that Mexicans are culturally different and so need educational programs that are suited to these differences (Sanchez 1967). This was not an unusual practice, since Americanization programs have affected most ethnically different people (Gonzales 1990; Sanchez 1966). Beginning in the nineteenth century, Americanization efforts were a common educational practice in cities filled with immigrants.

Many children were left behind academically because they could not understand the learning tasks given in English. The problem with Mexican-American children was not the fact that they spoke Spanish, but that teachers in the school system could not understand either their language or culture. This linguistic and cultural difference made authorities think that students were mentally retarded, so they were placed in special classes (Valencia 1991). By ignoring different cultural standards and educational needs, schools were adding to the confusion and disorientation of the students who already were lost in this new world. The words of the student quoted earlier on marginality elaborate on this problem:

> I remember in the fifth grade studying Spanish and when we had to do class conversations out loud it was always traumatic for me. Most of the kids in my class were Anglo, so when I spoke Spanish I was careful not to have an accent, so I would not be laughed at. Perhaps I should have showed more will power, but it's awfully damned hard when even the teacher snickers. This kind of experience gave me a shyness I have never been able to get rid of. Instead of mastering the language, it was, instead, taken away from me and replaced by the knowledge that Columbus discovered America and that Indians were savages.

Countless incidents of this nature have been cited throughout the Southwest to underscore the institutional insensitivity and damaging nature of such mistreatment (U.S. Civil Rights Commission 1971; Valencia 1991).

In time, as for millions of other members of minority groups through generational change, the improved learning levels came with familiarization with the Anglo culture. However, what sets Mexican Americans apart from the others is the almost steady influx of Mexicans into the United States throughout this century. This regular "human infusion" has replenished and regenerated fading Mexican cultural attributes; that is, Mexican culture spans the generations because there has been constant cultural immigration to remind even the assimilated ones of the Mexican presence.

Insensitive Educational Practices

An integral aspect of cultural imperialism was the ethnocentric attitude of teachers. It is important to note that most teachers felt they were helping the children learn American culture, even if it meant disparaging Mexican culture. This misguided and insensitive attitude infected the classroom atmosphere and promoted a poor self-image among the students (Valencia 1991). But matters did not end there, for many teachers harbored other feelings and showed them in insults and physical abuse. How could anyone learn when made to feel slow, dirty, and deficient because someone else thought it was true? The imperialist basis of these attitudes was often explicit: "A teacher, asked why she had called on 'Johnny' to lead five Mexicans in orderly file out of a schoolroom, explained: 'His father owns one of the big farms in the area and . . . one day he will have to know how to handle the Mexicans.' Another teacher, following the general practice of calling on the Anglos to help Mexican pupils recite in class, said in praise of the system: 'It draws them (the Americans) out and gives them a feeling of importance'" (Parsons 1965:219).

Socioeconomic forces dictated the above treatment, but cultural insensitivity was a part of it, too. Other educational areas were similarly affected by this attitude. There is a gross underrepresentation of Mexican Americans among teachers. In the Southwest, about 17 percent of students in the 1970s were Mexican-American, but only 4 percent of their teachers were Mexican American. In addition, the curriculum emphasized the value of the dominant group and denigrated the minority one. For instance, public school history books often ignore the Mexican-American War and the Treaty of Guadalupe Hidalgo, and this omission gives the impression that the Southwest was always a part of the United States. Many critics have questioned the lopsided nature of this "quest for truth" and what it does to the identity formation of a child. To complicate matters, coming from a different historical tradition, Mexican Americans have found it difficult to identify with dominant cultural themes.

> I'm sitting in my history class,
> The instructor commences rapping,
> I'm in my U.S. history class,
> and I'm on the verge of napping,
> The Mayflower landed on Plymouth Rock.
> Tell me more! Tell me more!
> Thirteen colonies were settled.
> I've heard it all before.
> What did he say?
> Dare I ask him to reiterate?
> Oh why bother.
> It sounded like he said,
> George Washington's my father.
> I'm reluctant to believe it,
> I suddenly raise my mano.
> If George Washington's my father,
> Why wasn't he Chicano?

The preceding verse by Richard Olivas (included in Romano-V 1968) shows that at least some students were aware of the discrepancies in cultural cues and images being fed to them; more militant students would question why monocultural education is useful if we are a nation of immigrants.

Those who overcame the learning barriers were usually very bright or lucky, and often felt that they had to turn their backs on their culture (Rodriguez 1988). Notwithstanding these successes, there were additional obstacles that further restricted the development of their innate potential. Poor counseling, ability tracking, and the biased attitudes and behavior of other students toward them are some of the hindrances. For example, thousands of students have been counseled into vocational or trade courses, even if they were capable of professional career training. Congressman Edward Roybal and Dr. Julian Nava, two notable graduates of Roosevelt High School in East Los Angeles, were successful despite counseling advice to pursue a career as a body-and-fender worker and an auto mechanic, respectively. This advice, unfortunately, is rooted in the centuries-old belief that Mexicans (and Indians) are "good with their hands" and nothing else. One fact that allowed these practices to continue, making them seem reasonable on the part of the dominant group, was that few Chicanos had risen to higher status positions in the 1960s.

Color: Inter- and Intragroup Racism

Ethnocentrism

The Chicano experience in the United States took place in the context of a society preoccupied with racial distinctions. Critics of the Mexican-American War noted the racist implications of the conquest (Acuna 1988), and soon thereafter the United States was almost dissolved in a war focused on slavery. A century after the Civil War, "people of color" were still subject to discrimination and social, economic, and even legal sanctions against their progress. This situation, of course, was not unique to the United States.

In the aftermath of the 1846 war until the 1910 Mexican Revolution, conditions and practices of racism permeated Anglo-Mexican relationships. The Mexican was considered an Indian, looked the part, and was held in low esteem just like the American Indian (Menchaca 1993). Mexican racial attitudes and practices from the colonial era still played a role in this new context; one faced a double dose of racism if he or she was Indian racially and Mexican (Spanish!) culturally. This reality persisted for many decades after the 1910 Mexican Revolution; however, some significant and far-reaching changes were introduced and they continued to ebb and flow for most of the century. Mexican immigration simultaneously increased the population and regenerated Mexican culture in many major cities of the Southwest. Faced with this steady influx and changes in the economy that led to stagnating conditions for wage workers, many Anglo Americans became angry and grumbled that this is what kept them from progressing and made their culture static (Melville 1994). Thus, the embers of past racism have been fanned into an intense anti-foreign, anti-immigrant sentiment, diverting attention from major macrostructural changes.

Behind all these developments was ethnocentrism, an attitude that exists in all cultures, but operates at its most dangerous levels within societies having a subordinate minority population. "The belief that one's own customs, language, religion, and physical characteristics are better or more 'natural' than those of others is termed ethnocentrism. Minor and minute cultural and physical differences may often be given exclusive attention to prove the inferiority of another people" (Wagley and Harris 1958:258). A cultural (and often a racial) group feeling good about itself can represent a benign form of ethnocentrism. But malignant ethnocentrism leads one to focus on the alleged inferiority of others as an excuse to curtail their movement or freedom.

Ethnic minorities in the United States have encountered a type of malignant ethnocentrism that has frequently turned into racism. After socioeconomic changes rearrange society, and cultural rationales solidify the barriers for status inequalities, then racial prejudice and discrimination is invoked to instill feelings of inferiority and mobilize institutions to keep minorities subjugated.

Although the experience varied for each ethnic minority in the United States, there were some clear similarities. Emphasis on racial features is one of them. Another is the use of racial standards as a justification for economic exploitation. At first the goal was simple—one human group benefiting at the expense of another—but it soon grew, for ethnocentrism finds many avenues to create and maintain status and distance between groups. However, it should be understood that such feelings and actions to gain and maintain economic advantages are not consciously formulated. Rather, the rationale is probably developed subconsciously to assuage the dominant group's conscience; it is a subtle form of racism, or "aversive" racism, that still affects attitudes, if not behavior (Dovidio et al. 1992). Racist practices were initiated in the colonial period, and these customs were elaborated upon and exacerbated in the modern period. Many downtrodden people carry racist perceptions of themselves, even without white people leading the way.

Roots of Prejudice and Discrimination

Prejudicial attitudes gave rise to discriminatory behavior. To anchor Mexicans in the lowest positions, the dominant group prejudged their behavior negatively (prejudice) and set up social barriers (schools, housing, and so on) to impede their social mobility (discrimination). Thus, discrimination is prejudice turned into action. In a very short time, dominant group members believed Mexicans were so obviously inferior, that their subordinate status was really of their own doing. Mexican workers are seen as irresponsible, lazy, and undependable. There is, therefore, a ready association between Mexicans and menial labor (Simmons 1973). Such imagery, similar to that used with regard to black slaves (and later sharecroppers), was widely disseminated in American society at the time of the Mexican-American War; the discrimination extended to the point of denying the Mexican Americans citizenship (Menchaca 1993). Even white ethnic groups have had trouble overcoming barriers that for a long time prevented their advancement. Mexicans have had to wait even longer. Indeed, the problem was a dual one for Mexicans: The dominant group believed in their inferiority and rejected them, and many Mexicans learned to agree with the dominant group's verdict and internalized a negative self-image (Bernal and Knight 1993; Phinney 1995). Few people understood that racial ideologies resulted from the colonial encounter of Europeans with people from Africa, America, and Asia. Europeans justified their political and economic domination on the grounds that they were dealing with inferior races (Frazier 1957). As one observer has remarked, "Color is neutral; it is the mind that gives it meaning" (Bastide 1968:34). Unfortunately, this meaning has been far more sinister for Mexicans and other people of color than it has for European whites.

Class relationships were at the root of racial policies in the countries that emerged in the Americas, "particularly those with capitalist economies" (Melville 1994:88). Such policies eventually generated sociopsychological problems, including poor self-esteem, self-hatred, and marginality. The strain of gaining social acceptance made Mexicans in the United States work harder and longer than the average citizen. The Mexican experience was a continuation of a United States colonial pattern that began with the Indians. For most, it was also a continuation of the discrimination suffered under the ethnic elite of Mexico. During the Mexican-American War, Senator John C. Calhoun said: "I know further, sir, that we have never dreamt of incorporating into our union any but the Caucasian race—the free white race. To incorporate Mexico, would be the very first instance of the kind of incorporating an Indian race; for more than half of the Mexicans are Indians, and the other is composed chiefly of mixed tribes" (Weber 1973:135; see Menchaca 1993). The historical sequence and context of color discrimination against Chicanos thus began with the Indians but included subsequently the importation of African slaves, the inclusion of Mexicans after the 1846 war, the enticement of cheap Chinese labor from Asia, and large-scale southeastern European immigration in the late nineteenth century.

"Pigmentocracy"

Anglos often used to insist that a light-skinned Mexican is Spanish rather than Mexican. This was based on their conviction that Mexicans are very dark (Simmons 1973). Anglo feelings of superiority were so pernicious that only lighter-hued Mexicans might escape the worst effects of racism, and even "swarthy" Spaniards were looked down upon (Almaquer 1994). "The term 'racism' can be considered shorthand for the phrase 'pejorative social discrimination based on phenotypic (observable biological) characteristics'" (Melville 1994:92). According to Americo Paredes (1978), a professor of folklore, the superiority syndrome is ethnocentrism perfected: A strong nationalist inclination that diminishes other people's sense of self-respect in many ways, such as always making the "good guys" Anglos and the "bad guys" Mexicans (and other people of color) in motion pictures (Noriega 1992).

Although this was the pattern of racism, it must be underscored that many American leaders and groups fought against this practice. The civil rights struggles in the United States have generally found progressive elements leading the way in this regard. The 1964 Civil Rights Act is an example of this type of striving for equality. Nonetheless, such hard-won victories were few and far between for most of our history, as the majority groups' attitudes remained mired in the past even as they toned down overt racism (Dovidio et al. 1992).

Cultural imperialism was easy to practice with racial cues, and once activated, the worst attitudes and behavior of the dominant group often emerged. Sometimes just hearing the ethnic group's language, as in the case of lighter Mexicans, would be enough of a catalyst. In large part these visual and linguistic "markers" are responsible for hindering Mexican entrance into the social mainstream of the United States. Often the degree of assimilation or white appearance of the minority-group member does not matter to the white middle class. A Mexican is still a Mexican no matter how refined in speaking English or stylishly dressed. In fact, in early legal cases, the interplay between physical appearance and cultural habits played havoc in the courts, and in one instance led to a strange ruling: "White Mexican students . . . could be segregated only if they did not speak English" (Menchaca 1993:598). The social and political environment thus cursed the Mexican in many ways, both within and from without (Stowell 1974).

Institutional Racism

Branding with prejudicial words and labels might affect any minority group, but in the case of Mexican Americans it was accompanied by stronger discriminatory actions. No doubt this began in the period after the Mexican-American War (1848), when anti-Mexican feeling prevailed. In time these feelings and actions became built into the structure of society. Thus, the "authorities"—law enforcement officers particularly, but others, too—did not wait for Mexicans to go wrong but acted precipitately to keep a tight rein on the population and asked questions afterward (Morales 1972). As in the earlier colonial confrontation, the struggle over resources—land, labor, and wealth—and "social power" (Melville 1994:97) was an important reason for this behavior.

Racist ideology, and later, institutions, operated to prevent Mexican acquisition and retention of land and wealth. Their poverty was then frequently used, in a vicious circle, to justify continued mistreatment. As recently as the early 1960s, a Los Angeles police chief remarked that "poor people who are of darker skin are under greater suspicion of committing crime—even more so if they communicate in a 'foreign' language. . . . It seems just, however, to say that Mexicans are unmoral rather than immoral since they lack a conception of morals as understood in this country. Their housing conditions are bad, crime is prevalent and their morals are a menace to our civilization. They are illiterate, ignorant and inefficient and have few firm religious beliefs" (Morales 1972:33). Imagine how these words translated into attitudes and actions toward Mexicans on the part of the rank and file police officers, as reported not only in Los Angeles but also in other regions of the Southwest (U.S. Civil Rights Commission 1971).

Mexican-American efforts to obtain rights blocked by institutional racism had occasional success, especially in the celebrated cases involving segregated schools: The Lemon Grove (Alvarez 1987) and the *Mendez v. Westminster* cases (Gonzalez 1990; Menchaca 1993). Nevertheless, the well-structured program of suppression required only periodic supervision for maintenance (Simmons 1974). As mentioned earlier, schools and teachers were instruments that fostered this arrangement. Most other societal sectors were interwoven with racial standards that were implicitly or even explicitly aimed at the exclusion of ethnic minorities. Earlier generations of ethnic minorities who had learned these lessons socialized their children with the stain of second-class citizenship even before they might experience it themselves.

Public Barriers

Racism continued in social realms outside the school. The community swimming pool might be especially reserved for Mexicans and blacks on a set day. There were even reports that the pool was drained and refilled for white use for the remainder of the week; while this placated Anglo racists, it probably was a symbolic draining of a small proportion of the water. In addition, lighter-hued Mexicans might be welcomed on "regular" days if they could "pass." More often, it was a mixed affair, as this example shows: "In 1939, it was revealed that, although the swimming pool at Chaffey Junior College was used on an integrated basis during the academic year, when it was open to the general public during the summer, Chicanos were allowed to use it only on Mondays" (Acuna 1988).

A similar experience awaited Chicanos at the movie theater (Taylor 1934), where sometimes the front rows or whole balcony was known as the "Mexican" section (Menchaca 1995). One Texas town limited the types and amount of ice cream a minority person might buy. Even something as mundane as a haircut was touched by racism: In 1945, it was revealed in the U.S. Senate hearings that Chicanos from McCarney, Texas, had to travel forty-five miles in order to get a haircut because Anglo barbers refused to cut their hair and because Chicanos could not legally become barbers in McCarney (Guzman 1974). A Texas barber had earlier explained his understanding of this practice: "'No, we don't wait on Mexicans here. They are dirty and have lice, and we would lose our white trade. The Mexicans also have venereal diseases, most of them, but of course some whites do, too. The Mexicans go to their own barber shop. The Negroes barber each other'" (Taylor 1934:250).

Reactions to Mistreatment

Social discrimination, along with inadequate education and unfair political practices such as poll taxes and gerrymandering, built up a backlog of resentment among Chicanos. Many Chicanos developed acute self-hatred and came to despise their ethnicity and all that it seemed to signify (Moore and Pachon 1985). However, the resistance and resilience of many more is of at least equal importance.

Chicano resistance in reaction against racism erupted in the nineteenth century in forms such as social banditry and has continued to the present. Some incidents were minor scrapes involving a handful of people, while others took the form of major riots and protests where hundreds, even thousands participated (Mazon 1983). The so-called pachuco riots of the early 1940s in Los Angeles, one of several major race riots taking place in American cities in that time, is a modern example of this stand against racist persecution. On that occasion Mexican Americans grouped together for defensive purposes, as the community was subjected to angry attacks by both authorities and civilians, and rioting continued for several days. Anglos singled out for confrontation youth who wore the zoot suit, as younger Chicanos had begun to dress that way.

Zooters and sailors battle.

Originally, the zoot-suit dress and label applied across class and ethnic lines to all those who dressed in this particular style, but on this occasion, it became equated with Chicanos (Guzman 1974). At first, only "zoot-suit pachuco" types were beaten by armed mobs, then anyone Mexican, and finally any other easily recognizable ethnic minority.

The attacks on members of the Chicano community met strong resistance and even counterattacks over several days. Despite the violence, however, there were no deaths associated with the strife (Mazon 1983). The authorities, overlooking the actions of the predominantly white mobs, tended to blame the entire episode on the Mexican Americans. Captain E. Duran Ayers, chief of the Foreign Relations Bureau (!) of the Los Angeles County Sheriff's Department, summed up the dominant public attitude toward the affair: "The biological basis is the main basis to work from. . . . This total disregard for human life has always been universal throughout the Americas among the Indian population" (Morales 1972:41). These events showed, if nothing else, that the Chicanos were not docile people and would fight back when pushed. Chicanos salvaged a certain amount of pride and dignity from this, and Anglo authorities grudgingly afforded a new respect for a group that stood up for its rights (Mirande 1989).

Returning Mexican veterans from World Wars I and II reinforced the battle against racist institutions (Melville 1994). They were not content with first-class citizenship in the front lines and second-class citizenship at home. Discrimination was particularly resented since Mexican Americans were the United States' most highly decorated ethnic minority (Morin 1966). Consequently, they steadily challenged the racist policies that often characterized real estate operators, restaurants, movie theaters, and other establishments.

Negative Imagery. The institutional discrimination was reinforced by the proliferation of derogatory images of Chicanos, and labels such as "greaser" and "Mecskin." One early book about Mexican travel has these words: "There are two things I could never understand, why the Lord made mosquitoes and Mexicans" (Stowell 1974:116). Claims to superior status are often accompanied by a vocabulary of insult to flaunt and fortify the power dominant groups have amassed. The early labels were joined by "beaners," "wetbacks," "chili chokers," "tacos," "chukes," "half-breeds," and many others (Kirk 1979). Ironically, poorer whites who lived near Mexicans, often sharing similar poverty conditions, were usually the ones who used the labels. Although they were just as destitute, they felt relieved to have someone below them, a practice that was also present in certain areas of the South, between poor whites and blacks.

There were also more sophisticated ways of negatively portraying an ethnic minority. These carried more weight because social-science writers and other academicians created them to rationalize the experiences of the ethnically defined underclass. Mexicans were described as lazy, dumb, dirty, bloodthirsty savages, immoral, breed-like-rats, culturally deficient, and a host of other demeaning stereotypes. While social scientists now have purged their own remarks of such racist imagery, the legacy lives on elsewhere. One need only look to Hollywood movies and recent television programs to document such stereotyping. In films, Mexican (as well as Indian) characters often were distorted and were mostly a bad sort. They were usually portrayed in a lowly status such as gardener, waiter/waitress, baby-sitter, janitor, or an underworld role such as bandit, terrorist, or gang member. If given a higher status, it was often as a dictator or leader of a global crime syndicate, and for females, the sinister femme fatale. Moviegoers far removed from real Mexicans came away thinking the worst of the people (Noriega 1992).

Similarly disparaging images were fed daily to national television audiences. Misinformation on racial and cultural characteristics was common. Advertising especially showed very demeaning images, and viewers learned how to be racist even without knowing any Mexicans (Martinez 1973). One blatant example was a deodorant commercial that depicted Mexicans as reeking of body odor.

Reverse Racists

Chicanos have over time adjusted to this treatment and fashioned a self-protective shell to become "reverse racists," even toward other racial minorities. Put-down words such as "gringo," "paddy," "*gavacho*" (meaning foreigner, used initially toward the French), and "*bolillo*" (a hard-crusted loaf of white bread) were hurled back at whites. More sophisticated Chicanos have labeled Anglos as aggressive, competitive, money hungry, exploitative, and insensitive. This racist attitude was probably one of the adaptive mechanisms Mexican Americans used to survive with some self-dignity. In contrast, the lower classes in Mexico are much more tolerant of those who are racially different, possibly because that segment of the Mexican population is racially mixed. Lest we forget, even after immigration to the United States, intragroup racism persisted among Mexicans, with the darker-hued people still treated shabbily.

In addition, intragroup relationships have also been affected by generational distance from Mexico. To some degree, Mexicans in the United States have mistreated and verbally abused Mexican immigrants on the basis of cultural attributes, calling them "*chuntaros*," "*mojados*" (wetbacks), "T.J.s" (from Tijuana, and suggesting riffraff border residents), and so on. On occasion, Mexican-American leaders have made an effort to reduce this animosity (Weber 1973). According to Samora, economic causes lay behind this friction: "the hiring of cheap alien labor has [had the effect] of pitting Mexican Americans against Mexicans" (Samora 1971:130). Immigrant Mexicans reacted by calling Mexican Americans "pochos," "*agringados*" (having gringo traits), and "cholos."*

Although the labels aim at cultural phenomena, the terms are implicitly racist. The more Mexican-looking (Indian!) may resent those who are lighter and thus more employable by Anglo standards; often a great deal of time and energy has been expended in worry and concern over job prospects. Racial attitudes probably did, in fact, play a role in

---

*An earlier definition of this word throughout Latin America meant someone in cultural transition, such as a native acculturating to the Hispanic mode, but the word is now used to describe a Chicano subcultural, street-gang style; perhaps it is also indicative of the transition from Mexican to Anglo-American culture.

Anglo hiring practices (Reisler 1976). Another source of intraethnic conflict is the contrast in backgrounds. Mexican immigrants compare their socioeconomic status to the status they had in Mexico, whereas the Mexican Americans born in the United States compare their status with that of Anglos. The relative advantages and disadvantages that each group perceives may thus affect their self-images and attitudes toward one another (Dworkin 1971).

Roots of Intragroup Racism

Not all Chicano racism is attributable to experiences in the United States, nor does it stay at the inter- or intragroup level. Families have been known to favor the *guero* (light-skinned) child over the darker *prieto* offspring. This appears to be a Spanish colonial practice that has carried over into the present day. In New Mexico, there is clearly a defensive attitude about being part Indian. Intermarriage with Indians is looked down upon, and, when it does occur, the children of the union are stigmatized with the terms *lobo* (wolf) or coyote (Kluckholm and Strodtbeck 1961). Many who were lighter in color called themselves Spanish and sought to marry Anglos, often looking down on their own group in order to gain the allegiance and respect of Anglo acquaintances (Simmons 1974).

However, having a light skin did not guarantee that this would happen, for a light complexion was not necessarily equated with better socioeconomic conditions; many poor Mexicans were very white. In addition, darker-skinned Mexicans sometimes sought a status change through intermarriage. Generally it is true that Mexicans have attempted to emulate whites, if only because opportunities for social mobility were increased in this way. Nevertheless, there was always a certain amount of pragmatic switching. The distinction between Indian and Hispanic features in certain individuals is difficult to make. These individuals are, therefore, able to claim to be of either Spanish or Indian descent, depending on the group of people they are dealing with (Gonzales, N. L., 1967).

Thus, at the end of this period, the Chicano community still faced tremendous problems stemming from racial discrimination. Barriers to advancement in employment and social standing continued; the mass media ignored Chicanos at best and disparaged them at other times; for too many, the vacillation over self-image led inexorably to self-hate; and even more within the community had incorporated an intrapsychic mode of self-repression. However, resistance to these conditions had also survived and even grown, and the stage was set for change.

Chapter 9

Breakup and Transformation of the Social Order

Contact: Civil Rights Ferment

Shaping the Chicanos

From the time of its incorporation in the United States, the Mexican-American community has encountered forces that bred change in its lifeway and expectations. The Civil War and Reconstruction, the settling of the West, the rise of industrial capitalism and urbanization, labor unions and economic crises, and two world wars affected Chicanos along with other Americans, although in different ways. Social and economic discrimination and policies aimed at coerced assimilation afflicted them in common with other ethnic minorities, again, in different ways. Continuous contact with Mexico uniquely affected the Chicano people, at once affording more cultural stability and also exposing them, more than most other Americans, to the revolutionary ideas of the late nineteenth and early twentieth centuries. This was especially true in the 1910 revolution and its aftermath (Knowlton 1975).

The Chicanos were not passively buffeted about by these social forces. Many fought their way against great odds into the middle-class mainstream of American society. Others, with equal vigor, resisted the social pressures to "Americanize and abandon traditional ways." Followers of both strategies won victories, large and small, in pushing for equality and justice. As Rendon (1971:2–3) has noted in rebutting the notion that the events of the 1960s were without precedent, "It is closer to the truth to say that there has always been a Chicano revolt. That is, the Mexican American, the Chicano, as he calls himself and his Carnales, brother and sister Chicanos, has never ceased to be a revolutionary all the while he has suffered repression."

Modern Chicano resistance to unequal treatment is rooted in the legacy left to the community from colonial times (Vigil 1978; Alvarez 1973). What Romano-V. (1973:54–55) has labeled the "seemingly endless decades" of Mexican and Mexican-American involvement in labor uprisings against unjust exploitation is an example of the continuity of the Chicano's quest for social justice, "conflict which involved literally tens of thousands of people of Mexican descent and which at one time spread to eight different states in the Union—conflict which was met with massive military counteraction." Of course, not all these events were full-blown affairs like social banditry that captured the public eye. They were more often localized, sporadic, spontaneous eruptions, such as a group of people gathered around a jail, clamoring for release of a prisoner unjustly detained; workers from railroads, mines, or farms organizing to improve living conditions; or political rallies to support a candidate who reflects Chicano interests. Chicanos participated in many of these activities in unison with other members of American society.

In their own way, Chicanos have carried a banner of protest throughout this century. Spontaneous and sporadic efforts improved living and working conditions. This evolved into a self-conscious organizational discipline that brought public attention to the plight of the Chicano population. Only when repressive actions were stepped up did resistance issues and programs decline. In some instances such activities were crushed completely. Nonetheless, despite temporary slowdowns, each revival of resistance brought on renewed discussion and planning in Chicano leadership circles (Romano-V. 1968). Early efforts at resolving basic contradictions were made, and many leaders worked to spread their insights, programs, and goals. Social and political recommendations varied from moderate to radical, but it is clear that previous generations of Chicanos did not passively accept their socioeconomic situation. For example, one study of the Chicano youth movement mentions how those who started organizing in the 1930s later helped the present generation toward similar goals (Gomez-Quinones 1978).

Beginning in the late nineteenth century, *mutualistas* (mutual aid societies) were established for self-help purposes, often promoting the sense of ethnic unity and mission for other activities. Chicanos pooled their resources and helped each other economically by, for example, providing low-interest loans and low-cost funeral and insurance benefits. Subsequent groups followed these self-help patterns, also. For example, Mexicans and Chicanos have begun operating *tandas*, rotating credit associations, based on *confianza* (trust) (Velez-I. 1983). Moreover, they have broadened the goals to encompass other issues. Organizations such as the League of United Latin American Citizens (LULAC); the Community Service Organization (CSO); and G.I. Forum, are a few illustrations of this historical pattern (Marquez 1989). A recent biography of

Bert Corona and his career as a California activist clearly documents several decades of socioeconomic strife that pervaded Chicano communities (M. T. Garcia 1994). Corona's role predates the official Chicano movement and illustrates how there has been a continual struggle for improvement and justice. Such local and focused activities, when it was not yet possible or popular to organize on a larger scale, served a twofold purpose. First, they kept the light of protest burning during the quiet, incubating years. Second, these groups formed a core from which later organizations gained inspiration to continue the struggle.

Effects of Modern Urban Industrial System

Despite the historical precedents, the modern period is unique for several reasons. Modern technological systems have brought former peasants into the mainstream of work and urban growth. These developments are clearly evident in the Chicano experience. In 1930 nearly half of all employed Chicanos worked in agriculture; by 1982 this figure decreased to less than 7 percent. Between 1950 and 1990, the percentage of Chicanos living in urban areas increased from 66 percent to 94 percent (Meier and Ribera 1993). Previously, most of the world's people were locally organized and nationally controlled. Now the spread of capitalist enterprises and networks has developed what is in many ways an international social system and a global economy. In their drive to acquire raw resources and more workers, capitalist leaders have made a large part of the world's population more homogeneous, through, for example, the mass media. Thus, modernization has also meant ideological revision and, perhaps, congruence and conformity in thought. This experience has tended to pull the interests, concerns, and needs of modernizing people into the same orbit. What happens to one group or in one part of the world generally has repercussions on other groups and regions (Wallerstein 1974). Because of a system's macrolevel influences, observers are beginning to seek macrolevel solutions to conditions and problems. Chicanos are uniting with other groups that have similar interests. Labor resistance to exploitation offers an example: Labor unions, which have a heavy Chicano representation, are increasingly working together to develop strategies for socioeconomic and political change. More recently, Chicanos are uniting with other Latinos to fight for educational and political reform.

Precursors of Change

Three major developments helped to make the 1960s a watershed period within the Chicano movement and community. One was the inroads made by the black civil rights movement; another was the United States

government's efforts under President Lyndon Baines Johnson to eliminate poverty in the nation (Harrington 1962); and the third was the Vietnam War and its consequences. Each operated to restimulate the ethnic
solidarity struggle, which at this time snowballed into the first relatively
united national Chicano effort. The achievements of the black civil rights
movement sparked renewed organization in the Chicano community,
often modeled in large part on earlier black campaigns. The political
power mustered by the civil rights campaigns also paved the way for
stronger ties between Chicano leaders and national political organizations. The presidentially endorsed War on Poverty led to new job opportunities in the Chicano community and to the recruitment of Chicanos in
government and the universities on a scale never previously reached.
This, in turn, had two effects: It increased the number of highly visible
middle-class Mexican Americans, and it brought Chicano intellectuals
into contact with the activist social reformers and revolutionists then concentrated in the universities. The War on Poverty soon worked as a catalyst to awaken the political actions of barrio dwellers and their
sympathizers (Romo 1990). The war in Vietnam brought to the Chicano
community the same dissension it sparked elsewhere in the nation.
Newly radicalized Chicano students were quick to note the discrepancy
between their community's underrepresentation in the social, political,
and economic power structure and their overrepresentation in war casualty statistics.

Chicanos generated their own leadership and methods aimed at
problems unique to them. By the late 1950s, discontent within the Chicano population became noticeable, especially within the CSO. The CSO,
formed in Los Angeles in the 1940s, began with a concerted effort to reg-
ister voters and win elections. With some early successes, especially in
advancing the career of Congressman Edward Roybal, CSO eventually
became a community agency that provided social services (Moore and
Pachon 1985). With the increasing support of the Chicano community,
the first steps to social change could now be effected (Dunne 1967). The
main goal of the CSO was to prod government into alleviating serious
social problems. Through political networking, Roybal focused on civil
rights and immigrant cases, which helped generate community interest
and support. After some moderate successes, especially in breaking down
some of the housing covenants in segregated areas, CSO settled into a
role primarily as a service provider, while remaining important in helping to prepare new leaders (Gomez-Quinones 1990).

LULAC, organized in the 1920s by World War I veterans primarily
to combat prejudice, also built a platform to aid Mexican integration into
the body politic (Marquez 1989, 1993). With some moderate shifts in orientation over the decades, LULAC has now expanded considerably. Nevertheless, the organization still remains moderate to conservative in its

approach to political issues. For instance, LULAC now generally follows a middle-of-the-road path that champions community programs, but with the acceptance of corporate support.

The G.I. Forum was founded by World War II and Korean War veterans who pushed for equal access to economic and political opportunities. Because of the inroads the G.I. Forum made, it was able to develop a southwestern regional organization that later expanded its goals to include educational issues. At present it still plays a role in electoral politics as well as other matters. During the 1960s War on Poverty, both the G.I. Forum and LULAC helped start Project SER (Service, Employment and Redevelopment) programs throughout the Southwest (Gomez-Quinones 1990).

The G.I. Forum gained support among Chicanos, and one of the premier politicians, Congressman Henry B. Gonzalez from San Antonio, Texas, was one of its strongest supporters. Gonzalez had a long and varied career in Democratic politics in local, state, and national arenas. Always a champion of the poor and dispossessed, he has remained outspoken to the present. Beginning as a probation officer, he rose through the elective ranks, winning city, state, and national offices and showing remarkable ingenuity in capturing votes from several sectors, especially Latinos and blacks. Recognized as a "New Deal" Liberal, he has nonetheless at times angered Chicano activists with the stance he has taken on some issues. Nevertheless, he and others in the 1970s were instrumental in bringing together all Latino congressmen into an organization called the Hispanic Congressional Caucus.

Cesar Chavez was one Chicano who learned how to organize in the CSO. Chavez's successful attempt to organize farm workers was helped considerably after the United States' Mexican bracero program ended in 1964, which had long been a goal of labor and liberal political forces (Menchaca 1995). Under this program the United States government had officially recruited and sanctioned use of Mexican workers in a guest-worker arrangement, which made it more difficult for Chavez to mount a unionization campaign. Thus, the United Farm Workers union, founded by Chavez and Dolores Huerta, focused first on American-born or naturalized Chicanos. Generally they were more familiar with the union idea and working conditions in the United States, and presumably they were easier to organize. In addition, their extended exposure to conditions and consumer standards in the United States may have driven them to improve on their underclass role. A contemporary commentator noted: "It is a paradox that the termination of the Bracero Program is the only way in the long run of helping Mexican as well as American workers" (Nelson 1966:17). However, the continued immigration of undocumented laborers and community opposition to suppression of the immigration later led Chavez to alter this strategy and attempt to orga-

Union leader Cesar Chavez surrounded by farm workers.

nize the immigrant workers as well. The UFW initiated strikes and boy-
cotts against farm growers, singling out lettuce and grapes as the products to avoid. Chavez emphasized nonviolence as a strategy and,
following the tactics of such previous leaders as Mahatma Gandhi, went
on several fasts to bring attention to the farm workers' cause (Griswold
del Castillo and Garcia 1995). Chavez is gone now, but the farm workers'
struggle continues under UFW leadership to this day, with gradual success despite strife and many obstacles (Griffith and Kissan 1995). Additionally, the Farm Labor Organizing Committee (FLOC), founded in
1967, has expanded the struggle to improve migrant farm worker life in
the Midwest (Valdes 1991). They have recently succeeded in negotiating
an agreement with Campbell Soup and Campbell's tomato and cucum-
ber growers in Ohio and Michigan to improve working conditions
(Barger and Reza 1994).

Another example of an idea put into practice was the Reis Lopez
Tijerina land-grant movement, a collective demand for the return of a

UFW co-founder Dolores Huerta (left) *joins in prayer for Cesar Chavez outside the
Monterey County jail in Salinas, California, in 1970. Chavez was jailed for
violating a court injunction prohibiting a lettuce boycott. Mrs. Ethel Kennedy
(right) marched to the rally with hundreds of Mexican field workers before
attending the Mass and visiting Chavez in jail.*

Tijerina and followers petitioning Governor Fages of Arizona.

Patsy Tijerina joins the protest and torches a sign.

communal land grant. Communal land grants from the Spanish crown, historically more common in northern Mexico (including present day New Mexico) than in the other colonies, were given to groups of petitioners, each made up of at least ten families from a pueblo. The grant was to enable the petitioners to establish a farming community (Gardner 1970). Following the takeover by the United States in the last century, such lands fell under new ownership. Tijerina, an evangelical Protestant minister, and his followers had been active in attempts to reclaim title to these lands that once belonged to early Mexican settlers. The efforts became much more militant in 1966 when Tijerina and many members of his Alianza armed themselves in a highly publicized series of "re-occupations" and other protests (Nabokov 1969; Oboler 1995). Detailing the abrogation of Chicano land and cultural rights, and basing their program on the 1848 treaty ending the Mexican-American War, they subsequently took a memorial signed by thousands of Chicanos to Mexico to hand over to President Lopez Mateos. The document demanded the Mexican president intercede with the United States government to fulfill the terms of the Treaty of Guadalupe Hidalgo. These efforts ended in failure, with Tijerina and his followers being arrested on numerous charges related to the protests. Literally hundreds of Alianza members were involved in these activist incidents and protracted legal processes. Although no land grants were obtained, the national eye was riveted on New Mexico. Chicano activists, of course, were encouraged by this stirring of the national memory. Many Chicanos rallied behind these goals. The demonstrations led by Chavez, Tijerina, and others raised the social consciousness of Chicanos to the point where they planned further actions (Swadesh 1973).

As a result of exposure to urban life, many Chicanos were caught up in rising expectations common to that segment of the population. This is best understood as a change in attitude toward a desire to improve life's material rewards. Previous expectations were low, for Chicanos had inherited a meager standard of living with little hope for the future. The post-World War II years were good for the economy in general, and many Chicanos similarly benefited. Movement from the barrios and into a higher social status broke the pattern of low expectations. One middle-aged man, comparing the economic difference between the time of his youth and the 1960s, noted that: "'Now you see bread lying in the streets. When I was a boy you never saw bread in the streets'" (Grebler, Moore, and Guzman 1970:343). Thus, with one dream fulfilled, there is a rising expectation for the satisfaction of previously unheard-of possibilities. Chicanos who experienced this feeling grouped together in order to have their wishes recognized and met (Romero 1979). The urbanization process was responsible for bringing Chicanos into the center stage of national life.

Nature of Inequality

Urbanization brought Chicanos into contact with other people, some of whom had been similarly relegated to a life of low status and poverty. In spite of the differences among all of them, there were some who began to perceive that strong threads held them together. Complementing this new mood of national interethnic awareness were the first attempts to draw parallels with colonized peoples in the Third World of the Americas, Africa, and Asia. Many Chicanos began to view their situation as that of an "internal colony." Inherent in this assessment was the fact that colonial systems throughout the world share certain common features. Since Chicanos were either Indians, and thus the original inhabitants of this hemisphere, or Mexican settlers before the United States expansion into Mexican territory, it was necessary to explain their presence in the United States in a framework other than that applicable to other immigrants or poor ethnic minorities. Like so many people in other parts of the world, they were integrated into a new society by a war of conquest. Thus, they became an internal colony, within which barrio life was affected at all levels (Barrera, Munoz, and Ornelas 1974; Moore 1973; Mirande 1987). Although far from uniform throughout the southwestern states, the basis of such a belief is this: As indigenous residents of the area, Chicanos were involuntarily incorporated into the United States; thus, contemporary ethnic relationships are colored by these beginnings.

In understanding this important fact, Chicano leaders began to develop new insights and gain increasing strength, with the goal of building alliances with other similarly affected peoples. Although some leaders never completely embraced this concept of human solidarity, preferring instead a strict La Raza nationalist program, many came to believe that similar conditions (or contradictions) necessitated coordination among the "powerless."

Conflict: 1960s Chicano Movement

Movement Background

What has become known as the Chicano movement was born, or at least was for the first time widely acknowledged, in the 1960s. However, it is difficult to pinpoint exactly how the movement started or who initiated it; there were too many contributors—students, teachers, community activists, intellectuals or old "pols" (experienced political insiders)—and too many key issues (Rendon 1971; Munoz 1989; Gomez-Quinones 1990). The Chicano movement "was a creative and revivalist cultural surge, it was a civil rights struggle, it was an effort for political recognition and economic rights by middle-class elements, and it had intimations of an incipient national liberation struggle" (Gomez-Quinones 1978:29).

No single date marks the beginnings of the Chicano movement. One can safely state, however, that most of the widespread activity was unleashed in the mid-1960s as the Chavez farm workers and Tijerina Alianza (Alliance) gained momentum. In a remarkably short period of time, many organizations and activities had blossomed (Meier and Ribera 1993). These groups focused their energies mostly on the issues and conditions that were discussed in the earlier stages. The farm union fought to correct injustices against workers, and the Alianza sought the return of treaty-guaranteed land; both issues, land and labor, are at the center of this historical account. Other organizations brought attention to another core problem: the lack of resources and wealth among the Chicano population. Some groups concentrated their efforts on a single sector, such as education or politics. Others, with varying success, confronted most social conditions that blocked Chicano development.

Groups and Actions

The earlier reform groups were joined by others. The Crusade for Justice in Denver, led by Corky Gonzales in the mid-1960s, was a broadly based thrust for community control, mainly economic and political (Gomez-Quinones 1991; Marin 1975). Under his leadership, links were established with other groups throughout Colorado and later into other areas of the Southwest. Gonzales forged strong bonds within the network he had assembled under the rubric of "cultural nationalism" and self-determination.

The Brown Berets emerged in 1967 from a group of young students who worked for the VISTA program, a government-sponsored initiative to resolve urban problems. As the foremost militant unit within the Chicano movement, the Berets were instrumental in organizing protests and demonstrations attacking educational policies and police practices, often with the assistance of young barrio gang members and other disaffected youth who reveled in direct action. For example, they were one of the primary organizers of the largest of the Chicano Moratoriums. The Chicano Moratoriums of the 1970s were nominally anti-Vietnam War but took on a broader front, addressing the whole social system (Munoz 1989; Morales 1972). Internal struggles for leadership and differences over issues, as well as infiltration by police agents, led to the Berets disbanding in 1972. They are still recognized, however, as a group that shook the political establishment, including many moderate and middle-class Chicanos (Acuna 1988).

United Mexican American Students (UMAS) and other Southwest student organizations, such as Mexican American Youth Organization

(MAYO) in Texas, helped generate university student involvement in all areas, exerting demands to establish Chicano Studies programs and effective minority student recruitment. The activities of these and similar student groups later led to the formation of the National Association of Chicano Studies (NACS), a faculty and student organization that has subsequently expanded in size and strength. They were key leaders, along with the Brown Berets, in planning and executing the Los Angeles high school walkouts aimed at improving education (Gomez-Quinones 1978; Munoz 1989). Later, as participants in a youth conference sponsored by Corky Gonzales in Colorado, MAYO merged with other student organizations to form the Movimiento Estudiantil Chicano de Aztlan (MEChA) with local affiliates throughout the Southwest. MEChA is still in existence today, with some campus units continuing the direct and confrontational actions of the 1960s, while others now act principally as social clubs, with only occasional efforts at protecting special programs for minority students when challenged.

The political goal of Jose Angel Gutierrez's La Raza Unida Party (United Peoples Party) in Texas was to build an independent third-party throughout the country (Shockley 1974; Garcia and de la Garza 1977; Garcia 1989). This brash move stemmed from a series of successful local election campaigns in small towns in Texas. For a while, Raza Unida gained adherents throughout the Southwest, but ultimately, like most other third-party movements in the United States, it collapsed. The dominant political parties, both Democrat and Republican, were able to undermine the "nationalist" appeal of Raza Unida's platform. Nevertheless, this attempt at a third party encouraged Chicanos for the first time to think of a national, coordinated campaign to participate in the political system. This experience was invaluable, in the sense that subsequent events gained impetus from their example.

Catolicos Por La Raza (Catholics for the People) demanded somewhat tumultuously that the church be made responsive to the needs of the Spanish-speaking poor (Acosta 1973). In the past, the Catholic church usually could take for granted the faithful participation of the Mexican population in religious affairs. Thus, when Catholic activists joined the movement and demanded that the church respond to the social and economic needs of the barrio communities, church leaders stiffened in opposition to such disobedient and unruly behavior. Only after some priests had become involved in the farm-workers movement and anti-Vietnam War protests in the United States, did the church became more responsive. (Interestingly, this coincided with the Theology of Liberation movement among Catholic priests in Latin America.)

Actually, the Catholic church had generally initiated and supported, with moderate success, social and cultural programs addressing poverty and social isolation. The Catholic Youth Organization (CYO) provides a prominent example of these efforts. Due to the American dictum of the separation of church and state, the church seldom played an overt role in political organizing in the Chicano communities. It wasn't until after the 1960s that community-based units such as United Neighborhood Organization (UNO) in Los Angeles and Communities Organized for Public Service (COPS) in San Antonio were formed with participation of church leadership. Although strong numerically, usually such groups concentrated on tangible local issues—for example, reducing auto insurance rates and gang violence—and have only recently expanded to focus on political candidates and their platforms, and thus political change.

An example of the momentous events of the period is provided by the 1968 walkouts in which several thousand students boycotted classes. This incident is important for several reasons: It was the first major urban confrontation in the largest Chicano-populated area in the nation. It was coordinated by numerous groups—teachers, students, and community activists—and afterward, other individuals and organizations of various ideological shades rallied to their defense (Munoz 1989). Most importantly, the event and subsequent developments sparked debate and action not only on the educational front but in a number of different areas. However, education was the pivotal rallying issue. The public educational system historically served to oppress the Chicano population, both culturally and economically. Students subject to this treatment soon became part of the struggle (Gomez-Quinones 1978). Two high school student leaders at that time wrote that "the situation created a climate . . . where students started questioning things. . . . Schools are supposed to service the community and they weren't. Rather, they were more like prisons in the community. They were just doing custodial things as far as keeping students together" (Santana and Esparza 1974:1).

Consciousness-Raising

The reform activities show how far-reaching contacts brought many groups into conflict with the social system. Furthermore, these were not merely sporadic, apolitical confrontations, but well-organized challenges to the power brokers. Participation in the movement allowed adolescents as well as adults the opportunity for positive identity formation, for loyalty to an ideological position is a normal part of that process. Protest activity served a psychological purpose in assuaging the effects of inferiority and marginality. Militancy became the rallying banner for those who confronted Anglo-American institutions. As noted previously, Chicanos challenged every sector, although the extent and nature of the challenges varied from community to community (Knowlton 1975). A small number of groups even advocated taking up arms and went on a spree of terrorist bombings.

The groundswell also enveloped less militant organizations. One was the Association of Mexican-American Educators (AMAE), a moderate group that championed educational reform. Although accused of adhering to an "establishment" orientation, many in this group helped organize the students (Ericksen 1970:59). Some of the more radical teachers, such as Sal Castro, a major leader and spokesman of the walkouts, led the way for change. However, even the less-threatening suggestions of the AMAE moderates created suspicion in the eyes of the authorities. Both moderate and radical elements were in open conflict with the system at different levels. "In fact . . . the differences between them are less important than the similarities that bind them" (Garcia and de la Garza 1977:43).

An old-line (1959) political group, the Mexican-American Political Association (MAPA), steadily evolved under Bert Corona into a more militant organization as the movement spread (Garcia and de la Garza 1977; Gomez-Quinones 1978). The original goals of MAPA were rather moderate, for they stressed ethnic identity, direct electoral politics, and electoral independence. Centered around the personage of Edward Roybal, MAPA had tired of the Democratic party's nonchalant attitude toward the always reliable Mexican voting bloc. The campaign work of MAPA helped elect Roybal to Congress, where he became an influential leader until retiring in 1991. MAPA still plays a role in the state politics of California (Gomez-Quinones 1991).

Countless individuals and groups remained in the background but contributed immensely to the cause. For example, the Mexican-American Action Committee (MAAC) was founded in 1966 in Los Angeles by young professionals who spanned the political spectrum but agreed on one goal: social action. Because of or despite this ideological diversity, by 1968 they were responsible for helping other groups and causes that caught the public eye. Members of the MAAC played instrumental roles in MEChA, the Brown Berets, the high school walkouts, and various educational and political reform actions. Among the participants of this group were individuals who subsequently became political officials, several prominent activists, and even local judges who got their start in politics during this time.

Step-Up in Militancy: Aztlan Nation

The formation of the southwestern regional body known as Movimiento Estudiantil Chicano de Aztlan (MEChA; the Chicano Student Movement of Aztlan) emphasized the increasingly common use of the word "Aztlan." This ancient Aztec name for the Southwest came to symbolize the Chicano destiny (Chavez 1984). Student groups, meeting in Denver in 1969, developed a historically based type of nationalism (El Plan Espiritual de Aztlan, 1970). Their goal of an Aztlan nation was one instance of the recurrent call for Chicano separatism. (Other examples are the Sonora Immigration in 1856, the San Diego Plan in 1914–1915, and the Sinarquistas in the 1940s.) However, separatism in this case meant more than a return to earlier, perhaps indigenous, sociocultural traditions. It also implied the use of modern resources and techniques for community control and development (Garcia, I. 1989). One of the spokesmen, Rodolfo "Corky" Gonzales (1967:3), wrote an epic poem that explained an aspect of the Chicano dilemma, as this excerpt shows:

> I am Joaquin,
> Lost in a world of confusion,
> Caught up in a whirl of a
> gringo society
> Confused by the rules,
> Scorned by attitudes,
> Suppressed by manipulation,
> And destroyed by modern society.
> My fathers
> have lost the economic battle
> and won
> the struggle of cultural survival
> and now
> I must choose.

Gonzales, the poet-politician, chose a separatist Aztlan. Others resolved the dilemma by working for cultural retention but a fairer economic integration, to obtain what they viewed as the best of two worlds. Still others sought total social and economic equality for Chicanos in the United States, with or without the retention of distinct cultural traditions. This divergence in strategies in some ways characterizes the ways in which the two major political parties have responded to the Chicano population. Democratic leaders have generally espoused the need for social and economic programs to help the less advantaged members of the minority community. However, the strings attached to this advocacy often entail that Chicanos forgo cultural and nationalistic goals and follow an assimilationist path as strict "Americans." Republicans, on the other hand, have only recently attempted to woo Chicanos, but the enticement for support is that Chicanos buy into "corporate" America and all that this entails, including the interventionist policies of the United States government in Central and Latin America, as well as other parts of the troubled world. Nevertheless, part of the Chicano population is attracted to Republican conservatism and its emphasis on family moral values. Thus, the Chicano vote has become a "swing" vote in the United States, with presidential candidates often becoming involved in what has been termed "fiesta politics" (Moore and Pachon 1985).

The Chicano reform movements were viewed with suspicion by much of the American public, who often misinterpreted the self-determination efforts of Chicanos as attacks on democracy, and by the political and economic elite, who correctly viewed them as a threat to some of the privileges they controlled.

August 29 Moratorium

Various actions were taken to stem the new wave of Chicano self-determination. Throughout the Southwest there were dozens of incidents, but one example will suffice here. On a hot summer day, August 29, 1970, the largest Chicano demonstration of the period took place. The peaceful marchers were protesting the Vietnam intervention policies of the United States, and in particular the high Chicano casualty rate there (Mirande 1987). Over twenty thousand people from throughout the Southwest congregated at an East Los Angeles park for a rally. After a short time, sheriff's deputies broke it up (Morales 1972; Sanchez 1978). When the police lined up to intimidate the protesters, some monitors attempted unsuccessfully to hold the crowd back. Nevertheless, several hundred policemen drove the people from the park. In the aftermath, some people rioted, destroying over a million dollars in property on Whittier Boulevard, a main thoroughfare. Three people were killed, including Chicano reporter Ruben Salazar, and hundreds of others arrested (Shorris 1992). Scores of people were harassed, and one leader, Corky Gonzales, was apprehended and jailed because he "suspiciously" was carrying $300 in cash (Marin 1975:114).

A program of indoctrination was a major thrust of the counter-measures to this and other events. The media, politicians who preached "law and order," local and federal law enforcement officials, the court system, and other functionaries began to offer a negative assessment of the social ferment. At times their criticisms were correct. More often, however, they missed the mark. They characterized public protest as un-American and unlawful, despite protest organizers' efforts to ensure legal compliance at rallies and meetings. Some government leaders considered even minor differences of opinion to be an attack on the United States. A Mexican-American congressman, generally regarded at the time as a liberal, nevertheless felt it necessary to disavow any ties to the protests: "It may well be that I agree with the goals stated by the militants; but whether I agree or disagree, I do not now nor have I ever believed that the end justifies the means" (Gonzalez 1974:260). That the protest organizers had never suggested otherwise, and had in fact maintained discipline until police intervention, was apparently lost on the national leadership. The Brown Berets, prominent among the organizers of the protest, began to lose support and popularity in its aftermath (Acuna 1988). Nevertheless, the event on August 29 turned out to be a major turning point for the Chicano movement.

Comparisons with Other Groups and Counterreactions

Chicanos were not alone in their protests during this time for other groups, blacks and Indians in particular, were taking issue with similar features of the social structure. As a result, many minority group members began to perceive the social-class roots of inequality and injustice (Gomez-Quinones 1978). They were joined by white radicals in articulating and acting out their criticisms of government actions.

Developments tended to undermine the social movements. For example, many Chicanos, particularly those who were moderate or more conservative, were co-opted into various institutional networks, thus dulling the sharp edge of the movement. Some observers viewed this as a deliberate plan and pointed to the aftermath of the 1968 walkouts. The school board had established a community group, the Educational Issues Coordinating Committee (EICC), which succeeded in excluding the militants involved in the protests. Thus, those who governed the schools solidified their position of power over the Chicano community (Munoz 1974). In other situations authorities also supported Chicano groups favorable to the status quo in order to counter advocates of social change—thus creating intragroup fighting and slowing progress (Foley et al. 1977). In short, cooptation and accommodation worked in tandem to blunt the tip of the social movement. What one pundit referred to as the politics of putting someone into your hip pocket was very much the order of the day. Indeed, it is safe to state that the Democratic party picked up what pieces were left and helped redirect much of what energy remained in the Chicano community; often this meant keeping a moderate lid on social ferment in order to play it safe.

Furthermore, the Chicano organizations that were making the most headway attracted another type of law enforcement attention. Like other militant organizations, these groups were infiltrated by undercover agents, or agents provocateurs, who managed to disrupt and misdirect them. One way they did this was to encourage internal conflicts between the organizational leaders (Munoz 1974). These provocateurs became full-time "militants" (with long hair, beards, and other visible paraphernalia) in order to redirect the movement into negative activities. David Sanchez (1978:6), former prime minister of the Brown Berets, had this to say about the problem: "The infiltrators were one of the main reasons why the Brown Beret organization was so often mis-

A scene from one of the series of Chicano Moratoriums from 1970 and 1971.

Marchers claiming racial pride.

Rioting after the Moratorium and the death of Ruben Salazar, a Chicano newspaper man, at the Silver Dollar.

interpreted and misrepresented. The infiltrators served as agitators of violence!" Intimidation, harassment, and arrests characterized this period.

Factionalism and Aftermath of the Conflict

As in most historical periods of ferment, there were also intragroup struggles. In addition to the macrolevel contradictions, there were microlevel differences that set Chicano against Chicano. Sometimes these conflicts were as heated as those occurring in the national arena (Gomez-Quinones 1978). Not surprisingly, Chicanos argued with one another over the ideology and methods that would best effect change. Programs for change ranged from total assimilation to white middle-class America to separatism, and they were vociferously debated at national conferences or in smaller units such as college MEChA chapters. Almost as much energy was expended in these intragroup conflicts as in united actions. Many people and organizations were casualties as a result. Besides the disintegration of some worthwhile organizations, the toll was often that Chicanos were alienated from each other and worse, from themselves. Intragroup conflicts had some good aspects, though, as indicated by Gomez-Quinones (1978:5): "Factionalism is a part of development, positive or negative; if positive it strengthens progressive ideological clarity and organizational coherence. Negative factionalism causes confusion and weakens organization."

In summary, the 1960s movement made its mark. The process is still unfolding, and so, of course, is a proper understanding of it. Aiming for the structural and political overhaul of the establishment, movement activists assuredly missed their mark. However, mass protest did have some positive outcomes. One such gain was in the learning and experimentation that transpired and the knowledge that people thus acquired. With this insight they might be better prepared for another day, or perhaps be able now to more successfully penetrate the closed political system that drove them to such extreme measures. However, Munoz (1974:120) pointed out the movement's shortcomings, which were largely due to "the lack of a critical analysis on the part of Movement leadership of the nature of Chicano oppression." Clearly, a careful assessment of the impact of this conflict is in order.

Change: 1970s and Beyond

State of the People

It is difficult to speak of an aftermath of the Chicano movement and the conflict surrounding it, for both the movement and the conflict continue in abated fashion. There were certainly initial victories as there were also setbacks. Some measures have withstood the test of time and blossomed. Even with major changes and improvements, many of the conditions that gave rise to the movement are still present—for example, underrepresentation of Chicanos in social, economic, and political positions of leadership; discord between the community and local authorities; and lower-than-average income and education. The dramatic headlines of the 1960s are gone and an air of general normality has returned to the Chicano community, although activism still erupts periodically to address unresolved issues. However, the norms have changed, although in many instances only subtly, with Chicanos now having more direct participation in the political process.

The movement has altered the consciousness of Mexican Americans with a ferment that began after WW II but peaked in the civil rights era. The highly publicized assertions of Chicano rights and cultural legacies have led some in the community to goals similar to those stemming from the Mexican Revolution: that "the people refuse all outside help, every imported scheme, every idea lacking some profound relationship to their intimate feelings, and that instead they turn to themselves" (Paz 1961:147). Others have built on the earlier militancy in more traditionally American reform efforts, directing their energies toward fuller Chicano participation in the benefits of the larger society. As Samora and Simon noted (1977:227), Chicanos have learned the maxim of American democratic politics that "the wheel that squeaks the loudest gets the most grease." (They have also learned its corollary of what happens when one begins to seriously threaten the ruling elite, as the old Asian adage has it: the nail that sticks out gets hammered.) Others have sought to redirect the focus of the 1960s to even more far-reaching efforts, including critical analyses of the basic structures of society and socioeconomic stratification. Finally, there are still a few who continue to attribute Chicano problems to Chicanos themselves.

Chicanozaje

The development of Chicanozaje or Chicanismo, as it is sometimes called, is the most pervasive sign of the altered consciousness of Mexican Americans. The term "Chicano" was seized upon by militants, especially youths, in the 1960s to express disdain for their "hyphenated" status as Mexican Americans and to reconnect with their Mexican heritage. While many in the Mexican-American community rejected the term, associating it with the vulgarities of street life, its use spread until even establishment figures, white middle-class leaders included, had adopted it. In recent years more sophisticated objections to Chicanozaje have been raised; including those who argue that a "noble savage" interpretation of Chicano culture must be resolutely avoided, as there are still many unresolved problems to be addressed and many cultural traits still in gestation. This viewpoint, however, downplays the importance of the all-encompassing scope of the word "Chicano," which covers the diversity of Mexican-American lifestyles (Gomez-Quinones 1978).

Generally, Chicanozaje includes a historical awareness of the Chicanos' role as oppressed members of society. Chicanos stress the acts of being (how the past shaped them) and becoming (how they will shape the future). Equally important, they now realize that their past is a complex one of multiple heritages both ancient and new, made up of Indian, Spanish, Mexican, and Anglo elements (Campa 1993; Bacalski-Martinez 1979). The historical record shows that a succession of different identities reflects the laboring role and social status of the people at different time periods, suggested in the categories and in the passage of time from indigenous to peasant to immigrant.

Moreover, this complex, multiple background was taken off the shelf to which it had been consigned, full of negative influences, and was now extolled as a positive virtue. Much of this regeneration of cultural awareness aided political developments and maturation (Gutierrez, D. 1995). Chicano students and activists made pilgrimages to Mexico to recapture their "lost" heritage. Through these contacts, the Mexican government has become informed of this interaction. Mexican leaders in high positions helped establish cultural and student exchange programs to reconnect with the vast territory of the north. For a while, a strong current of international, albeit informal, cooperation began to take shape, with each group showing interest and involvement in the political situation in their respective countries. In large part, these activities comprised a move to rekindle ties with the territory and people stripped from Mexico over one hundred years ago. This striving was exemplified by wave after wave of immigration as Mexicans returned to their native land. (However, this immigration has elicited quite different reactions since the recent economic crisis in Mexico and increases in unemployment in the United States. Anti-immigrant attitudes in the 1990s have become more widespread and fueled political debates in the United States, especially in the Southwest.)

Because of their complex background, a whole range of cultural variation is possible for Chicanos. Some can favor the European side, others the Indian, or they can move in between, seeking the cultural style that fits them (Bernal and Knight 1993; Sanchez 1976). Chicanozaje thus expands the boundaries of the age-old mestizaje tradition of Mexico. It is a fluid, dual cultural membership that gives a deeper meaning to the term "Chicano." This fluid sense of identity has been referred to as "personas mexicanas" (the many identities of Mexicans): "Pigeonholing oneself with just one ethnic identity may have been appropriate during earlier phases of our American and international history, but our current period of introspection is drawing us together into a 'global village'. . . It is incumbent on all of us to think multiculturally and transnationally; to become 'border crossers'" (Vigil 1997:2).

Chicano Arts

Both aspects of Chicanozaje, the past and the future, are apparent in the blossoming of Chicano arts since the 1960s. Contemplative artists incorporated a change of consciousness. In very profound and complex ways, the processes of acculturation through several historical eras have helped generate various cultural influences, which Chicanos can claim for inspiration. With the modest support cultural pluralism is now receiving in the United States, this regenerative and innovative quality has grown. Contemplative artists have incorporated into their art a consciousness of political change. Poets, writers, filmmakers, and muralists are known to create and maintain this state of mind. East Los Angeles

Mestizaje heritage.

Chicano painters and muralists, and others as well, have interpreted the cultural-historical legacies of barrio dwellers. By creating a work of art, they have brought a new awareness and focus to the people's experiences. They have especially reflected the interests and concerns of the people and neighborhoods where this art is found, showing the pride, anger, and futility in the faces of its characters. The murals draw especially from historical inspirations such as the Mexican Revolution and the Indian legacies, thus reminding viewers of the rich past and revolutionary potential of the Chicano people (Cockcroft and Barnet-Sanchez 1993; Griswold del Castillo, McKenna, and Yarbro-Bejarano 1991).

This type of consciousness-raising can be found in several areas of expression. For example, the Teatro Campesino (Rural Workers Theater) began as a medium to inform farm workers and others about the 1965–1970 grape boycott (Broyles 1990; Broyles-Gonzales 1994). Later it

A scene from Zoot Suit *by Luis Valdez at the Center Theatre Group / Mark Taper Forum in Los Angeles.*

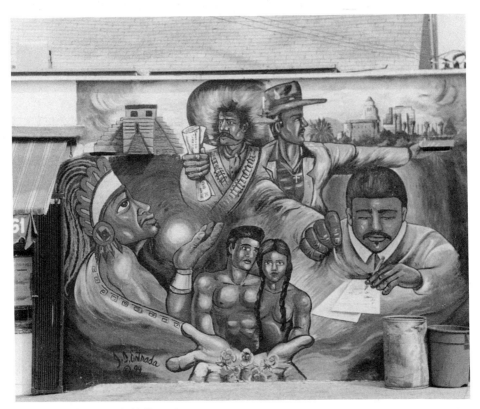

Cultural heritage and diversity.

became a model for teatro groups for youth throughout the nation. These theater groups used dramatic interpretation to expose the conditions of the Chicano people. Theater in the Southwest has always served to entertain and instruct, and so it became an effective means of raising cultural and political awareness (Bacalski-Martinez 1979). Teatros have combined humor and satire to portray the multiple Chicano heritage. In this manner, a consciousness is generated. People laugh, cry, or feel pain at the same moment, as if they were all of a similar mind. "All of the dramatic techniques used by the teatro were directed toward depicting the political situations and offering alternative solutions. The goal of the techniques was to produce immediate empathy in order to motivate action. They were symbolic of what 'ought' to have been done in reality" (Garcia 1978:40). The original Teatro Campesino, led by Luis Valdez, presented the successful play *Zoot Suit*, and later *La Bamba*, which familiarized audiences with Chicano urban experiences. Culture Clash, a more recent theater group, has continued this tradition of political education.

Educational Transformations

Similar changes are taking place in the Chicano educational experience. From Operation Head Start to the university, teachers and students are comparing notes on the past and present (Samora and Simon 1977). In this exchange, each learns from the other. Since most of the teachers were middle class in the midst of the movement, students regularly reminded them of community needs. As a result, teachers found themselves responding to subtle pressures, even though they may have left the barrio years before. Eventually, many of these same students became teachers and helped reshaped the learning landscape. Student awareness was also altered as teachers presented knowledge previously unavailable to them. Garfield High School in East Los Angeles exemplifies this change, as students now compete on an equal basis with all other city students in mathematics and other college-prep courses. Students have embraced a new social concern, as initially heralded by El Plan de Santa Barbara in the 1970s, continuing to call for the university to serve the community (Gomez-Quinones 1978).

One program offered by reformers was for bilingual education, an idea that garnered increasing support from Anglo officials. According to experts, Chicano educational liabilities have stemmed from a cultural, and specifically, a linguistic source. To correct this, schools were to give equal time and attention to English and Spanish. Thus, Chicanos and others would learn to appreciate their culture and language. Gradually, it was reasoned, the sense of Chicano inferiority engendered by traditional schooling would give way to a positive attitude

Defending bilingual education.

toward themselves and education, and traditional Anglo ethnocentrism would begin its demise.

Government-supported experimental bilingual education programs began to tackle the "cultural" problem. It is no coincidence that most of these programs were started at the height of the movement in the 1960s (de la Garza 1979; Valencia 1991), although even reformist notions based on cultural criteria were previously considered too radical. After the programs were initiated, however, it was too late to rescind them. Both Anglo and Chicano educators found that the bilingual programs in large part improved student school performances (U.S. Commission on Civil Rights 1975); recent evidence generally supports this position (Trueba 1991). Parents and community leaders strongly supported bilingual education, for they had participated in its creation and implementation. The battle is not over, however. Counterattacks on bilingual education are mounting, as critics (sometimes including parents) underscore how these programs slow learning in English and retard integration into American society. An "English-language-only" movement has also gained national media attention. In spite of these attacks, research continues to show the success of bilingual education programs.

During the late 1980s and the early 1990s, student groups began again to struggle for educational reform. In large part, this reclamation

Protest to save old Mexican pueblo of Los Angeles.

effort was headed by a new generation of Chicano students. Most of these leaders and participants came from the "1.5 generation"—immigrants who arrived in the United States as children, and were raised in a bilingual and bicultural setting (Vigil 1997). UCLA students mobilized in the spring of 1993 to push for a separate Chicano Studies department. The students were motivated by their frustration with decades of neglect and undermining of the interdisciplinary Chicano Studies program and major. Moreover, their anger was aggravated by the fact that UCLA Chancellor Young announced his intent to reject an enhanced status for Chicano Studies shortly after the death of Cesar Chavez. A coalition of student, faculty, and community activists went on a hunger strike to convince the university's administrators that this change was long overdue. Public and media attention focused on this event, which ended with a partial victory for the activists; a new Chicano Studies department was established and named the Cesar Chavez Center.

Revolution or Reform?

While reforms made a contribution, some claim that leaders of these efforts exploited the Chicano movement (Munoz 1989; Gutierrez 1995). Rocco (1974:168) has argued that "this type of effort accepts and legitimizes, thus reinforcing, the institutions and processes through which demands are made." Thus, it is said, while such reforms and others—the Southwest is now dotted with Chicano agencies and centers—have ameliorated suffering in Chicano communities and afforded the opportunity for more familiarity with dominant institutions, they have also allowed the same institutions to "co-opt" community leaders; indeed, it may be argued that some of these leaders come to the table "pre-co-opted," and thus are motivated primarily by self-interest. Activist critics are quick to point out that in most instances, reformers' purse strings are not in the hands of Chicanos.

So far only the reform efforts within a cultural nationalist framework have been discussed. Other factors and forces also were important, as Chicanos were committed to improving their overall standard of living—schools, jobs, and so on—and they worked hard for these goals. Nevertheless, it seems that the spirit of the times and primary impetus for change was culturally based. Leaders tended to emphasize cultural rights as a precondition leading to advances in other areas, such as in the political arena. This orientation has remained strong in the Chicano community, as even the Brown Berets enjoyed a brief resurgence in the late 1980s and early 1990s.

While cultural transformations were under way, some weak (even barely perceptible) class and color changes occurred. The spirit of the Mexican Revolution was instrumental in this slight stirring since cultural nationalists drew on the egalitarian revolutionary ideas of such leaders as Emiliano Zapata, Pancho Villa, and Ricardo Flores Magon. This imagery and call to action has continued its appeal with time and was renewed by the Zapatista army revolt in Chiapas in 1994. In contrast, there is still a strong ideology that possessions and material wealth are more important than people (Rocco 1974). The movement gave hope for future generations, but the 1970s put brakes on those aspirations. In fact, for a while, especially in the 1980s "Decade of the Hispanic," it was thought that sheer demographic increases in the population would force changes; later, one observer quipped, "now that the Decade of the Hispanic is over, what do we do now?" Moreover, recent events show that Chicanos have tended to acquiesce to the conservative atmosphere of the 1980s and 1990s, even as major increases in Chicano political representation occur (Gomez-Quinones 1990; De La Garza and De Sipo 1996). For example, in 1996, there were more than fifty-four hundred elected and appointed officials nationwide, and in California, the fastest growing Mexican/Latino state in the nation, representatives in the state legislature have increased from seven in 1991 to thirteen in 1996. With these changes, however, many have joined the Republican party while others, now secure in the middle class, have identified with conservative forces in the Democratic party who shun social programs for the disadvantaged. Even organizations with long records of activism have formed commercial alliances with very conservative business firms in return for contributions to their social programs.

One significant outcome of the lull in progressive changes was the efforts on the part of Latino politicians to organize a national Latino network, primarily comprised of Chicanos and Puerto Ricans, but inclusive of other Spanish-surname, Spanish-speaking pressure groups. NALEO (National Association of Latino Elected and Appointed Officials) successfully attempted in the late 1970s to establish a common meeting ground for lobbying for Latino issues, such as political underrepresentation, low average income and education levels, and so on. NALEO then broadened its agenda and took on the work of encouraging immigrants throughout the country to become naturalized citizens. Interestingly, former Congressman Edward Roybal from Los Angeles was instrumental in starting this group, just as he was with the CSO in the late 1940s and MAPA in the late 1950s.

Another move, led by Willie Velasquez from Texas, was to coordinate a region-wide voter-registration drive. The Southwest Voter Registration Education Project (SVREP) successfully targeted Mexican-American districts with low registration and voter-turnout patterns, and increased the size of the voting bloc over the years. Gradually, the organization gained a wider appeal among Chicanos and won respect from established politicians, who, of course, want to facilitate access to the Chicano vote. Much of this activity was aided by the Voting Rights Act in 1965, which was expanded in 1975 to include language minorities.

Equally important to the push was the work of the Mexican American Legal Defense and Education Fund (MALDEF) and the National Council of La Raza (NCLR). MALDEF had formed in the early 1970s to assist local agencies and organizations in providing services to the community. As it grew in stature and expanded its base, it eventually focused on political issues. One of them was to challenge political district boundaries, which historically had gerrymandered Chicanos to dilute their vote, a widespread practice throughout the Southwest. In Los Angeles, MALDEF, along with other plaintiffs, succeeded in getting the courts to redraw county supervisory district lines to better reflect the large, concentrated Mexican-American neighborhoods. Not one of the five supervisors was Chicano (or other minority), and none was female. In a subsequent election to fill a vacant seat on the Board of Supervisors, then Los Angeles City Councilwoman Gloria Molina won and her victory became a cause celebre. The National Council of La Raza (NCLR), begun in 1968, has become recognized as a Washington, D.C., lobby force for Latino issues. While there is some disagreement on just who NCLR represents, there is no doubt that its presence in the nation's capital has placed Latino national concerns in the forefront.

Chicano Power!

The Tomas Rivera Center, a California-based think tank named after a deceased Chicano scholar and prolific writer, has more recently contributed to the movement toward reform with a series of studies and initiatives aimed at policy formulation and implementation on such pressing issues as education, politics, and economic conditions.

Social Class and Gender Equality

The median family income of the Spanish-surnamed population in 1969 was $7,080 and that of the Anglos $10,750—a sizable gap (Briggs, Fogel, and Schmidt 1977). Ten years later, Chicano family income was still about 70 percent of that for whites, or $11,742 as opposed to approximately $16,000 (Thurow 1979; Daniels 1991). By 1990, Chicano families earned an average of $21,025 versus $33,142 for non-Hispanic families, that is, only two-thirds as much (Segura 1992). Moreover, the 1990 census showed that while family incomes had improved, 25 percent of Chicano families were still below the poverty line (Meier and Ribera 1993). In Los Angeles between 1969 and 1985, there was an overall increase in poverty, with almost all of it stemming from the Chicano population (Moore and Vigil 1993; Ong 1988). Statistics also indicate that Mexican male workers in the late 1980s earned only 57 percent of the earnings of white males (Reimers 1992). Even controlling for generational change and social mobility to the middle class through skilled and white-collar occupations, there is still a relative gap in income. Several researchers have emphasized the persistence of discrimination as the primary barrier (Bean and Tienda 1987; Romero 1979).

A national issue that has been steadily gaining attention in recent decades deals with equal opportunity for women, another class factor (Hondagneu-Sotelo 1994). Chicanas (Mexican-American women) are very much involved in that struggle, and in fact their role affects important cultural and socioeconomic dimensions (Del Castillo 1990; Melville 1980). In the 1980s there was a tremendous jump in Chicana participation in the labor force, more than double the rate for women generally (Segura 1992). Since historical conditions have relegated Chicanos to the lowest positions, Chicanas are even more disadvantaged than non-Chicana women (Gonzales 1979). In 1969, the earnings of working Chicanas averaged only a third of those of white female workers. This discrepancy in wage levels has diminished but it does still exist; in 1990, Chicanas earned much less than non-Hispanic women (Meier and Ribera 1993). Average earnings for 1990 were: Chicanas, $8,110, versus non-Hispanic women, $11,245 (Segura 1992); however, the pay gap for men was even larger: Chicanos, $12,107, versus non-Hispanic males, $21,267. The wage gap for Chicanas is largely due to the usual restriction of Chicanas to low-wage, low-status jobs, such as domestic and agricultural work, which offer little opportunity for promotion (Hondagneu-Sotelo 1994; Segura 1990). Chicanas and women from Mexico, like their male counterparts, are part of a "transnational" reservoir of labor, adding further to the importance of migration and immigration to any discussion of social-class issues (Ruiz and Tiano 1987; Martinez and McCaughan 1990).

However, the Chicano movement as a whole has been hesitant to address gender issues and problems of male domination. When Chicanas raised the issue of gender inequities, some movement activists responded by arguing that feminist concerns diverted attention from the "real" issues of racism and class exploitation. Chicano intellectuals "interpreted the condition of Mexican men and women to be synonymous; gender was irrelevant in determining life experience and power" (Orozco 1990:12). Feminism was also viewed to be Anglo, middle-class, and bourgeois, and Chicanas were thus denounced as being traitors to "la causa" (Oboler 1995). This resulted in many Chicanas initially being reticent in voicing their demands. Slowly and inexorably, however, a more concerted feminist perspective developed to generate increased information and insights to fill the ethnohistorical gap of knowledge about the obviously neglected half of the Chicano people.

Confronting these difficulties, Chicanas have fought for equality and justice within their community organizations. Demands have included welfare rights, rehabilitation programs for *pintas* (female ex-convicts), safeguards against male violence, access to birth control, and the right to refuse forced sterilization (Oboler 1995). One Chicana, Francisca Flores, played a major role in politics and other Chicana issues by founding the California League of Mexican American Women (Meier and Ribera 1993).

The heroine of the classic labor film *Salt of the Earth* underscores the Chicana plight with these angry and insightful words (aimed not only at her husband but presumably at all minority men): "Do you feel better having someone lower than you? Whose neck shall I stand on to make me feel superior? And what will I get out of it? I don't want anything lower than I am. I'm low enough already. I want to rise. And push everything up with me as I go." Chicanas and other minority women are actively pursuing the end of their position as "twice a minority" (Melville 1980).

United States, Mexico, and Undocumented Immigrants

Chicano economic inequality is intertwined with the continuing saga of "as the United States goes, so goes Mexico!" Recent events illustrate the growing complexity of problems resulting from multinational corporate entanglements. For example, in an effort to escape from United States labor unions and environmental restrictions, many corporations (known as multinationals because they transcend national boundaries and move to whatever nation provides the cheapest workers) have built plants (*maquiladoras*) just across the Mexican border, to tap the cheap source of labor (Fernandez 1977). Many of these maquiladoras, to gain added advantage from wage disparities, employ mostly women, who in Mexico as here, tend to receive lower wages than men. Maquiladoras have increased urban growth, with the rise of "sister" border cities along the United States–Mexican boundary (Arreola and Curtis 1993). On the Mexican side, residents might earn only 20 to 30 percent of what they would for comparable work in the United States (Price 1973; Gann and Duignan 1986). As an upshot of these economic ties and transactions, social relations and cultural exchanges between Americans and Mexicans on both sides of the border have multiplied exponentially. A whole new literature devoted to the phenomena of "border culture" has arisen, with some observers even coining a new regional term, MexiAmerica (Alvarez 1995:4). Both sides of the border have become more important, as northern Mexico now is the source of many agricultural products targeted for U.S. communities (Heyman 1991; Alvarez 1990).

In addition, in 1993 Mexico joined the United States and Canada to form a North American Free Trade Agreement (NAFTA), thus further-

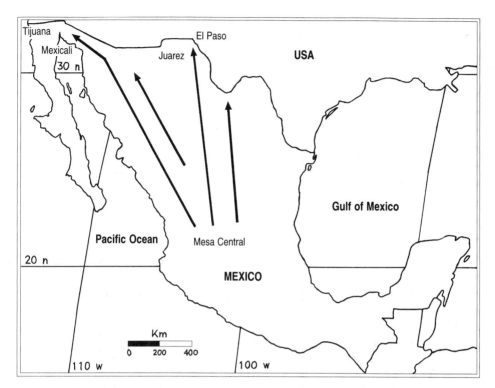

Immigration routes in the 1960s.

ing the economic integration of the nations, but also adding uncertainty to workers' futures on both sides of the border. Organized labor expressed concerns that NAFTA would lead to loss of jobs in the United States, and environmentalists feared increased pollution because of less stringent regulations in Mexico. In January of 1994, as NAFTA took effect, the Zapatista Army of National Liberation (or EZLN, Ejercito Zapatista de Liberacion Nacional) dramatically surfaced in one of the neglected indigenous, peasant regions of southern Mexico to challenge the Mexican government (Collier and Quaratiello 1994). Their demands for attention and access to resources included mention of NAFTA. The latter was a strategy to shake the Mexican government and bring correctives to the serious state of underdevelopment in the region. Such a reaction serves to underscore the importance of macrostructural developments in transnational economic growth and globalization, including large-scale and continuing migration.

The 1970s witnessed the largest presence of undocumented Mexican workers in the United States, anywhere from 2 to 12 million (Cornelius 1978), and this transnational process continues to the present with the figures remaining more or less the same for the 1980s and

1990s. Previous periods of high immigration were the 1920s, the 1950s, and the 1960s. Significantly, in each immigration wave in this century, most of the newcomers originated in the same central and northern regions and states. Recently, however, there are many more urban dwellers from these regions, and a much larger number of indigenous peasants from southern Mexico (and Central America) have begun to alter the figures (Cornelius and Bustamante 1989).

These workers fill the low-paid, unskilled jobs no one else desires and, indeed, provide important services; and as earlier, they often settle in whatever open spaces are available near work locations (Chavez 1992). Some observers have duly noted that these jobs are low paying. More important is the labor force's "flexibility and disposability" to fit a fluid and volatile economic system subject to periodic recessions and downturns (Cornelius and Bustamante 1989). In fact, "such labor is regarded simply as a windfall to a greedy minority of U.S. employers intent on protecting or enlarging their profit margins; a subsidy to middle-class U.S. consumers who do not want to pay more for their restaurant meals, clothing, agricultural produce, and personal services; and a social safety valve—an employment-welfare program—for Mexico" (Cornelius and Bustamante 1989:26). In this assessment, economic restructuring in the U.S. and consumer demands have made a reliance on immigrant labor that much more important (Massey et al. 1987).

Immigration has nevertheless become a focus of concern for many people, including government officials, and some of the solutions to the "problem" have betrayed continuing attitudes of a discriminatory nature. For example, in the 1970s, Congressman Peter Rodino presented a bill that would allow employers to ask for place of birth identification from anyone "appearing" to be Mexican. Obviously, such a measure would infringe on the civil rights of millions of Mexican Americans born in the United States. To resolve this difficulty, one naive apologist suggested that native Mexicans could wear badges. Congressional struggles over this issue mirrored the national mood until the Immigration Reform and Control Act (IRCA) was passed in 1986. The passage of IRCA was intended to resolve this problem but failed to do so. Meanwhile, anti-immigrant fervor has reached a panic level, especially with the passage of state and federal legislation curtailing services to noncitizen immigrants. This disposition has engulfed affirmative action and other hard-won civil rights laws and regulations to fan a general mood of antipathy toward ethnic minorities.

For the first time in American history, there are as many noncitizen Mexicans (and other Latinos) as there are registered Mexican voters in the United States. This means that numerical superiority cannot translate into political power unless all Latinos, documented and undocumented, participate in the political process. NALEO and SVREP, noted

above, are striving toward this goal and expend much energy on inform-
ing unregistered Latinos of the importance of voting in the United
States. Democrats and Republicans alike are watching these developments with increasing interest, knowing that in certain sections of the
nation—mainly in the Southwest, Midwest, and Florida—Mexicans (and
Latinos) can influence election outcomes. In fact, the degree of observation will certainly increase in light of the recent 1996 elections in a
Republican stronghold of Orange County, California, where a Chicana
defeated a hard right-winger in a close contest. The event caused a furor
on several levels, not least because of the discovery that a small number
of the newly naturalized Mexicans had voted prematurely, before being
sworn in.

Integral to these political changes are the legal issues surrounding
immigration. As noted, since the 1970s, different attempts have been
made in Congress to control the tide of immigration. During the 1980s,
Cesar Chavez and the UFW supported immigration reform proposals
that resulted in the passage of IRCA in 1986. However, many Chicano
activists challenged this legislation, some aspects of which they considered racist and discriminatory. Nevertheless, Chavez argued that IRCA
would improve working conditions by allowing undocumented immigrants to unionize (Griswold del Castillo and Garcia 1995).

Currently, the debate continues on various political fronts as to
whether American labor will benefit from IRCA in keeping down the
competition from foreign labor. Employers' efforts to screen job appli-
cants with proof of citizenship or legal resident alien registration cards,
a part of IRCA stipulations, is also proving to be a difficult task. Further,
the movement of large numbers of immigrants, legal and undocumented,
continues. Fewer undocumented immigrants applied for legal residence
under IRCA than some observers expected, but enough (about 3.8 million) to demonstrate that making a home in the United States is important. Recently, the Mexican government has moved in the direction of
binationality, allowing immigrants to maintain Mexican citizenship
with full rights while also becoming American citizens.

The renewed interest on the part of the Mexican government to
keep ties with the millions of Mexicans who reside on this side of the border is a recent development. Previously, Chicano leaders and intellectuals had firmed up a connection for mostly cultural and educational
purposes. However, it is apparent today that both Chicano and Mexican
leaders realize that a continuing flow of information and exchanges is
essential to political situations on both sides of the border. Testimony to
the importance of this budding relationship is seen in the electoral campaign visit made by Cuauhtemoc Cardenas, the loser by a close margin
in the contested 1988 Mexican presidential election. The subsequent
postelection visit of the Mexican President Salinas was also, in part, an

Service workers organize.

attempt to curry favor with the Mexican population, in both Mexico and the United States.

Growing Chicano Strength

The resistance mounted against IRCA, although unsuccessful, nevertheless shows the increasing strength of the Chicano community. Chicanos are increasingly outspoken in American politics and more adept at forming alliances with liberal whites and others. Earlier demonstrations of this resolve is the successful (but short-lived) outcome of the United Farm Workers' call for a boycott of California grapes and lettuce—farmers eventually recognized the union and California enacted progressive farm labor laws. While most of these changes were partially turned back in the 1980s, UFW continues to attract attention and support for migrant workers. Similarly, the third party thrust of La Raza Unida at times influenced local elections—even winning several—and since then, Chicano elected and appointed officials have increased in number at all levels of government. The Catholic Church has successfully organized barrio families into large neighborhood groups such as Communities Organized for Public Service (COPS) in San Antonio, The Organization of the Northwest (TON) in Chicago, and the United Neighborhood Organization (UNO) in Los Angeles. Increasingly, the large and vocal immigrant community has become a part of this community-based organizing. The 1992 Los Angeles upheavals were characterized as a poor-people's rebellion, and many of the participants were Mexican or Latino, which shows the intense disenchantment of part of this population.

Both small and large demonstrations of discontent and strength have by no means overcome all institutional discrimination against Chicano leadership, and factionalism among Chicano politicians has also interfered with advances. Still, the few protests and eruptions are sufficient to prove that a growing awareness and sophistication in tactics and strategy is being amassed in dealing with the barriers and obstacles in U.S. society.

Indeed, there is ample reason to expect Chicano consciousness and political influence to continue to blossom. Two cabinet-level officers, Henry Cisneros from Texas and Federico Pena from Colorado, played a vital role in the administration of President Bill Clinton in the 1990s. The Chicano population is also increasing rapidly and by early in the next century will be the largest minority group in the United States. Some observers are predicting that the Chicano population of Los Angeles will soon grow sufficiently to make California the first "minority-majority" state in the contiguous United States. The continuing massive immigration from Mexico will not only enlarge the Chicano population in the United States, but it will strengthen the links between the Chicano community and Mexico (Rocco 1974; Gomez-Quinones 1978). Moreover, it will add luster to Chicanozaje imagery (Ramirez 1985).

Of great significance to this growth in numbers and rise in consciousness is the understanding associated with "macrostructural identities." In other words, there may have been cultural differences among the earliest Mexicans, such as Aztecs varying from Tarascans or Mayas, but nearly all of them became peasants in the Spanish era and remained so in the subsequent Mexican period. Later, with further regional and worldwide economic and political revampments, regional variation among peasants from places such as Oaxaca, Yucatan, or Morelos became blurred when they joined the massive migrations of the twentieth century (Kearney 1996). Thus, macrostructural identities of indigene (Indian), peasant, and immigrant characterize the lives of the bulk of the Mexican people, even while holding cultural identity constant.

The legacy of the Chicano movement has not yet been worked out. Former activists have taken different routes since the halcyon days, with a few still carrying the banner of confrontation and change. Most of these participants, however, were forced to adjust to the realities and demands of everyday life where job and family duties loom largest. The latter have sought to fashion new strategies for change within the social system,

Homeboys mural in east Los Angeles.

The barrios today.

with the realization that a long-term commitment is necessary. Thus, the process of change is weaving a newly distinct, yet diverse, pattern (Lux and Vigil 1979).

As might be expected, many hazards can accompany such a complex process. There still persists, for example, the problem of marginality; some people are unable to function adequately in any culture, much less become creative cultural innovators. Many variants to this situation of conflict and confusion reflect a type of "multiple marginality" (Vigil 1988) in which economic forces predominate. High dropout rates, learning difficulties, self-image problems, drug and alcohol use and abuse, and family strains are among the offshoots of these conditions. For example, the barrio problems with gang warfare stem from many sources, but one cannot explain the life-style of cholo gang members without considering cultural criteria. As previously noted, the cholo or chola is marginal to both Mexican and Anglo cultures and is mainly a street-raised person. Some have patterned a life based on *la vida loca*— the crazy life. This is a subcultural model that over the years has become so institutionalized that "crazy" acts are accepted as normal. Considering the conditions that created this *vato loco* (crazy dude) tradition, it is no wonder that many who feel wronged by society believe it is the only way to survive in the United States. In recent years, problems asso-

Cholo montage.

ciated with this lifestyle have spiraled almost out of control, partly because society's solution for these multiple problems has largely emphasized suppression at the expense of prevention and intervention. However, it must also be noted that the majority of those who appear to be cholos are "wannabes" who follow a less destructive path, cruising with the cholas, getting high, and generally presenting an image of urban Chicano cool. Many simply dress and behave like cholos because it is stylish and the "in thing" to do.

Chicanos: Nativist Acculturationists

The Chicano community on the whole has sought a more rewarding route in insisting that something positive is linked to their background. Those favoring the label "Chicano" have chosen a name that stems from indigenous sources; and when a generic label is needed, "Latino" is favored over "Hispanic," the latter promoted by the federal government for all Spanish-speaking, Spanish-surnamed Americans. Using the label "Chicano" (and "Latino") is partly a declaration of independence, of the desire to no longer be treated as a second-class citizen. It challenges the stereotype that Chicanos are inferior or culturally deprived (de la Garza 1979). The term "Chicano" implies pride in a background of many and mixed heritages and the versatility to widen one's sociocultural persona. This orientation of nativist acculturation, in which the dominant cultural mode is learned and the native style kept, will help to lead American citizens away from ethnocentrism (Vigil and Long 1978). "Biculturalism is of tremendous advantage . . . for it carries with it . . . the ability to pick and choose constructively and eclectically from two different and useful cultures" (Arvizu 1974:125–26).

This pattern is based on cultural democracy: everyone's way of life is right and proper (Ramirez 1985, 1976). Specifically, it finds strength in multiplicity, the "personas mexicanas" (the many faces of Mexicans) that makes for a people (Vigil 1997). As a socioculturally diverse population within the United States and perhaps leading the Western Hemisphere in this regard, Chicanos are in the forefront of this new age of "panhuman" awareness, in which a global economy requires, minimally, an open mind to the development of a global culture.

References

Acosta, O. Z. 1973. *The revolt of the cockroach people*. San Francisco: Straight Arrow Books.

Acuna, R. 1984. *A community under siege*. Los Angeles: UCLA Chicano Studies Research Center.

_____. 1988. *Occupied America*, 3d ed. San Francisco: Canfield Press.

Almaquer, T. 1974. Historical notes on Chicano oppression: The dialectics of racial and class domination in North America. *Aztlan*, Spring and Fall.

_____. 1994. *Racial fault lines: The historical origins of white supremacy in California.* Berkeley: University of California Press.

Alvarez, R. R., Jr. 1987. *Familia.* Berkeley: University of California Press.

_____. 1990. Mexican entrepreneurs and markets in the city of Los Angeles: A case of an immigrant enclave. *Urban Anthropology* 19,1–2:99–124.

_____. 1994. Changing patterns of family and ideology among Latino cultures in the United States. In *Handbook of Hispanic cultures in the United States: Anthropology*, ed. T. Weaver. Houston: Arte Publico Press.

_____. 1995. The Mexican-US border: The making of an anthropology of borderlands. *Annual Review of Anthropology* 24:1–24.

Alvarez, R. 1973. The psycho-historical and socioeconomic development of the Mexican-American people. In *Chicano, the evolution of a people*, eds. R. Rosaldo, R. A. Calvert, and G. L. Seligman. Minneapolis: Winston Press.

_____. 1976. The psycho-historical and socioeconomic development of the Chicano society in the U.S. In *Chicanos: Social and psychological perspectives*, 2nd ed., eds. C. A. Hernandez, M. J. Haug, and N. N. Wagner. St. Louis: C. V. Mosby Co.

Alverez, J. H. 1973. A demographic profile of the Mexican immigration to the United States, 1910–1950. In *Chicano: The evolution of a people*, eds. R. Rosaldo, R. A. Calvert, and G. L. Seligmann. Minneapolis: Winston Press.

Arreola, D. D. and J. R. Curtis. 1993. *The Mexican border cities: Landscape anatomy and place personality.* Tucson and London: University of Arizona Press.

Arroyo, L. E. 1977. Industrial and occupational distribution of Chicana workers. In *Essays on la mujer*, eds. R. Sanchez and R. M. Cruz. Los Angeles: University of California, Chicano Studies Center.

Arvizu, S. F. 1974. Education for constructive marginality. In *The cultural drama*, ed. W. Dillon. Washington, DC: Smithsonian Institution Press.

Bacalski-Martinez, R. R. 1979. Aspects of Mexican American cultural heritage. In *The Chicanos: As we see ourselves*, ed. A. Trejo. Tucson: The University of Arizona Press.

Balderama, F. 1995. *A decade of betrayal.* Albuquerque: University of New Mexico Press.

Barger, W. K. and E. M. Reza. 1994. *The farm labor movement in the Midwest: Social change and adaptation among migrant farmworkers.* Austin: University of Texas Press.

Barker, G. C. 1972. *Social functions of language in a Mexican-American community.* Tucson: University of Arizona Press.

Barrera, M., C. Munoz, and C. Ornelas. 1974. The barrio as an internal colony. In *La causa politico: A Chicano politics reader*, ed. F. C. Garcia. Notre Dame, IN: University of Notre Dame Press.

Bastide, R. 1968. Color, racism, and Christianity. In *Color and race*, ed. J. H. Franklin. Boston: Houghton Mifflin Co.

Bazant, J. 1977. *A concise history of Mexico from Hidalgo to Cardenas, 1805–1940.* New York: Cambridge University Press.

Bean, F. D. and M. Tienda. 1987. *The Hispanic population of the United States.* New York: Russell Sage.

Bellah, R. N., et al. 1985. *Habits of the heart.* New York: Harper and Row.

Bernal, M. E. and G. P. Knight, eds. 1993. *Ethnic identity: Formation and transmission among Hispanic and other minorities.* New York: State University of New York Press.

Bogardus, E. 1934. *The Mexican in the United States.* Los Angeles: USC Social Science Series, no. 8.

Briggs, V. M., Jr. 1973. *Chicanos and rural poverty.* Baltimore: Johns Hopkins University Press.

Briggs, V. M., Jr., W. Fogel, and F. H. Schmidt. 1977. *The Chicano worker.* Austin: University of Texas Press.

Broyles, Y. 1990. Women in El teatro campesino. In Cordova, T., N. Cantu, G. Cardenas, J. Garcia, and C. M. Sierra, eds., *Chicana voices: Intersections of class, race, and gender.* Austin: A National Association for Chicano Studies Publication.

Broyles-Gonzales, Y. 1994. *El teatro campesino.* Austin: University of Texas Press.

Buriel, R. 1984. Integration with traditional Mexican American culture and sociocultural adjustment. In *Chicano psychology,* eds. J. L. Martinez, Jr. and R. Mendoza. New York: Academic Press.

Bustamante, J. 1978. Commodity migrants: Structural analysis of Mexican immigration to the United States. In *Views across the border: The United States and Mexico,* ed. R. S. Ross. Albuquerque: University of New Mexico Press.

Camarillo, A. 1979. *Chicanos in a changing society: From Mexico pueblos to American barrios in Santa Barbara and southern California, 1848–1930.* Cambridge: Harvard University Press.

Campa, A. 1973. The Mexican-American in historical perspective. In *Chicano: The evolution of a people,* eds. R. Rosaldo, R. A. Calvert, and G. L. Seligmann. Minneapolis: Winston Press.

_____. 1993. *Hispanic culture in the Southwest.* Norman: University of Oklahoma Press.

Cardenas, G. 1977. Mexican labor: A view to conceptualizing the effects of migration, immigration and the Chicano population in the United States. In *Cuantos somos: A demographic study of the Mexican American population,* eds. C. Teller, L. Estrada, J. Hernandez, and D. Alvirez. Austin: University of Texas Press, Center for Mexican American Studies.

Cardoso, L. A. 1980. *Mexican emigration to the United States.* Tucson: University of Arizona Press.

Castaneda, A. 1974. Melting potters vs. cultural pluralists: Implications for education. In *Mexican Americans and educational change,* eds. A. Castaneda, et al. New York: Arno Press, Inc.

Castaneda, C. 1968. *The teachings of Don Juan: a Yaqui way of knowledge.* Berkeley: University of California Press.

Chavez, J. R. 1984. *The lost land: The Chicano image of the Southwest.* Albuquerque: University of New Mexico Press.

Chavez, L. 1992. *Shadowed lives.* Ft. Worth, TX: Harcourt Brace.

Chavira-Prado, A. 1994. Latina experience and Latina identity. In *Handbook of Hispanic cultures in the United States: Anthropology*, ed. T. Weaver. Houston: Arte Publico Press.

Chinas, B. 1983. *The Isthmus Zapotecs: Women's roles in cultural context.* Prospect Heights, IL: Waveland Press.

Cline, H. F. 1963. *Mexico: Revolution to evolution 1940–1960.* New York: Oxford University Press.

Coatsworth, J. H. 1988. Patterns of rural rebellion in Latin America: Mexico in comparative perspective. In *Riot, rebellion, and revolution: Rural social conflict in Mexico*, ed. F. Katz. Princeton: Princeton University Press.

Cockcroft, E. and H. Barnet-Sanchez. 1993. *Signs from the heart: California Chicano murals.* Albuquerque: University of New Mexico Press.

Cockcroft, J. D. 1968. *Intellectual precursors of the Mexican Revolution, 1900–1913.* Austin: University of Texas Press.

———. 1986. *Outlaws in the promised land.* New York: Grove Press.

———. 1990. *Mexico: Class formation, capital accumulation, and the state.* New York: Monthly Review Press.

Collier, G. and E. L. Quaratiello. 1994. *Basta!: Land and the Zapatista rebellion in Chiapas.* Oakland, CA: Institute for Food and Development Policy.

Cordova, T., N. Cantu, G. Cardenas, J. Garcia, and C. M. Sierra, eds. 1990. *Chicana voices: Intersections of class, race, and gender.* Austin: A National Association for Chicano Studies Publication.

Cornelius, W. A. 1978. *Mexican migration to the United States: Causes, consequences, and U.S. responses.* Cambridge: Center for International Studies.

Cornelius, W. A. and J. A. Bustamante, eds. 1989. *Mexican migration to the United States: Origins, consequences, and policy options.* San Diego: Center for U.S.-Mexican Studies, University of California.

Cumberland, C. C. 1968. *Mexico: The struggle for modernity.* Oxford: Oxford University Press.

Daniels, C. 1991. *Chicano workers and the politics of fairness.* Austin: University of Texas Press.

De Anda, R. M., ed. 1996. *Chicanas and Chicanos in contemporary society.* Boston: Allyn and Bacon.

de la Garza, R. O. 1979. The politics of the Mexican Americans. In *The Chicanos: As we see ourselves*, ed. A. Trejo. Tucson: University of Arizona Press.

———. 1984. *The Mexican American electorate.* San Antonio, TX: Southwest Voter Registration Education Project.

———. ed. 1987. *Ignored voices: Public opinion polls and the Latino community.* Austin: Center for Mexican American Studies, University of Texas.

de la Garza, R. and L. De Sipo, eds. 1996. *Ethnic ironies: Latino politics in the 1992 elections.* Boulder, CO: Westview Press.

de La Torre, A. and B. M. Pesquera, eds. 1993. *Building with our hands: New directions in Chicana research.* Berkeley: University of California Press.

de Leon, M. 1970. The hamburger and the taco: A cultural reality. In *Educating the Mexican American*, eds. H. S. Johnson and W. I. Hernandez. Valley Forge, PA: Judson Press.

Del Castillo, A. R., ed. 1990. *Between borders: Essays on Mexicana / Chicana history*. Encino, CA: Floricanto Press.

Diaz-Guerrero, R. 1975. *Psychology of the Mexican*. Austin: University of Texas Press.

_____. 1978. Mexicans and Americans: Two worlds, one border . . . and one observer. In *Views across the border: The United States and Mexico*, ed. R. S. Ross. Albuquerque: University of New Mexico Press.

Dinnerstein, L. and D. M. Reimers. 1988. *Ethnic Americans: A history of immigration*. New York: Harper & Row.

Dovidio, J. F., et al. 1992. Cognitive and motivational bases of bias: Implications of aversive racism for attitudes toward Hispanics. In *Hispanics in the workplace*, eds. S. B. Knouse et al. Newbury Park, CA: Sage Publications.

Dunne, J. G. 1967. *Delano*. New York: Ambassador Books, Ltd.

Dworkin, A. G. 1971. Stereotpes and self-images held by native-born and foreign-born Mexican-Americans. In *Chicanos*, 1st ed., eds. N. N. Wagner and M. J. Haug. St. Louis: C.V. Mosby Co.

El Plan Espiritual de Aztlan. 1970. In *Educating the Mexican American*, eds. H. S. Johnson and W. J. Hernandez. Valley Forge, PA: Judson Press.

Emiliano, R. 1976. Nathuatlan elements in Chicano speech. In *Grito del sol*, ed. O. I. Romano-V. Berkeley, CA: Tonatiuh International, Inc.

Ericksen, C. A. 1970. Uprising in the barrios. In *Educating the Mexican American*, eds. H. S. Johnson and W. J. Hernandez. Valley Forge, PA: Judson Press.

Escobar, E. 1998. *Race, police, and the making of a political identity: Police-Chicano relations in Los Angeles, 1900–1945*. Berkeley: University of California Press.

Fernandez, R. A. 1977. *The United States-Mexico border*. Notre Dame, IN: University of Notre Dame Press.

Foley, D. E., et al. 1977. *From peones to politicos: Ethnic relations in a south Texan town, 1900 to 1977*. Austin: University of Texas Press, Center for Mexican American Studies.

Forbes, J. D. 1973. *Aztecas del norte: The Chicanos of Aztlan*. New York: Fawcett Books.

Foster, G. 1987. *Tzintzuntzan: Mexican peasants in a changing world*. Prospect Heights, IL: Waveland Press.

Frazier, E. F. 1957. *Race and culture contacts in the modern world*. New York: Alfred A. Knopf, Inc.

Galarza, E. 1964. *Merchants of labor*. Santa Barbara, CA: McNally & Loftin, Publishers.

_____. 1971. *Barrio boy*. Notre Dame, IN: University of Notre Dame Press.

Gamio, M. 1969. *Mexican immigration to the United States*. New York: Arno Press, Inc. (originally published in 1930).

Gann, L. H. and P. J. Duignan. 1986. *The Hispanics in the United States: A history*. Boulder and London: Westview Press.

Garcia, F., ed. 1988. *Latinos and the political system*. Notre Dame: University of Notre Dame Press.

Garcia, F. C. and R. O. de la Garza. 1977. *The Chicano political experience*. North Scituate, MA: Duxbury Press.

Garcia, G. H. 1990. *Hispanic Hollywood—The Latins in motion pictures*. New York: Citadel Press.

Garcia, I. 1989. *United we win: The rise and fall of La Raza Unida Party*. Tucson: University of Arizona Press.

Garcia, J. C. 1978. Teatro Chicano and the analysis of sacred symbols: Towards a Chicano world-view in the social sciences. In *Chicano perspectives on decolonizing anthropology*, ed. S. F. Arvizu. Berkeley, CA: Tonatiuh International, Inc.

Garcia, M. T. 1989. *Mexican Americans*. New Haven: Yale University Press.

_____. 1994. *Memories of Chicano history: Bert Corona*. Los Angeles: University of California Press.

Gardner, R. 1970. *Grito: Reis Tijerina and the New Mexico land grant war of 1967*. New York: Harper & Row, Publishers.

Gibson, M. and J. Ogbu. 1991. *Minority status and schooling: A comparative study of immigrant and involuntary minorities*. New York: Garland Publishing, Inc.

Glick, L. B. 1966. The right to equal opportunity. In *La Raza: Forgotten Americans*, ed. J. Samora. Notre Dame, IN: University of Notre Dame Press.

Gomez-Quinones, J. 1978. *Mexican students por La Raza: The Chicano student movement in southern California, 1967–1977*. Santa Barbara, CA: Editorial La Causa.

_____. 1990. *Chicano politics: Reality and promise, 1940–1990*. Albuquerque: University of New Mexico Press.

_____. 1994a. *Roots of Chicano politics, 1600–1940*. Albuquerque: University of New Mexico Press.

_____. 1994b. *Mexican American labor: 1790–1990*. Albuquerque: University of New Mexico Press.

Gonzales, N. L. 1967. *The Spanish-Americans of New Mexico*. Albuquerque: University of New Mexico Press.

Gonzales, R. 1967. *I am Joaquin*. Denver: Crusade for Justice.

Gonzales, S. A. 1979. The Chicana perspective: A design for self-awareness. In *The Chicanos: As we see ourselves*, ed. A. Trejo. Tucson: University of Arizona Press.

Gonzalez, G. 1990. *Chicano education in the era of education*. Philadelphia: The Balch Institute Press.

_____. 1994. *Labor and community: Mexican citrus worker villages in a southern California county, 1900–1950*. Urbana: University of Illinois Press.

Gonzalez, H. B. 1974. Response to Chicano militancy. In *Readings on La Raza: The twentieth century*, eds. M. S. Meier and F. Rivera. New York: Hill & Wang.

Gordon, M. 1964. *Assimilation in American life*. New York: Oxford University Press.

Grebler, L., J. W. Moore, and R. C. Guzman 1970. *The Mexican-American people*. New York: The Free Press.

Griffith, B. 1948. *American me*. Boston: Houghton-Mifflin Co.

Griffith, D. and E. Kissan. 1995. *Working poor: Farmworkers in the United States*. Temple: Temple University Press.

Griswold del Castillo, R. and R. A. Garcia. 1995. *Cesar Chavez: A triumph of spirit*. Norman and London: University of Oklahoma Press.

Griswold del Castillo, R., T. McKenna, and Y. Yarbro-Bejarano, eds. 1991. *CARA: Chicano art: Resistance and affirmation*. Los Angeles: Wight Art Gallery, University of California, Los Angeles.

Gutierrez, D. 1995. *Walls and mirrors: Mexican Americans and the politics of ethnicity*. Berkeley: University of California Press.

Guzman, R. 1974. The function on Anglo-American racism. In *Readings on La Raza: The twentieth century*, eds. M. S. Meier and F. Ribera. New York: Hill & Wang.

Hansen, N. 1981. *The border economy, regional development in the Southwest*. Austin: University of Texas Press.

Harrington, M. 1962. *The other America*. New York: The Viking Press, Inc.

Hass, L. 1995. *Conquest and historical identities in California, 1769–1938*. Berkeley: University of California Press.

Herrera-Sobek, M. 1985. *Beyond stereotypes: The critical analysis of Chicana literature*. New York: Bilingual Press Inc.

Heyman, J. 1991. *Life and labor on the border: Working people of northeastern Sonora, Mexico, 1886–1986*. Tucson: University of Arizona Press.

Hinojosa-Ojeda, R. 1994. The political economy of Latino employment and income. In *Handbook of Hispanic cultures in the United States: Anthropology*, ed. T. Weaver. Houston: Arte Publico Press.

Hoffman, A. 1974. *Unwanted Mexican Americans in the Great Depression*. Tucson: University of Arizona Press.

Hondagneu-Sotelo, P. 1994. *Gendered transitions: Mexican experiences of immigration*. Berkeley: University of California Press.

Inkeles, A. 1977. Quoted in R. Toth. Americans' traits: Steady amid change. *Los Angeles Times*, September 20.

Katz, F., ed. 1988. *Riot, rebellion, and revolution: Rural social conflict in Mexico*. Princeton: Princeton University Press.

Keefe, S. and A. Padilla. 1987. *Chicano ethnicity*. Albuquerque: University of New Mexico Press.

Kirk, R. C. 1979. "Honk if you're fatalistic": Chicanos and the problem of Anglo stereotypy. In *Social problems in American society*, eds. J. M. Henslin and L. T. Reynolds. Boston: Allyn and Bacon.

Kluckholm, F. R. and F. L. Strodtbeck, 1961. *Variations in value orientations*. Evanston, IL: Row, Peterson and Co.

Knouse, S. B., P. Rosenfeld, and A. L. Culbertson. 1992. *Hispanics in the workplace*. Newbury Park, CA: Sage Publications.

Knowlton, C. S. 1975. The neglected chapters in Mexican-American history. In *Mexican-Americans tomorrow*, ed. G. Tyler. Albuquerque: University of New Mexico Press.

Lewis, O. 1959. *Five families: Mexican case studies in the culture of poverty*. New York: Harper & Row, Publishers.

Linton, R. 1975. One hundred per cent American. In *Introducing anthropology*, eds. J. R. Hayes and J. M. Henslin. Boston: Holbrook Press, Inc.

Lux, M. and M. E. Vigil. 1979. Return to Aztlan: The Chicano rediscovers his Indian past. In *The Chicanos: As we see ourselves*, ed. A. Trejo. Tucson: University of Arizona Press.

Macias, A. 1982. *Against all odds: The feminist movement in Mexico to 1940*. Westport, CT: Greenwood Press.

Madsen, W. 1964. *The Mexican Americans of south Texas*. New York: Holt, Rinehart Winston.

Marger, M. N. 1994. *Race and ethnic relations*. Belmont, CA: Wadsworth.

Marin, C. 1975. Rodolfo "Corky" Gonzales: The Mexican-American movement spokesman 1966–1972. In Early southwestern minorities, ed. M. P. Servin, *Journal of the West* XIV:4.

Marquez, B. 1993. *LULAC: The evolution of a Mexican American political organization*. Austin: University of Texas Press.

Martinez, C. 1976. Community mental health and the Chicano movement. In *Chicanos: Social and psychological perspectives*, 2nd. ed., eds. C. A. Hernandez, M. J. Haug, and N. H. Wagner. St. Louis: C. V. Mosby Co.

Martinez, E. and E. McCaughan. 1990. Chicanas and Mexicanas within a transnational working class. In *Between borders: Essays on Mexicana / Chicana history*, ed. A. R. Del Castillo. Encino, CA: Floricanto Press.

Martinez, T. 1973. Advertising and racism: The case of the Mexican American. In *Voices*, ed. O. I. Romano-V. Berkeley, CA: Quinto Sol Publications.

Massey, D., et al. 1987. *Return to Aztlan*. Berkeley: University of California Press.

Mazon, M. 1983. *The zoot-suit riots: The psychology of symbolic annihilation*. Austin: University of Texas Press.

McWilliams, C. 1968. *North from Mexico—the Spanish-speaking people of the United States*. Westport, CT: Greenwood Press, Inc.

Meier, M. S. and F. Ribera. 1993. *Mexican Americans / American Mexicans: From conquistadores to Chicanos*. New York: Hill and Wang.

Melville, M. B. 1978. The Mexican-American and the celebration of the Fiestas Patrias: An ethnohistorical analysis. In *Chicano perspectives on de-colonizing anthropology*, ed. S. F. Arvizu. Berkeley, CA: Tonatiuh International, Inc.

_____, ed. 1980. *Twice a minority: Mexican American women*. St. Louis: C. V. Mosby Co.

_____. 1994. "Hispanic" ethnicity, race and class. In *Handbook of Hispanic cultures in the United States: Anthropology*, ed. T. Weaver. Houston: Arte Publico Press.

Menchaca, M. 1993. Chicano Indianism: A historical account of racial repression in the United States. *American Ethnologist* 20(3): 583–603.

_____. 1995. *The Mexican outsiders: A community history of marginalization and discrimination in California*. Austin: University of Texas Press.

Mirande, A. 1987. *Gringo justice*. Notre Dame, IN: University of Notre Dame Press.

Mirande, A. and E. Enriquez. 1979. *La Chicana*. Chicago: University of Chicago Press.

Monroy, D. 1990. *Thrown among strangers: The making of Mexican culture in frontier California*. Berkeley: University of California Press.

Montejano, D. 1987. *Anglos and Mexicans in the making of Texas, 1836–1986.* Austin: University of Texas Press.

Monto, A. 1994. *The roots of Mexican labor migration.* Westport, CT: Greenwood Press.

Moore, J. W. 1973. Colonialism: The case of the Mexican American. In *Introduction to Chicano studies*, eds. L. I. Duran and H. R. Bernard. New York: Macmillan, Inc.

_____. 1978. *Homeboys.* Philadelphia: Temple University Press.

_____. 1991. *Going down to the barrio: Homeboys and homegirls in change.* Philadelphia: Temple University Press.

Moore, J. and H. Pachon. 1985. *Hispanics in the United States.* Englewood Cliffs, NJ: Prentice-Hall, Inc.

Moore, J. and J. D. Vigil. 1993. Barrios in transition. In *In the barrios: Latinos and the underclass debate*, eds. J. W. Moore and R. Pinderhughes. New York: Russell Sage Foundation, pp. 27–49.

Morales, A. 1972. *Ando sangrando.* La Puente, CA: Perspectiva Publications.

Morin, R. 1966. *Among the valiant.* Alhambra, CA: Borden Publishing Co.

Munoz, C. 1989. *Youth, identity, power.* New York: Verso.

_____. 1974. The politics of protest and Chicano liberation: A case study of repression and cooptation. *Aztlan*, Spring and Fall.

Murillo, N. 1976. The Mexican American family. In *Chicanos: Social and psychological perspectives*, 2nd ed., eds. C. A. Hernandez, M. J. Haug, and N. N. Wagner. St. Louis: C. V. Mosby Co.

Nabokov, P. 1969. *Tijerina and the courthouse raid.* Albuquerque: University of New Mexico Press.

Najera-Ramirez, O. 1994. Fiestas Hispanicas: Dimensions of Hispanic festivals and celebrations. In *Handbook of Hispanic cultures in the United States: Anthropology*, ed. T. Weaver. Houston: Arte Publico Press.

Negrete, L. A. 1974. Culture clash: The utility of mass protest as a political response. In *La causa politica: A Chicano politics reader*, ed. F. C. Garcia. Notre Dame, IN: University of Notre Dame Press.

Nelson, E. 1966. *Huelga.* Delano, CA: Farm Workers Press, Inc.

Noel, D. L. 1973. A theory of the origin of ethnic stratification. In *Ethnic conflicts and power: A cross-national perspective*, eds. D. E. Gelfland and R. K. Lee. New York: John Wiley & Sons, Inc.

Noriega, C. 1992. *Chicanos and film: Representation and resistance.* Minneapolis: University of Minnesota Press.

Oboler, S. 1995. *Ethnic labels, Latino lives: Identity and the politics of (re)presentation in the United States.* London and Minneapolis: University of Minnesota Press.

Ong, P. 1988. The Hispanization of L.A.'s poor. University of California, Los Angeles, School of Planning, photocopy.

Orozco, C. 1990. Sexism in Chicano studies and the community. In *Chicana voices*, eds. T. Cordova et al. Albuquerque: University of New Mexico Press.

Padilla, A. M., ed. 1995. *Hispanic psychology.* Thousand Oaks, CA: Sage Publications.

Paredes, A. 1978. The problem of identity in a changing culture: Popular expressions of culture conflict along the lower Rio Grande border. In *Views across the border: The United States and Mexico*, ed. R. S. Ross. Albuquerque: University of New Mexico Press.

_____, ed. 1993. *Folklore and culture on the Texas Mexican border*. Austin: University of Texas Press.

Parsons, T. 1965. Ethnic cleavage in a California school. Palo Alto, CA: Stanford doctoral dissertation.

_____. 1971. School and society: School bias toward Mexican Americans. In *Chicanos: social and psychological perspectives*, eds. N. N. Wagner and M. J. Haug. St. Louis: C. V. Mosby Co.

Paz, O. 1961. *The labyrinth of solitude*. New York: Grove Press, Inc.

Pena, M. 1985. *The Texas-Mexican conjunto*. Austin: University of Texas Press.

Penalosa, F. 1973a. The changing Mexican-American in southern California. In *Chicano: The evolution of a people*, eds. R. Rosaldo, R. A. Calvert, and G. L. Seligmann. Minneapolis: Winston Press.

_____. 1973b. Toward an operational definition of the Mexican-American. In *Chicano: The evolution of a people*, eds. R. Rosalda, R. A. Calvert, and G. L. Seligmann. Minneapolis: Winston Press.

Phelan, P., and A. L. Davidson, eds. 1993. *Renegotiating cultural diversity in American schools*. New York: Teachers College, Columbia University.

Phinney, J. S. 1995. Ethnic identity and self-esteem: A review and integration. In *Hispanic psychology: Critical issues in theory and research*, ed. A. Padilla. Thousand Oaks, CA: Sage Publications.

Portes, A. and R. L. Bach. 1985. *Latin journey: Cuban and Mexican immigration in the United States*. Los Angeles: University of California Press.

Poston, D., D. Alvirez, and M. Tienda. 1977. The high cost of being Chicano. *Human Behavior*, September.

Preciado-Martin, P. 1992. *Songs my mother sang to me*. Tucson: University of Arizona Press.

Price, J. A. 1973. *Tijuana: Urbanization in a border culture*. Notre Dame, IN: University of Notre Dame Press.

Ramirez III, M. 1976. Cognitive styles and cultural democracy in education. In *Chicanos: Social and psychological perspectives*, 2d ed., eds. C. A. Hernandez, M. J. Haug, and N. N. Wagner. St. Louis: C. V. Mosby Co.

_____. 1985. *Psychology of the Americas: Mestizo perspective on personality and mental health*. New York: Pergamon Press.

Reimers, David M. 1985. *Still the golden door: The Third World comes to America*. New York: Columbia University Press.

Reisler, M. 1976. *By the sweat of their brow*. Westport, CT: Greenwood Press, Inc.

Rendon, A. 1971. *Chicano manifesto*. New York: Macmillan, Inc.

Rios, S. 1978. An approach to action anthropology: The community project, C.S.U.S. In *Chicano perspectives on decolonizing anthropology*, ed. S. F. Arvizu. Berkeley: Tonatiuh International, Inc.

Rios-Bustamante, A. J., ed. 1977. *Immigration and public policy: Human rights for undocumented workers and their families*. Los Angeles: University of California, Chicano Studies Center.

Rippy, J. F. 1926. *The United States and Mexico*. New York: Alfred A. Knopf, Inc.

Rivera, G., Jr. 1974. Nosotros venceremos: Chicano consciousness and change strategies. In *La causa politica: A Chicano politics reader*, ed. F. C. Garcia. Notre Dame, IN: University of Notre Dame Press.

Rocco, R. A. 1974. The role of power and authenticity in the Chicano movement: Some reflections. *Aztlan*, Spring and Fall.

Rodriguez, R. 1988. *Hunger of memory: The education of Richard Rodriguez: An Autobiography*. New York; Toronto: Bantam Books.

Romano-V., O. I. 1968.The anthropology and sociology of the Mexican Americans: The distortion of Mexican American history. In *El grito*, ed. O. I. Romano-V. Berkeley, CA: Quinto Sol Publications.

_____. 1973. *Voices*. Berkeley, CA: Quinto Sal Publications.

Romanucci-Ross, L. and G. De Vos, eds. 1995. *Ethnic identity: Creation, conflict, and accommodation*. Walnut Creek, CA: AltaMira Press.

Romero, F. 1979. *Chicano workers: Their utilization and development*. Los Angeles: University of California, Chicano Studies Center.

Romo, H. 1990. *Latinos and blacks in the cities: Policies for the 1990s*. Austin: LBJ Library and the LBJ School of Public Affairs.

Romo, R. 1983. *East Los Angeles: History of a barrio*. Austin: University of Texas Press.

Rubel, A. 1966. *Across the tracks: Mexican Americans in a Texas city*. Austin: University of Texas Press.

Rueschenbeg, E. J. and R. Buriel. 1995. Mexican-American family functioning and acculturation: A family systems perspective. In *Hispanic psychology: Critical issues in theory and research*, ed. A. M. Padilla. Thousand Oaks, CA: Sage Publications.

Ruiz, R. 1980. *The great rebellion: Mexico, 1905–1924*. New York: Norton Press.

_____. 1992. *Triumphs and tragedy: A history of the Mexican people*. London: W.W. Norton and Co.

Ruiz, V. 1993. "Star struck": Acculturation, adolescence, and the Mexican American woman, 1920–1950. In *Building with our hands*, eds. A. De La Torre and B. M. Pesquera. Berkeley: University of California Press.

Ruiz, V. L. and S. Tiano. 1987. *Women on the U.S.–Mexico border*. Boston: Allen & Unwin.

Salas, E. 1990. *Soldaderas in the Mexican military: Myth and history*. Austin: University of Texas Press.

Saldana, D. H. 1995. Acculturative stress: Minority status and distress. In *Hispanic psychology: Critical issues in theory and research*, ed. A. M. Padilla. Thousand Oaks, CA: Sage Publications.

Samora, J. 1971. *Los mojados: The wetback story*. Notre Dame, IN: University of Notre Dame Press.

Samora, J. and P. V. Simon. 1977. *A history of the Mexican American people*. Notre Dame, IN: University of Notre Dame Press.

Sanchez, D. 1978. *Expedition through Aztlan*. La Puente, CA: Perspectiva Publications.

Sanchez, F. A. 1976. Raices Mexicanas. In *Grito del sol*, ed. O. I. Romano-V. Berkeley, CA: Tonatiuh International, Inc.

Sanchez, G. I. 1966. History, culture, and education. In *La Raza: Forgotten Americans*, ed. J. Samora. Notre Dame, IN: University of Notre Dame Press.

Sanchez, G. I. 1967. *Forgotten people: A study of New Mexicans*. Albuquerque: Calvin Horn Publishers (originally published in 1940).

_____. 1974. Educational change in historical perspective. In *Mexican Americans and historical change*, eds. A. Casteneda et al. New York: Arno Press, Inc.

Sanchez, G. J. 1993. *Becoming Mexican American: Ethnicity, culture and identity in Chicano Los Angeles, 1900–1945*. New York: Oxford University Press.

Sanderson, S. E. 1988. *The transformation of Mexican agriculture: International structure and the politics of rural change*. Princeton: University of Princeton Press.

Sands, K. M. 1993. *Charreria Mexicana: An equestrian folk tradition*. Tucson: University of Arizona Press.

Santana, D. H. 1995. *Acculturative stress: Minority status and distress*. In *Hispanic psychology*, ed. A. Padilla. Thousand Oaks, CA: Sage Publications.

Santana, R. and M. Esparza. 1974. East Los Angeles blowouts. In *Parameters of institutional change: Chicano experiences in education*. Hayward, CA: Southwest Network.

Scott, A. 1979. Anglos in city soon will reach minority status. *Los Angeles Times*, April 9.

Segura, D. A. 1990. Chicanas and triple oppression in the labor force. In *Chicana voices*, eds. T. Cordova et al. Albuquerque: University of New Mexico Press.

_____. 1992. Walking on eggshells: Chicanas in the labor force. In *Hispanics in the workplace*, eds. S. B. Knouse, P. Rosenfeld, and A. L. Culbertson. Newbury Park, CA: Sage Publications, pp. 173–93.

Selby, H., A. D. Murphy, and S. A. Lorenzen. 1990. *The Mexican urban household: Organizing for self defense*. Austin: University of Texas Press.

Shockley, J. S. 1974. *Chicano revolt in a Texas town*. Notre Dame, IN: University of Notre Dame Press.

Shorris, E. 1992. *Latinos: A biography of the people*. New York and London: W.W. Norton & Company.

Simmons, O. G. 1973. The mutual images and expectations of Anglo-Americans and Mexican Americans. In *Introduction to Chicano studies*, eds. L. I. Duran and H. R. Bernard. New York: Macmillan, Inc.

_____. 1974. *Anglo-Americans and change: Mexican Americans in South Texas: A study in dominant-subordinate group relations*. New York: Arno Press, Inc.

Soto, S. 1979. *The Mexican woman: A study of her part in the revolution*. Palo Alto CA: R&E Research Associates.

Spencer, M. H. 1977. *Contemporary economics*. New York: Worth Publishers, Inc.

Spindler, G. and L. Spindler. 1990. *The American cultural dialogue and its transmission*. London: The Falmer Press.

Starr, P. C. 1978. *Economics: Principles in action*. Belmont, CA: Wadsworth Publishing Co.

Stephan, L. 1991. *Zapotec women*. Austin: University of Texas Press.

Stowell, J. S. 1974. The near side of the Mexican question (1921). In *Perspectives on Mexican-American life*, ed. C. E. Cortez. New York: Arno Press, Inc.

Suarez-Orozco, C. and M. Suarez-Orozco. 1994. The cultural psychology of Hispanic immigrants. In *Handbook of Hispanic cultures in the United States: Anthropology*, ed. T. Weaver. Houston: Arte Publico Press.

Swadesh, F. L. 1973. The alianza movement: Catalyst for social change in New Mexico. In *Chicano: The evolution of a people*, eds. R. Rosalda, R. A. Calvert, and G. L. Seligmann. Minneapolis: Winston Press.

Tabler, H. W. 1988. Peasants and the shaping of the revolutionary state, 1910–1940. In *Riot, rebellion, and revolution: Rural social conflict in Mexico*, ed. F. Katz. Princeton: University of Princeton Press.

Tannenbaum, F. 1993. *Peace by revolution: Mexico after 1910*. New York: Columbia University Press.

Taylor, P. S. 1934. *An American Mexican frontier*. Chapel Hill: University of North Carolina Press.

Thurow, L. C. 1979. Hispanics closing income gap. *Los Angeles Times*, May 5.

Trueba, H. T. 1991. From failure to success: The roles of culture and cultural conflict in the academic achievement of Chicano students. In *Chicano school failure and success: Research and policy agendas for the 1990s*, ed. R. Valencia. London: The Falmer Press.

U.S. Commission on Civil Rights. 1970. *Mexican Americans and the administration of justice in the Southwest*. Washington, DC: U.S. Government Printing Office.

_____. 1971. Report 1: *Ethnic isolation of Mexicans in the public schools of the Southwest*. Washington, DC: U.S. Government Printing Office.

_____. 1975. *A better chance to learn: Bilingual-bicultural education*. Washington, DC: U.S. Government Printing Office.

Valdes, D. 1991. *Al Norte: Agricultural workers in the Great Lakes region, 1917–1970*. Austin: University of Texas Press.

Valdez, L. 1992. *Zoot-suit and other plays*. Houston, TX: Arte Publico Press.

Valencia, R. R. 1991. *Chicano school failure and success: Research and policy agendas for the 1990s*. London: The Falmer Press.

Vallens, V. M. 1978. *Working women in Mexico during the Porfiriato, 1880–1910*. San Francisco: R&E Research Associates.

Velez-I., C. G. 1979. Ourselves through the eyes of an anthropologist. In *The Chicanos: As we see ourselves*, ed. A. Trejo. Tucson: University of Arizona Press.

_____. 1983. *Bonds of mutual trust*. New Brunswick, NJ: Rutgers University Press.

_____. 1996. *Border visions: Mexican cultures of the Southwest United States*. Tucson: University of Arizona Press.

Vigil, J. D. 1978. Marx and Chicano anthropology. In *Chicano perspectives on decolonizing anthropology*, ed. S. F. Arvizu. Berkeley, CA: Tonatiuh International, Inc.

_____. 1988. *Barrio gangs: Street life and identity in Southern California*. Austin: University of Texas Press.

_____. 1990. Cholos and gangs: Culture change and street youth in Los Angeles. In *Gangs in America: Diffusion, diversity and public policy*, ed. R. Huff. Beverly Hills: Sage Publications.

Vigil, J. D. 1997. *Personas Mexicanas: Chicano high schoolers in a changing Los Angeles*. Ft. Worth, TX: Harcourt Brace Inc.

_____. Forthcoming. Time, place, and history in the formation of Chicano identity. In *Many Americas: Perspectives on racism, ethnicity, and cultural identity*, ed. G. Campbell. Missoula: University of Montana Press.

Vigil, J. D. and Long, J. M. 1981. Unidirectional or nativist acculturation?—Chicano Paths to School Achievement. *Human Organization* 40(3): 273–77.

_____. 1994. Social problems in urban Latino communities. In *Handbook of Hispanic cultures in the United States: Anthropology*, ed. T. Weaver. Houston: Arte Publico Press.

Villarreal, J. A. 1970. *Pocho*. New York: Doubleday & Co., Inc.

Wagley, C. and M. Harris. 1958. *Minorities in the New World*. New York: Columbia University Press.

Wallerstein, I. 1974. *The modern world-system: Capitalist agriculture and the origins of the European world-economy in the sixteenth century*. New York: Academic Press.

Weaver, T., ed. 1994. *Handbook of Hispanic cultures in the United States: Anthropology*. Houston: Arte Publico Press.

Webb, W. P. 1935. *The Texas Rangers: A century of frontier defense*. Austin: University of Texas Press.

Weber, D. J. 1973. *Foreigners in their native land*. Albuquerque: University of New Mexico Press.

_____. 1992. *The Spanish frontier in North America*. New Haven; London: Yale University Press.

Wolff, E. N. 1996. *Top heavy: The increasing inequality of wealth in America and what can be done about it*. New York: Twentieth Century Fund, New Press.

Wright, D. E., E. Salinas, and W. P. Kuvlesky. 1973. Opportunities for social mobility for Mexican-American youth. In *Chicanos and Native Americans*, eds. R. de la Garza, A. Kruszewski, and T. Arciniega. Englewood Cliffs, NJ: Prentice-Hall, Inc.

Zavella, P. 1987. *Women's work & Chicano families: Cannery workers of the Santa Clara Valley*. Ithaca: University of Cornell Press.

Zeleny, C. 1974. *Relations between the Spanish-Americans and Anglo-Americans in New Mexico*. New York: Arno Press, Inc.

Conclusion

A Look to the Future: 1990s Onward

The Intersection of History and Culture Change

To understand the Chicano people is to understand their history. It is to recognize that Chicanos have been shaped by a series of social systems. Each social system made its own imprint, adding a new and different piece to the complex mosaic that evolved under intense and strained culture change. The sequence was largely one of oppression and deprivation for the Chicano people. Thus Chicano achievements, if they are to be fully assessed, must be measured in the context of a series of ruling elites who imposed their will on the people.

Close to five centuries of conditioned learning and relearning have inscribed certain patterns and traits into the Chicano character. It is a unique character, indeed, because of the variety of situations and changes. In some instances, no sooner were new customs learned than there was a new array of alterations. This history created a psychology of conquest, exploitation, and oppression in Mexico, and the process was repeated for the Chicanos in the United States. In addition, many ways of thinking and acting were shaped by reactions to the several types of contact-conflict-change sequences (Naylor 1996). Successes were relatively few. Most importantly, the people and the culture had changed, adapted, and survived. On the most culturally observable level, it was a passage of ethnic influences and linkages, from Indian to Spanish to Mexican to Anglo, each having had its impact. Changing macrostructural identities accompanied these developments. These big changes brought about over-arching identities, as large groups of people were collapsed into one category (see Kearney 1996:174).

It is also equally important that peoples learn the correct lessons from their setbacks in history (Balibar and Wallerstein 1991). In this context, some adaptive traits surfaced to aid survival, such as: (1) a strong tradition of work productivity, although others have benefited from it; (2) a syncretic culture that is broad and deep and helps facilitate human interaction and understanding; (3) concern and support from family and friends in the face of adversity; (4) almost habitual striving for equality and justice; and (5) pride (recently rekindled) in the accomplishments of their indigenous forefathers. The persistence of Chicanos indicates that at least some correct answers have been learned. However, few would disagree that the Chicano community is also beset by a legacy of "wrong answers."

The Chicano community is a product of this history and broad macrostructural changes. Their original, relatively small local human energy system underwent a complex series of reorganizations associated with larger entities that gradually became global. This macrostructural experience is rooted in the indigenous landholding villages, which were transformed and reorganized by the Spanish into a peasantry more or less working the same land. Later descendants were uprooted completely and forced to migrate to modern industrial jobs. Quite a journey! The irony of indigenous peoples undergoing these changes under different European elites and mestizos and driven to reimmigrate to former ancestral lands (Aztlan) and be labelled "illegal aliens" cannot go unnoticed.

Such historical developments and macrostructural experiences have culminated in the present period. A people is both a product of what its forebears have undergone and a contributor to what its descendants will become. Not least, we have provided a framework for understanding the ways in which distinctive social and cultural patterns arose, thus clarifying the relationship between contemporary habits and their historical basis and avoiding the tendency of social scientists to assess minorities within a zero-time framework. However distant the link, the events of the past have always had an impact on the present (Brass 1992); put another way, to understand the present, one must back into the past.

Lessons from Each Stage: Continuity and Change

Something new was learned in each historical stage. Cultural revampments and the blending of traditions progressed through the centuries to create a rich cultural tapestry. The pre-Columbian period supplied the foundation for all that followed. Attachment to old lifeways, especially to certain egalitarian and familial practices, has persisted in attenuated form to the present. Foods that evolved during that period still comprise the staples of most Chicano households, and ancient motifs are prominent in the arts and folklore of the modern community. Most obvious in this indigenous heritage is the racial and physical appearance of a large portion of the Chicano people.

The arrival of the Spaniards began the colonial period. Under oppressive and exploitative conditions, the Mexican people endured three hundred years of underdevelopment, with most becoming part of a macrostructural peasant category. Amassing Indians into the larger, more complicated economic system of Spanish colonial and other subsequent stages has had devastating effects. This is an inheritance that still affects many Chicanos' habits and beliefs. Overt racism and intraracial color preferences stemmed from this period, together with a landholder-peon social relationship that continues to hinder egalitarian movements. Technological improvements were also introduced by the Spanish, as were the spiritual values of the Catholic Church (which at times ameliorated oppression), but the major legacy of the Spanish period was a social structure based on racial and class inequality. In addition, some of the most long lasting and deeply rooted cultural recombinations—e.g., the syncretic Mexican Catholic religious practices and ideology—stem from this time period.

Eventually there was a movement by some Mexicans to break free of this oppression. During the period of Mexican independence and nationalism, the people became more assertive and began to act on new insights. Chicanos still celebrate that independent spirit with annual Cinco de Mayo (Fifth of May) and Dieciseis de Septiembre (Sixteenth of September) parades, and the desire for control over their own destiny is reflected in the many community action and political groups. However, old influences and habits tend to die hard. New ruling elite groups emerged, some recast from the old ones and others comprised of the new power brokers, to insist that former practices need not change so rapidly or completely. A strain between adhering to the old and adapting to the new resulted, and conflict arose between those trying to "keep the natives down" and growing numbers of "disenfranchised workers fighting for autonomy."

While the Mexican people were in the throes of this awakening, the modern era was thrust on them. This period of time was doubly confusing; accommodating and integrating indigenous and Spanish heritages was made difficult by the imposition of a new (American) social order in the northern frontier areas, with its own set of standards. The modern period also soon led to a reconstitution of peasants into immigrants, integrated into an even larger, denser economic system and a new macrostructural identity. Nevertheless, the early interactions and adjustments included experimentation with and learning of new patterns; increasing awareness of the influence of the old patterns; and a broader understanding and acceptance of a very complicated and convoluted multidimensional world. In the beginning, many were caught in the unusual dilemma of reconciling the unresolved problems of the indigenous and peasant identities and at the same time learning to integrate the new vistas of their externally imposed modern role as immigrants (Kearney 1996). Despite this quandary, many experimented, learned from mistakes, and moved on in a never-ending cycle of resistance, protest, and organization. All of these activities and developments were accelerated in the United States. When more people immigrated in the aftermath of the 1910 Mexican revolution, bringing new ideas with them, the transition from peasantry was quickened. Eventually, a predominantly urban Chicano community flexed its political and economic muscles in the 1960s. Simultaneously, its rural component was also engaged in a militant assertion of economic rights.

Contemporary Stage—Growing Awareness

As a result of events since the mid-1960s, Chicanos have reached a new plateau in which they can learn from previous stages and gain further insights into the complicated nature of a background of multiple cultural influences and macrostructural identities. However, they must not per-

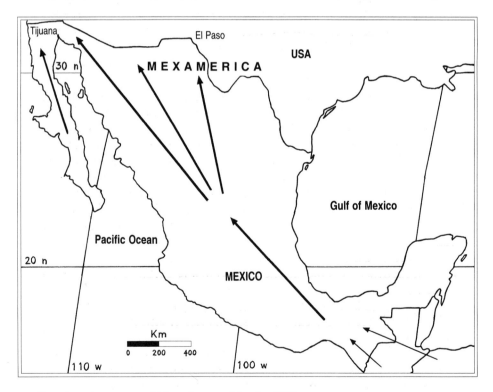

Immigration routes shift and expand in the 1990s.

ceive each cultural antecedent or identity as separate, but rather must incorporate all the experiences into one fabric; it is a variegated cloth of intragroup diversity. The present makeup of the population, in fact, reflects this diversity. For example, immigrants often come from Indian peasant communities as bilinguals from Mexico (i.e., speaking both a native language and Spanish) and quickly adjust to English, becoming trilinguals.

The Chicano population faces a hopeful, if potentially difficult, future. While past events have taken their toll, Chicanos have nonetheless gradually advanced. Because of their high birth rate and the steady flow of Mexican immigration, they are soon to become (with other Latinos) the nation's largest minority group; and significantly, the population will include a critical mass of first-generation Mexicans. Moreover, the border region has taken on a life of its own, and the cultural and economic exchanges between Mexicans and Anglo Americans in this region has increased such that many now refer to the region as Mex-America (Alvarez 1995; Velez-Ibanez 1996; Martinez 1996). However, the economic strains and political unrest in Mexico have begun to take center stage. NAFTA, "narcopolitics," Zapatistas in Chiapas, and the weakening of PRI (Institutional Revolutionary Party, which has ruled Mexico since the 1920s) are just a few of the crises that symbolize the turmoil and dissension of modern Mexico. Coupled with a downturn in the American economy and the intensification of anti-immigration hysteria, these developments will continue to have a major impact on Chicanos/Mexicanos in the coming years, especially tempered by the dual citizenship that Mexican immigrants will enjoy. These facts loom larger when taken alongside the continuing movement to organize other Spanish-speaking groups (Puerto Ricans, Cubans, and other Latin Americans) into a Hispanic or Latino national network; especially since the current anti-immigrant (Latino) climate is helping close ranks among them. Despite historical-cultural differences among Latinos, this is considered a politically expedient goal, given some of the shared commonalities of colonized people, particularly in the midst of the ferment and flux that characterizes Latin America politics and the region's growing importance to United States interests.

Geopolitical considerations and economic exchanges with Latin America will bolster the trend toward cultural democracy, even as the United States grudgingly acknowledges the importance of bilingual and multicultural learning programs. With the rise of ethnic consciousness, Chicanos are becoming more accepting and comfortable with their racial and ethnic heritage. The prospects for participating more fully in American life are increased with this foundation of confidence and certainty. In the 1990s, for example, organizations and leaders were able to increase naturalization rates and shepherd a higher voter turnout than

1990 Chicano Moratorium (20 year anniversary): Return of the Indigenous!

1995 Chicano Moratorium (25 year anniversary): Return of Zapata!

1995 Chicano Moratorium: We are all Zapatistas!

in earlier years. In turn, fuller participation places Chicanos on the
threshold of realizing their political power and thus further strengthening their cultural rights. While such advances and inroads are significant, there is still room for improvement; for example, the educational
performance of Chicanos still lags behind that of the majority population
(Valencia 1991).

Beginning in the aftermath of World War II, there has been a steady
increase of Chicanos in the middle-income sectors, a process that has
gained even more headway since the 1960s. The accompanying mush-
rooming economic clout adds immeasurably to Chicanos' growing influence. Millionaires, entrepreneurs, business magnates, and national-level
political leaders are more common today than at any time in the past. For
many of these successful individuals and groups, it often happens that
assimilation to the dominant culture goes hand-in-hand with socioeconomic mobility. This has been a choice for many, especially in earlier
decades when some people equated Mexican culture with being poor.
Today, however, there are many additional choices for an acculturation
route. It appears that Chicanos/Mexicanos are increasingly opting for a
bilingual/bicultural style and identity, an orientation that I have referred
to as "personas mexicanas," the many faces of Mexicans (Vigil 1997). In
short, feeling comfortable in drawing from multiple heritages in one's presentation of self is becoming more fashionable and practical. Some Chicano millionaires followed this strategy by establishing businesses
among their own ethnic group; Anglo-Americans along the border have
tried to accommodate this orientation to capture the ethnic trade.

Whatever cultural route is taken, however, social mobility will
undoubtedly expand, as a growing number of peasants-turned-immi-
grants strive to reach the American dream. Despite some activists'
charges that having social aspirations translates into "selling out" your
people, it is clear that Chicanos have tired of a life of scarcity and want.
This is especially the case now, when the stigma of being Mexican has
lessened. Many Chicanos feel that their time for power and influence has
come. Thus, affluence is a much sought-after goal. However, affluence for
many is a relative thing. Coming from an immigrant or peasant background, some families feel successful if they move out of the barrio and
into a nearby tract home in a suburban area. Self-interest drives others
to seek a much higher status and income. In contrast, some of these individuals have also elected to help advance the "causes" of Chicanos. Lest
we forget, however, the gap between rich and poor in the United States
has widened in the last decade, and Chicanos are still disproportionately
represented in the lower-income sectors.

It is clear that when a higher income level is reached, more doors
open—or are broken down. The civil-rights struggle has made a difference, even though tensions remain and few can rest on their laurels and

allow the reversal of affirmative action. Many race-based problems still persist. In the past, racial discrimination was blatantly practiced, and it still is in many sections of the Southwest. Relaxation of barriers has come faster in urban areas, at least in the sense that they are now subtle and covert or apply mostly to poorer people. Chicanos are slowly destroying many racial and cultural myths that have hindered their participation in mainstream America. Although they still have a long way to go, they continue to struggle—some publicly, others privately—to attain a level of parity in all areas of society.

Economic Forces and Human Expansion

The growing awareness associated with Chicano history and culture change must include consideration of the manner in which the economic sphere and its growth have dominated sociocultural features in each prior stage and the shift from one stage to the next. Each historical period has had a particular class-culture-color conformation, and each stage has terminated in a contact-conflict-change sequence. While all aspects of the sociocultural configuration are important, careful reading of Chicano history indicates clearly the priority of economic issues.

Many Third World peoples, as well as other ethnic minorities in the United States, have certain similarities with Chicanos because of the nature of the social-class system in most parts of the world (Harrison 1981). They share with Chicanos a history of exploitation of natural resources and human labor and also the propensity to fight for justice and equality. Who could argue with the fact that many indigenous peoples throughout the world have also undergone their own version of macrostructural identity transformations? Or that they will eventually join the tides of human migration presently enveloping the world?

Several other issues and characteristics are traced by highlighting each historical stage. People's needs were adversely affected throughout all the stages. Forced labor, loss of land, and inadequate incomes still cause malnutrition and other physical suffering. Moreover, economic exploitation has resulted in a growing sense of emotional and status deprivation (Wolf 1982, 1969). Gross inequality on the basis of class and color was mitigated by the spread of Enlightenment philosophy in the late eighteenth century, but discrimination diminished only slightly. The struggle for independence continued into twentieth-century Mexico (Cockcroft 1990), but for most people the sketchily conceived and unevenly implemented reforms have meant little. These people remain subject to colonial influences even as they strive to break free (Stoler and Cooper 1996). However, continued and more sophisticated resistance offers hope for the future. A question of growing concern is the volatile situation in Mexico, for the unraveling of an economy and political system there can both aid and hinder Chicano/Mexicano advancements in the United States.

In the United States, exposure to a modern urban industrial system uncovered a host of new realities, as many of the resultant problems often matched and paralleled some of the worst features of earlier periods (Handlin 1951; Yinger 1994; Walch 1994). This involved not just unfortunate working conditions but a nearly total disenfranchisement of the worker in the economy (Handlin 1951). Even the increased Chicano awareness resulting from independence could not fully comprehend or integrate all these transformations in the first phases of the modern period. Nevertheless, a persistent and socially conscious method of resistance arose. Many adaptive strategies were used to ensure individual and group preservation. In a wide-ranging reaction to change, Chicanos fought, retreated, regrouped, organized, and demonstrated (Gomez-Quinones 1990). They took various paths of national integration—assimilation, acculturation, cultural pluralism, and separatism, for example. Because of the range of cultural influences and regional differences both in Mexico and the U.S. Southwest, the adjustment and adaptation could not merely be gauged on the basis of generational change (i.e., first, second, and so on) for time and place in one's background figured prominently in the tempo and style of Americanization (Horowitz 1977; Vigil 1997). For example, the contrast between rural and urban populations, or the political contexts for immigrants in the 1920s as opposed to the 1990s affected the choice of acculturation strategies. The Chicano experience in the United States is further underscored by participation in the fight for labor unions and the dual effects of the 1910 Mexican Revolution and immigration. These effects include ongoing cultural regeneration and increased activism for ethnic rights and a strengthening of ideological influences for a more just society.

Sociocultural Change: The Sequence of Complexity

A summary of the growth in complexity and historical development of the Chicano people leads to a discussion of the dynamics of sociocultural change. Throughout this long time period, various facets of culture change took center stage. Sometimes it was acculturation that characterized the period, a broad process upon initial contact between two cultures in which change takes place in one or both cultures. Later, when one of the cultures successfully dominates the interactions, the subordinate culture has little choice but to assimilate. Still more regularly, a syncretic amalgamation of cultures would produce a new variant. In the modern period, a notion of cultural democracy or cultural pluralism came to the fore. It was a culture-change strategy that strove to incorporate various cultures and languages in a multilingual/multicultural

Urban Civilian Conservation Corps.

1995 Chicano Moratorium: Brown Berets resurface with the new generation.

◀ *The backside of the "projects" are in a state of industrial decay.*

orientation. Sometimes individuals or groups adopted this style by chance or because of the nature of the culture-contact situation. Currently, government policies have attempted to help lead this democratizing effort.

In this context, what similarities bind the stages together? What differences separate them? How does the trajectory of Chicano culture change and history compare with that of other peoples? In short, the changes in each realm—socioeconomic (class), sociocultural (culture), and sociopsychological (color) are rooted in "a world of those who have and those who have not" (Barkin 1994). During the age of discovery and exploration, European states expanded into the lands of Third World peoples. This was the beginning of colonial rule, and the process of the expansion of some human energy systems at the expense of the contraction of the many. Euroethnocentrism at its most extreme, malignant level insured that indigenous populations would be subjected to a subordinate, inferior status and station. Class, cultural, and racial imperialism was practiced with impunity, and changes over the centuries never fully righted the inequity (Root 1992; Arthur and Shapiro 1996; Balandier 1966; Horowitz 1977). When colonialism ended, neocolonialism took over, and so on with direct and indirect political control and various multitudinous forms of control. Through all these macroeconomic transformations and geopolitical realignments, the global economy emerged as the ultimate human energy system (Sassen 1991; Balibar and Wallerstein 1991; Sanderson 1995).

As noted, these macrohistorical changes led to new macrostructural identities; even the resistance to these intrusions embodied a larger network, such as peasant revolts and movements or current examples of immigrant rights groups and issues. The Chicano case is different from many others because it is sequential: One colonial structure was replaced by another, while a similar superordinate/subordinate relationship was retained. In each phase, a larger energy system materialized after struggles of various sorts and at different levels. Much of the ensuing ethnic conflict results from the disparity in wealth and resources. Whatever the general explanations for ethnic conflict—indeed, the condition can be traced from biblical times—it is clear that economic motives apply in this instance. In almost every major stage, colonization and native resistance to forced changes were based on economic factors. Either simultaneous to the conqueror's victory or immediately afterward, the effort to explain or rationalize the takeover occurred. This generally meant the creation and refinement of prejudicial attitudes and discriminatory behavior. The culture and race of the victor were established as superior and those of the vanquished as inferior. Thus, the conqueror's feelings of guilt were averted because the natives were considered subhuman, a lower form of cultural and racial life.

Structural Ideology

The social relations and cultural beliefs were the ideological glue that held these economic arrangements together (Andersen and Collins 1995). Adjustments and reactions to such oppressive systems have taken different turns. Some fought to preserve their way of life by cloaking resistance in cultural themes (Pedraza and Rumbaut 1996; Horowitz 1977).

Others avoided forced change by limiting contact with the new overseers. Whatever reaction strategies were used (and there were many local adaptations), one factor stands out: groups used to privileges and access to resources often discriminate to maintain advantages for themselves. Thus, discussions of *social* problems (poverty, crime, housing, education, and so on), *cultural* problems (linguistic, value, and belief barriers), *racial* problems (inferior treatment, institutional racism, prejudice, and discrimination), and *psychological* problems (inferiority and marginality based on social-cultural-racial factors) of low-income ethnic minorities are, in fact, generally about *economics-related* issues.

An historical assessment and understanding of the currents described above are necessary requisites in examining the social framework. Foley and coworkers (1977:48) write that "the notions of racial, cultural, and class superiority are so intertwined that they constitute one belief system." In many parts of the world, a "structural ideology" was created to preserve "structured inequalities." This ideology encompasses local, national, and international networks. According to Hewitt (1977), many of the world's ethnic struggles in the past were centered on these issues, causing over 10 million fatalities (in minor and major conflicts, from riots to extended wars) in the period from 1945 to 1970. The strife that presently characterizes the Middle East and the Balkans clearly reflects the same underlying notions.

In the United States, as in many other countries, the ideology of oppression is in conflict with that of liberation. Southern and eastern Europeans in the past underwent a type of "structural ideological" oppression when they migrated to the United States. Their different "white" racial stock and cultural background barred them from wider opportunities. They also developed strategies similar to those used by Chicanos—cultural pluralism, assimilation, separatism, and direct action—to achieve social equality. The sociocultural life of many groups, both nationally and internationally, is affected by their powerless position and the ideological processes that keep them there. Thus, we must write "a history of the modern world in which we spell out the processes of power which created the present-day cultural systems and the linkages between them" (Wolf 1969:261).

In writing that history, we might discover that social problems revolve around the issue of "haves vs. have-nots." This macrolevel analysis provides a clearer insight into a number of conditions affecting Chicanos, including economic competition among the poor and the cumulative effects of oppression in which intragroup frictions derive from the colonial period and intergroup conflicts from the contemporary situation. However, "the study of culture change must take into account three orders of reality: the impact of the higher [dominant] culture; the substance of native life on which it is directed; and . . . change resulting from the reaction between the two cultures" (Malinowski 1945:26; see also Spicer 1962; Rosaldo 1989). A compounding factor in our macrohistorical and macrostructural analysis is how *time, place,* and *people* have varied through the centuries, adding nuances and contours to culture-change dynamics and reformulations. Both colonized and colonizer are affected by this. All the more reason for the student of change to heed Samuel Ramos's warning (1962) against over-romanticizing the native experience: Which native experience?

Legacies of the Past: Patterns and Problems

Most of the social patterns outlined below evolved through several stages of change and major wars with other ethnic groups, an inheritance that compounds the problems of modern Chicanos. This complicated, interwoven experience of long duration is the backdrop for any discussion of poverty, educational attainment, social mobility, cultural marginality, social and racial inferiority, and a host of other personal and group problems. Many of these problems are compounded by persisting intragroup dynamics (e.g., Spanish racism toward Indians reflected in attitudes among Mexicans) in competition with intergroup realities (e.g., Anglo racism toward Mejicanos [both Spanish and Indians, and admixtures thereof]) that coexist side by side.

In the growth and enlargement of human energy systems, socioeconomic adaptations went hand in hand with other sociocultural changes in Chicano history. The family, education, religion, and other institutions have undergone a monumental upheaval in each stage. As noted previously, many surviving customs and traits were positive and beneficial. However, language and cultural values have been subjected to intense pressures. Individuals and groups either resisted accommodation to the dominant culture and fought for preservation of native traditions, or synthesized a compromise. These transformations have shaped a pattern that largely reflects a lower socioeconomic lifestyle. A closer examination of this pattern will be made only to dramatize the debilitating nature of a life of scarcity, for many Chicanos have reached middle- and upper-income levels by using positive adaptation strategies.

Today, the continuing immigration of Mexicans (and other Latinos) is creating a critical mass in some U.S. cities and regions to threaten the once dominant Anglo population; and most of the newcomers are part of the poor or low-income sector. Importantly, it is economic concerns that drive both immigration as well as the anti-immigration hysteria. At the cultural level, intragroup variances and contrasts muddle the picture, as generational change through the decades has resulted in different cultural styles among Chicanos and Mexicanos. No one knows where the cultural center (or amalgamation thereof) is anymore in this constantly shifting and repeatedly redefined population. Economic competition and jockeying for the upper hand is taking place at intragroup and intergroup levels in this cultural cauldron.

Historically, Chicanos have experienced a sense of inferiority and marginality. Racial and cultural imperialism supported the system of economic imperialism. Feelings of racial and cultural inferiority and marginality stem from both the Spanish and Anglo-American systems. Many other examples of a similar legacy of "prejudice" are found throughout the world (Brown 1995). Making people feel inferior because of how they look, speak, and/or act is clearly a mechanism to keep them socially immobile (Essed 1991). An additional handicap is the establishment of social norms that keep those who are racially and culturally different marginal to most of society's groups and institutions. They are caught between different social worlds (Andersen and Collins 1995). Therefore, the sharp and heated conflict between groups produces a marginal zone where sociopsychological ambiguities and anxieties arise (Stonequist 1937). Several human dimensions are part of this experience. Thus, a cultural identity can withstand the pressures of change up to a point, but can be fractured and broken as well (Leon-Portilla 1990). Economic marginality is closely linked to this problem.

An analysis of the cultural transformations under the Spanish and, later, the Anglos offers an example of this and underscores the similarities between the colonial and modern experiences, especially when race is factored in. In short, one can view it as a nested evolution of culture and race relations. Spaniards (Anglos) neither accommodated nor appreciated Indian (Mexican) culture. Almost without exception, the subordinate culture has adopted the culture of the aggressor. As a result, cultural change was largely glorification of Spanish (Anglo) culture and destruction of Indian (Mexican) culture. Despite this pressure to assimilate dominant ways, however, many natives took the creative approach of amalgamating their culture with that of the dominant group. Thus, they innovated a new cultural style: Mexican (Chicano), a blend of Spanish (Anglo) and Indian (Mexican) elements.

Some natives came to feel inferior because of this process. Other factors added to the burden: (1) They could not adjust to the Spanish (Anglo) mode; (2) The Spanish (Anglos) did not want them anyway; and (3) They were unable to fit into the new syncretist Mexican (Chicano) culture.

Lacking a definite strategy of adaptation, many became marginal to all three cultures—the dominant, subordinate, and syncretist versions.

Racism compounded these problems (van den Berghe 1967). Eventually, race became a passport to social mobility, with Indian (Mexican) features effectively barring social advancement (Brown 1995). A further complicating factor was the rise of the hybrid, mestizo race. This phenomenon created an interesting situation, particularly since Indians were considered inferior to the Spanish. Many mestizos, especially those who looked Spanish, followed the racist colonial ideology; many Indians followed this strategy by "passing" as mestizos. They attempted to change racial membership and thereby gain wider socioeconomic opportunities. Sometimes the goal included intermarriage with someone from the superior group. In the modern period, there is increasing intermarriage of Anglos and Mexicans, adding another touch to the mestizo tradition. Although feelings of inferiority or socioracial passing are still prevalent, it appears that a more confident and accepting attitude is emerging to underscore recent improvements in self-image. Notwithstanding these advances, and to reiterate, racism has generated a pronounced impact on almost every single facet of Chicano life (Menchaca 1993).

A whole series of other characteristics and habits stem from economic considerations, some firmly entrenched in the minds of observers and others bordering on speculation. For example, the recent "underclass" notion of William J. Wilson (1987) is in many ways an extension of the Oscar Lewis idea of the "culture of poverty" (Lewis 1959). Both of these explanations have been applied to Chicanos (and other ethnic minorities, mainly African Americans) who have experienced persistent and concentrated poverty. In large part, the explanation focuses on the customs and values that are passed from one generation to the next under situations of poverty and want. Although critics have questioned the use of such an "omnibus" construct to explain the life of the poor (Moore and Pinderhughes 1993; Leacock 1971), it is a condition that must be addressed because there are segments of the Chicano population that are mired in poverty. Currently, the indices of poverty are very high among them— e.g., income, housing, education, and so on. Some writers have suggested that the "working poor" is a more apt characterization, particularly with the "self-created" jobs fashioned by many immigrants.

Poverty is often associated with other social problems, such as the high incidence of deviance and crime. Among the poor, illicit and informal economies are known to aid survival. Drug trafficking, drug use and abuse, crime, and gangs, among other problems, are also clearly reflective of the current Chicano urban condition. Accordingly, if such behavior is to be eliminated, the process must begin with an economy that integrates the poor and marginal segments of our cities. Research suggests that lower-class and marginal groups often are forced to follow deviant paths to success, such as the drug market (Moore 1991, 1978).

Old customs were also transformed by this history of culture change. In retrospect, the somewhat more egalitarian social practices of the indigenous period were revamped in a negative way. Two examples will suffice, one on communalism and the other on gender relations, because they seem to be regularly mentioned by modern Chicanos. Envidia (envy) is often pointed out as one of the stumbling blocks that prevents Chicanos from helping each other and getting ahead. While indigenous times were less than perfect, it is clear that cooperation and a communal spirit prevailed then; and in many instances, it still does. Obviously, an economy based on agriculture benefits from this arrangement. In the changes since, particularly during peasantization, cooperative customs were joined by a competitive orientation. This is not an exclusively Chicano quality; it affects the poor generally. George Foster (1967:305) suggests in his theory of "limited good" that "if 'Good' exists in limited amounts which cannot be expanded, and if the system is closed, it follows that an individual or a family can improve a position only at the expense of others." It appears that the process of underdevelopment has encouraged envidia in the Chicano people. During the movements of the 1960s, for example, there was great rivalry and dissension among leaders and groups, regardless of the merits of the idea or program. Perhaps it is envidia that beclouds the senses, making people call one another "Tio Taco," or traitor, without considering their worthiness or honesty.

In gender attitudes and relations, the machismo syndrome is yet another example of the corruption of a trait under conditions of poverty. Machismo has a positive aspect: Males learn to protect family and home and become disciplined, responsible providers, as they once did during earlier times and still do under the supervision of mothers and sisters who value a strong, worthy person. Because oppressive conditions have been so bad, however, there is also a negative result, especially in the context of how females lost status and were devalued in the process of these changes. Many males seek an outlet through the indiscriminate sexual conquest of females (following the lead of the Spanish, and later mestizos), with the aim of lowering the females' status; escape from reality through alcohol and drug use; and fighting and even killing each other for relatively minor reasons. Both Spanish and Anglo-American oppressive experiences contributed to this propensity. Indeed, it may be a way (however unfortunate) for the downtrodden to relieve negative energy and create outlets for their anxieties and frustrations.

Residue of Centuries of History

If it is true that "differences in culture—tribal, peasant, civilizational—provide different modes whereby individual personalities acquire cultural identity" (King 1974:107), then it is equally correct that a cumulative effect pertains for a culture that has undergone a relatively rapid transition. It also is the case that this transition transversed through four cultural imprints, two major wars, and three macrostructural identities. A series of identities in contrasting places and at many levels is what characterizes this complicated history. Currently, Chicanos are still thinking and discussing what the nature of this identity would be. It might be wise to begin to embrace all of the influences and antecedents as a starting point. A multilingual and multicultural foundation of this sort would provide the wellspring for shifting identities or a hierarchy of identities, instead of just "one self per person" (Vigil 1997). With the expansion of human energy systems and the incorporation of a large portion of the human population within these dense networks, the clashes and comminglings of cultures and languages are upon us. Chicanos already know what this entails, and they appear poised to act on it. The orientation and identity taken by those individuals and groups that feel constricted depend on these key factors: the people, the time, and the place.

The residue of this complex cultural history remains in the Chicano people. In fact, in some ways the array of cultural styles is still with us, as literally thousands of indigenous peoples today make their way from peasantry to the modern world in the United States, following old paths or charting new ones as they join older generations. Still, many suffer mental conflict and anguish because of past and present conditions. Minimally, this book has addressed the root causes of this background to explain how the attitudes and behaviors of the people were shaped. The next step is to begin an examination of how these thoughts and habits might be revamped and reordered.

There is also a positive side to the Chicano legacy; the ability to survive by fashioning syncretic adaptive strategies to many changing conditions. This is the Chicano's core strength and is reminiscent of the Mexican adage, "From bad comes good." Knowing different cultures and languages, and amalgamations thereof, certainly outfits a person better for this complex, ever changing world (Ramirez 1985; Vigil 1997). The work ethic is still intact, the spirit strong, and a hope and optimism for an improved future predominates among the people. On the practical side, growing numbers and increasing political clout, fortified and motivated by a pride in ethnic awareness, will translate into a formidable force for change and empowerment.

References

Alvarez, R. R., Jr. 1995. The Mexican-US border: The making of an anthropology of the borderlands. *Annual Review of Anthropology* 24: 1–24.

Andersen, M. L. and P. H. Collins. 1995. *Race, class, and gender.* Belmont, CA: Wadsworth.

Arthur, J. and A. Shapiro, eds. 1996. *Color-class-identity.* Boulder, CO: Westview Press.

Balandier, G. 1966. The colonial situation: A theoretical approach. In *Social change: The colonial situation,* ed. I. Wallerstein. New York: John Wiley & Sons, Inc.

Balibar, E. and I. Wallerstein. 1991. *Race, nation, class: Ambiguous identities.* London: Verso.

Barkin, D. 1994. *Distorted development.* Boulder, CO: Westview Press.

Brass, P. R. 1992. *Ethnicity and nationalism.* Newbury, CA: Sage Publications.

Brown, R. 1995. *Prejudice.* Oxford: Blackwell Publications.

Cockcroft, J. D. 1990. *Mexico class formation, capital accumulation, and the state.* New York: Monthly Review Press.

Essed, P. 1991. *Understanding everyday racism.* Newbury Park, CA: Sage Publications.

Foley, D. E., et al. 1977. *From peones to politicos: Ethnic relations in a South Texas town, 1900 to 1977.* Austin: University of Studies.

Foster, G. 1967. Peasant society and the image of limited good. In *Peasant society: A reader,* eds. J. M. Potter, M. N. Diaz, and G. M. Foster. Boston: Little, Brown Co.

Gomez-Quinones, J. 1990. *Chicano politics: Reality and promise, 1940–1990.* Albuquerque: University of New Mexico Press.

Handlin, O. 1951. *The uprooted.* New York: Grossett & Dunlap, Inc.

Harrison, P. 1981. *Inside the Third World: The anatomy of poverty.* New York: Penguin.

Hewitt, C. 1977. Majorities and minorities: A comparative survey of ethnic violence. In *The annals of the American academy of political and social science,* vol. 433, ed. M. O. Heisler.

Horowitz, D. L. 1977. Cultural movements and ethnic change. In *The annals of the American academy of political and social science,* vol. 433, ed. M. O. Heisler.

Kearney, M. 1996. *Reconceptualizing peasantry.* Boulder, CO: Westview Press.

King, A. R. 1974. A stratification of labyrinths: The acquisition and retention of cultural identity in modern culture. In *Social and cultural identity: Problems of persistence and change,* ed. T. K. Fitzgerald. Athens: Southern Anthropological Society, University of Georgia Press.

Leacock, E. B., ed. 1971. *The culture of poverty: A critique.* New York: Simon & Schuster, Inc.

Leon-Portilla, M. 1990. *Endangered cultures.* Dallas: Southern Methodist University Press.

Lewis, O. 1959. *Five families: Mexican case studies in the culture of poverty.* New York: Basic Books.

Malinowski, B. 1945. *The dynamics of culture change.* New Haven, CT: Yale University Press.

Martinez, O. 1996. *U.S.-Mexico borderlands: Historical and contemporary perspectives.* Wilmington, DE: Scholarly Resources.

Menchaca, M. 1993. Chicano Indianism: A historical account of racial repression in the United States. *American* 20(3): 583–603.

Moore, J. W. 1991. *Going down to the barrio.* Philadelphia: University of Temple Press.

Moore, J. W., et al. 1978. *Homeboys: Gangs, drugs, and prisons in the barrios of Los Angeles.* Philadelphia: Temple University Press.

Moore, J. W. and R. Pinderhughes, eds. 1993. *In the barrios: Latinos and the underclass debate.* New York: Russell Sage Foundation.

Naylor, L. L. 1996. *Culture and change: An introduction.* Westport, CT: Bergin and Garvey.

Pedraza, S. and R. Rumbaut, eds. 1996. *Origins and destinies: Immigration, race, and ethnicity in America.* Belmont, CA: Wadsworth Publishing Co.

Ramirez, M., III. 1985. *Psychology of the Americas: Mestizo perspective on personality and mental health.* New York: Pergamon Press.

Ramos, S. 1962. *Profile of man and culture in Mexico.* Austin: University of Texas Press.

Root, M. P. O. 1992. *Racially mixed people in America.* Newbury Park, CA: Sage Publications.

Rosaldo, R. 1989. *Culture and truth.* Boston: Beacon Press.

Sanderson, S. E. 1995. *Civilizations and world systems: Studying world-historical change.* Thousand Oaks, CA: AltaMira Press.

Sassen, S. 1991. *The global city.* Princeton: Princeton University Press.

Spicer, E. 1962. *Cycles of conquest.* Tucson: University of Arizona Press.

Stoler, A. L. and F. Cooper, eds. 1996. *Tensions of empire: Colonial cultures in a bourgeois world.* Berkeley: University of California Press.

Stonequist, E. V. 1937. *The marginal man.* New York: Russell & Russell, Publishers.

Valencia, R. R., ed. 1991. *Chicano school failure and success: Research and policy agendas for the 1990s.* London: The Falmer Press.

van den Berghe, P. L. 1967. *Race and racism: A comparative perspective.* New York: John Wiley & Sons, Inc.

Velez-Ibanez, C. G. 1996. *Border visions: Mexican cultures of the Southwest.* Tucson: University of Arizona Press.

Vigil, J. D. 1997. *Personas Mexicanas: Chicano high schoolers in a changing Los Angeles.* Ft. Worth, TX: Harcourt Brace.

Walch, T., ed. 1994. *Immigrant America.* New York: Garland Publications, Inc.

Wilson, W. J. 1987. The truly disadvantaged. Chicago: University of Chicago Press.

Wolf, E. 1969. *Peasant wars of the twentieth century.* New York: Harper & Row, Publishers.

_____. 1982. *Europe and the people without history.* Berkeley: University of California Press.

Yinger, M. 1994. *Ethnicity: Source of strength? Source of conflict?* Albany: State University of New York Press.

Bibliography

Freidenberg, J. 1995. *The anthropology of lower income urban enclaves.* New York: Annals of the New York Academy of Sciences.

Memmi, A. 1965. *The colonizer and the colonized.* Boston: Beacon Press.

Mirande, A. 1983. *The Chicano experience.* Notre Dame, IN: University of Notre Dame.

Robinson, C. *With the ears of strangers: The Mexican in American literature.* Tucson: University of Arizona Press.

Wilkie, M. W. 1977. Colonials, marginals and immigrants: Contributions to a theory of ethnic stratification. *Comparative Studies in Society and History* 19:67.

Index